HISTORICAL GEOGRAPHY RESEARCH SERIES NO. 38

Negotiating Colonialism

Gaelic-Irish Reaction to New English Expansion
in Early Modern Tipperary, *c*.1541-1641

John Morrissey

National University of Ireland, Galway
University Road
Galway
Ireland

ISBN 1 870074 20 3

In memory of my mother

Contents

Figures

Preface

Gaelic resistance to English colonialism and the emergence of Irish nationalism have come under renewed academic scrutiny in recent years. A series of complexities and ambiguities inherent in both the British colonial project and Irish reactions to its various manifestations has been shown to underline a whole set of tensions within Ireland's colonial past. As part of this growing discourse, this work explores the contradictory notions of accommodation and resistance in the early modern period by examining one Gaelic-Irish family's encounters in the late sixteenth and early seventeenth centuries. Focusing on the experiences of the O'Dwyers of Kilnamanagh, in west County Tipperary in south-western Ireland, and set against the backdrop of the emergence of nascent forms of Irish nationalism, the work interrogates the intricate and intriguing Gaelic/English relations of the early modern period.

The work seeks to sift out the contested spaces of early modern Irish society in an effort to underline the fluidity and inherent contradictions of practices of domination and resistance in the formation and interaction of Ireland's cultural identities; identities whose intricacies and conflicts are so revealing and consequential for the understanding of the present. In locating the historical geographies of early modern Ireland, the central focus has been the explication of the complexities of both the practices of New English colonialism and subsequent Gaelic-Irish responses. A key challenge has been the conceptualisation of the emergence of contemporary society's intrinsic ambiguities, which mirror the contradictory essence of both the shared and bounded, political, economic and cultural spaces of Ireland's past.

John Morrissey

Galway

May 2003

Acknowledgements

In researching and writing this book I have built up a lengthy list of personal and intellectual debts that I now take pleasure in acknowledging. There are always, of course, so many colleagues, friends and family that support and influence one's thinking and writing that it is difficult to adequately and gracefully remember them. However, I've endeavoured to record sincerely below my thanks to a number of important people in my life, social, academic and otherwise, and my apologies to anyone I've unintentionally neglected to mention.

My thanks go first to Alan Lester for his discerning advice as editor of the HGRG research series, and for the affable and enjoyable learning experience of working with him. Thanks also for the comments of two anonymous referees whose input was most valuable. There are others, too, whose observations were challenging, constructive and ever encouraging at different stages of the production of this work. These include: Catherine Brace; Alex Gibson; David Harvey; Mark Hennessy; Gerry Kearns; Matthew Kurtz; Mike Leyshon; Denis Linehan; Catherine Nash; Simon Potter; Lindsay Proudfoot; and Ulf Strohmayer – thanks for all your ideas, energy and joy of conversation.

I'd like to show my appreciation, too, to the Publications Fund of National University of Ireland, Galway for subventing the publication costs of this work, and I'd like to also acknowledge the UK Economic and Social Research Council and Department of Geography at the University of Exeter for the two scholarships that allowed me to do the doctoral research upon which the work is based.

Finally, thanks to my family and friends who have supported me in so many respects over the years and challenged and taught me in ways that perhaps they never even knew! Thank you.

John Morrissey

Abbreviations and Conventions

Primary sources are referred to in the footnotes in abbreviated form, full details being presented in the bibliography. The following abbreviations are employed throughout:

A.F.M. | *Annals of the Kingdom of Ireland by the Four Masters* (7 vols.)

Cal. Carew MSS | *Calendar of the Carew Manuscripts, Lambeth, 1515-74* [etc.] (6 vols.. Vol. 5, *Books of Howth, Miscellaneous*, is abbreviated to *Bks. Howth, Misc.)*

Cal. Clarendon Papers | *Calendar of the Clarendon State Papers, Bodleian (5 vols.)*

Cal. Ormond Deeds | *Calendar of Ormond Deeds, 1172-1350 [etc.]* (6 vols.)

Cal. pat. rolls Ire., Hen. VIII-Eliz. | *Calendar of the Patent and Close Rolls of Chancery in Ireland, 1514-1575*

Cal. pat. rolls Ire., Eliz. | *Calendar of Patent and Close Rolls of Chancery in Ireland, 1576-1603*

Cal. pat. rolls Ire., Chas. I | *Calendar of Patent and Close Rolls of Chancery in Ireland, 1625-1633*

Cal. pat. rolls Ire., Jas. I | *The Irish Patent Rolls of James I*

Cal. S.P. Ire. | *Calendar of the State Papers relating to Ireland, 1509-1573* [etc.] (24 vols.)

Carte, *Ormond* | T. Carte, *History of the Life of James, First Duke of Ormond* (3 vols.)

Census Ire., 1659 | *A Census of Ireland, c.1659*

Civil Survey, County Tipperary	*The Civil Survey, A.D. 1654-1656, County of Tipperary* (2 vols.)
Egmont MSS	*Report on the Manuscripts of the Earl of Egmont* (2 vols.)
Fiants Ire., Hen. VIII-Eliz.	*The Irish Fiants of the Tudor Sovereigns, 1521-1558* [etc.] (3 vols.)
Hastings MSS	*Report on the Manuscripts of the late Reginald Rawden Hastings, Esq.* (4 vols.)
Hearth Money Records 1665-1666/7	*Tipperary's Families: Being the Hearth Money Records for 1665-6-7*

H.M.C.	Historical Manuscripts Commission, London
I.M.C.	Irish Manuscripts Commission, Dublin
N.A.I.	National Archives of Ireland, Dublin
N.L.I.	National Library of Ireland, Dublin
P.R.O.	Public Record Office, London
T.C.D.	Library of Trinity College, Dublin

Spelling and punctuation have been presented in original format in all quotations. The term *Gaelic-Irish* is employed expediently throughout to refer to the existing population in Ireland prior to the Anglo-Norman colonisation in the twelfth and thirteenth centuries. By the mid-seventeenth century, this 'group' continued to constitute the numerical majority of the island. Other terms used (and sometimes quoted) include 'Native Irish', 'Old Irish', 'Gaedhil', 'Gaelic' or 'Native'. *Old English* here means the Roman Catholic descendants of the Anglo-Norman colonisation. It was the designation most current in the late sixteenth and early seventeenth centuries (also referred to elsewhere as 'Anglo-Norman', 'Anglo-Irish', 'Anglo-Hiberni', 'English-Irish' or 'Sean Ghaill'). The grouping *New English* refers here to the Protestant English government officials, entrepreneurs and settlers of the post-Reformation period in Ireland (synonymous denominations include 'Newcomer', 'Planter', 'Nua Ghaill' and later 'Anglo-Irish').[1] The term 'Protestant', which contemporary Church of Ireland members used exclusively to refer to themselves, is applied here to mean adherents of both the established and dissenter churches. The denomination 'Catholic', frequently recorded as 'Recusant', 'Papist' or 'Romanist' in the sources, here refers simply to adherents of Roman Catholicism. Regarding place-names, all spellings have been modernised except when quoted, and contemporary usage has been adhered to in referring to the modern counties of Laois and Offaly as, respectively, Queen's County and King's County.

---

[1] For further discussion on the use of nomenclature in Irish historiography of the early modern period, see S.G. Ellis, 1999, 'The Collapse of the Gaelic World', *Irish Historical Studies*, vol. 31, no. 124, pp. 451-456. Cf. M. MacCarthy-Morrogh, 1986, *The Munster Plantation: English Migration to Southern Ireland 1583-1641*, Clarendon Press, Oxford, pp. 277-278 and T.W. Moody, 1976, 'Early Modern Ireland', in: T.W. Moody, F.X. Martin and F.J. Byrne (eds.), *A New History of Ireland III: Early Modern Ireland 1534-1691*, Clarendon Press, Oxford, pp. xlii-xliii

*This publication was grant-aided by the Publications Fund
of National University of Ireland, Galway*

In history, every man and woman, seen
through my mind, through centuries, is unreal.
I dream the dead into a living presence
and shape dead bones into a new design,
let speak again the ages' buried voices
and so defy the killing power of time.

'Neither apathy nor antipathy can bring out
the truth in history.' Only the engaged heart
and mind will face the drama of the dead

but who will solve it?
        I live and write in doubt
loving the heart-beat of this passionate art
still wondering what the years have done and said.[II]

[II] Extract from B. Kennelly, 'Who Will Solve It?', quoted in: T.B. Barry, R. Frame and K. Simms (eds.), 1995, *Colony and Frontier in Medieval Ireland*, Hambledon Press, London, p. x

Chapter 1

Cultural Interaction in Early Modern Ireland

> This enterprize of Cashel I have mentioned the first of any in
> Munster, because it was the first attempted, merely by the fury of the
> populace, occasioned by impolitick acts of cruelty, exercised without
> a just distinction between the innocent and the guilty; a practice
> attended with very unhappy consequences in the course of the
> troubles of Ireland – *Thomas Carte, describing the outbreak of the*
> *1641 rebellion in County Tipperary* [1]

Carte conveys above a foreboding sense of the profound effect the 1641
rebellion would come to have on the emergence of the Irish nation, the
interaction of its social and cultural elements, and the tragic conflict of its
competing identities. The apparent abrupt manifestation of insurrection,
however, masked a series of specific and interrelated developments occurring
in a society that was imagined and negotiated in complicated and often
contradictory ways. By interrogating the evolving responses of Gaelic-Irish
society to New English colonial activities in the late sixteenth and early
seventeenth centuries, this work explores the diverse and conflicting 'voices'
of accommodation and resistance that cut across the sites, or settings, of cultural
interaction in early modern Ireland. Employing the example of the Gaelic-Irish
O'Dwyers of Kilnamanagh in west County Tipperary, it considers the fluid
nature of contemporary practices of colonialism and resistance, and demonstrates
the fundamental ambiguities of both the shared and bounded political, economic
and cultural spaces of early modern Ireland.

Themes of Contestation

The date *c*.1541 provides a convenient starting point from which to examine
themes of contestation in early modern Ireland following the reassertion of
crown control in the mid-sixteenth century. 1641, and the outbreak of a
rebellion which has been represented as a watershed in Irish history, constitutes
the end-point of the narrative. The intervening one hundred years or so
constitutes a hugely significant, formative period in the emergence of the

1

shared spaces, conflicting polities and contested identities of early modern Ireland. This work seeks initially to elucidate the various intricacies of pre-1641 Irish society, particularly the Gaelic-Irish knowledge and appreciation of political and economic realities and the subsequent level of both sophistication and contradiction fundamental to their responses to contemporary practices of English colonialism. Using the example of County Tipperary and the Gaelic-Irish O'Dwyers, it shows how the piecemeal nature of New English government ensured a significant level of integration with the existing population, which was negotiated principally by the upper levels of society sharing economic and social terms of reference. The O'Dwyers of Kilnamanagh provide a wonderful example of the complexities of the Gaelic-Irish response. The survival of a rich array of documentary evidence, gleaned from an eclectic range of sources,[2] enables a detailed exploration of their contradictory encounters with new and evolving colonial practices, which mirror in many ways the experiences of Gaelic Ireland more broadly in its complex interactions with the expanding New English administration of the early modern period.

The illumination of the transitional character of pre-1641 society is followed by an exploration of the contestation of identity politics in contemporary Ireland, the emergence of geographies of resistance and the subsequent breakdown of relations between 'natives' and 'newcomers' in late 1641. Fundamental notions of New English superiority and differentiation are argued to have constituted an integral feature of early modern Irish society that limited economic and social integration. This served ultimately to re-constitute the process of survival and accommodation as a polarised struggle between the basic groups of 'Irish Papist' and 'English Protestant', as delineated in the Civil Survey of the mid-seventeenth century.[3] By interrogating the manner in which society was transcended by a framework of New English exclusivism (which was itself being constructed in the early modern period), the work explores how the mobilisation of an increasingly 'othered' Catholic Irish identity and reaction occurred within an over-arching context of 'difference'.

One of the key challenges of researching and writing this work has been to account for the fundamental complexities and contradictions of Gaelic/English relations in the early modern period. Departing in many ways from earlier nationalist accounts implicitly imbued with fundamental assumptions of English colonial subjugation and Gaelic struggle, this work attempts to sift out the diverse, interlocking and conflicting practices of accommodation and resistance which cut across society in a multiplicity of ways. This is posited as a prerequisite to further elucidating the complex and contradictory reasons for the breakdown of social order in the late 1630s and subsequent outbreak of the 1641 rebellion. In essence, the work endeavours to engage the complex interconnections and conflicting voices of Gaelic and English worlds in the early modern period and advocates the premise that Ireland's contemporary cultural geographies can be (re)presented in the context of a broader historical discourse which explicitly celebrates notions of heterogeneity, fluidity and contradiction. In presenting my own narrative account of developments in early modern Ireland, I have had to situate myself in the tradition of writing historical geography in, or of, Ireland, and in order to present this work in that context (and particularly for those unfamiliar with the sub-discipline in Ireland), a brief exploration of relevant aspects emanating from Irish historical geography follows below.

Irish Historical Geography of the Early Modern Period

> Much remains hazy about the Irish past, and anyone trying to find his way about must feel at times like an early English newcomer floundering among Irish swamps and essaying the art of bog-trotting.[4]

Facing any reader of Irish historical geography of the early modern period is a wealth of studies, both national and regional, relating to a range of themes regarding the development and dynamics of contemporary Irish society. Considerable debate exists concerning numerous aspects of the English colonial project in Ireland, ranging from the nature and agenda of the expansion of English state control to the extent and degree of Gaelic-Irish and Old English response. Studies of Irish historical geography have been traditionally concerned with the cultural landscape over time. This concept of a 'cultural landscape' is of course an ambiguous term, implicitly rather than explicitly expressed in work which unproblematically delineates the visible scene as a representative manifestation of a given culture.[5] Comprehensive overviews such as Orme's *Ireland* and Aalen's *Man and the Landscape in Ireland* represent interpretations of the development of this cultural landscape from pre-history to the present day.[6] These works, in addition to those of the two dominant figures of Irish historical geography, Estyn Evans and Jones Hughes,[7] are situated within what Graham and Proudfoot describe as "the several traditional perspectives of Irish historical geography", exhibiting "a diversity of intellectual influences but simultaneously ... a marked insularity of explanation".[8] This 'marked insularity of explanation' is especially evident in studies with little or no reference to the context of developments outside Ireland. Throughout this work, the incorporation of a wider geographical context to consider contemporary circumstances in Britain and the Continent has aided both my own understanding of affairs in Ireland and the presentation of the broader significance of key developments therein during an age of flourishing European networks of ideas and material practices.

Many studies of Irish historical geography have concentrated on the workings and physical form of colonial development, and have also tended to concentrate on specific themes – such as the material culture of Gaelic Ireland and the socio-economic effects of the plantation of Ulster.[9] Two edited works, Nolan's *The Shaping of Ireland* and Smyth and Whelan's *Common Ground*, present a chronological interpretation of various historical geographical themes in Ireland.[10] Useful and informative chapters therein include Smyth's use of the 1659 poll tax returns to build up a picture of Irish society in the mid-seventeenth century, which identifies general trends in population and settlement that provide an over-arching context to the specific and localised setting of this work's research area of Kilnamanagh.[11] Smyth's other works, specifically on Tipperary, form an important 'historical geography' of population, settlement and other socio-economic patterns in the county,[12] and, together with other similar historico-geographical accounts of areas elsewhere in Ireland by Duffy and others, constitute an appropriate point from which to build my own exploration of the intricacies of Gaelic/English relations in the early modern period.[13]

The enduring legacy of the empirical tradition of writing Irish historical geography is evident in works that continue to seek to 'reconstruct' 'cross-sectional' historical geographies of Ireland' past.[14] Many such accounts, however, implicitly adopt the position of imparting an uncontested and singular (e.g., usually using the definitive article 'the') 'historical geography'.[15] Other narratives, too, are often presented with reference to narrowly 'descriptive' empirical material and writ large in unproblematic assumptions respecting 'colonial subjugation' and 'cultural agency'.[16] Relations between the native population and newcomers from Britain, for example, are often posited as exploitative and 'colonial', incorporating simplified and untheorised notions of Self and Other.[17] Such a fostering of rudimentary relationships precludes an

4

elucidation of the more complicated, fluid and contradictory interconnections of the spaces of colonialism in early modern Ireland.

It is important to note that in recent years some works by Irish geographers have "departed radically from the conventional certainties of colonial oppression which imbued [earlier] work", and these writings have significantly informed this work.[18] Graham, Proudfoot, Smyth and others have all offered significant re-conceptualisations of the cultural geographies of Ireland's past to account for its diversity of experience.[19] In geography's 'sister' disciplines, too, such as history and archaeology, there have been a number of re-examinations of aspects of early modern Irish society which have apprised this work.[20] Indeed, much current work in Irish historical geography has been done in conjunction with other disciplines (due in part, of course, to the small and often marginalised nature of geography departments in Ireland).[21]

In considering, however, the implications and context of 'doing' historical geography in, and of, Ireland, it seems that despite notable interests and efforts in broadening both the geographical imagination and indeed research 'field' there is nevertheless a kind of broader 'academic' status quo. This serves to marginalise those works that seek to "question the conventional intellectual categories through which the modern world has been interpreted and conceptualised"[22] or aspire to theorise and explore the nuances and contradictions that are so revealing of the complexities and conflicts of the social and cultural geographies of Ireland's past. In McCarthy's recent review of the 'nature' of historical geography in Ireland, for example, he implicitly bounds what is "traditional historical geography" by discussing the "impact" of 'new' cultural geography.[23] One way in which this can perhaps ultimately be surmounted is to situate one's narrative in broader theoretical and conceptual literature (as follows below) that engages notions of particularity, heterogeneity and contradiction and in so doing serves simultaneously to marginalise the idea of a singular narrative historical geography of Ireland, nationalist or otherwise.

Narrating Early Modern Ireland

[S]electivity and subjectivity permeate the writing of historical narratives from the selection of facts to the combining of those facts into a story. Assessing historical narratives is also a subjective exercise. Recognition of this selectivity and subjectivity does not lead to the despair of relativism but rather to the emancipation of scholarship from prevailing conformities.[24]

Wishart underlines above the essential importance of explicitly recognising the selectivity and subjectivity of archival research as a prerequisite to representing the past. In his coherent analysis of historical scholarship, he concludes that by choosing to bring on board the postmodernist critique of conventional historical representation "[a]t last we might be able to put the objectivist fallacy to rest, opening the possibility for many legitimate interpretations of the past".[25] The orientation of such a position would appear particularly pertinent in the case of Ireland, whose cultural geographies and histories have been so dogmatically represented since the early modern period. These 'narratives' have been shown to mask an overwhelming politics of position, predicated fundamentally from the vantage points of the 'coloniser' and the 'colonised'.[26] Hoppen, for example, notes that

> [s]ince at least the seventeenth century almost every group with an axe to grind has thought it imperative to control the past in order to provide support for contemporary arguments and ideologies.[27]

Irish historiography, since the partition of the island in 1921, has been inevitably inflected by the search for the various representative origin-legends, or origin-myths, of the past that were necessary for the construction of contemporary ideas of nationality and identity, consonant with the establishment of two separate states.[28] Graham observes the nature of the two basic, polarised representations that consequently emerged as broadly one of a powerful Gaelic-Catholic metanarrative – identified throughout the Republic of Ireland and in large parts of Ulster – opposed by a non-linear, Protestant narrative, reflective of a confused identity and unimagined representative landscape within Northern Ireland.[29] The question of the legitimacy, appropriateness and relevance of these representations has remained "an abiding area of contestation".[30] As Meinig earlier observed, the study of aspects of colonialism "tends to engage our emotions and thereby become enmeshed in polemics and coloured by political controversy".[31]

The dichotomy of perspective in recent years has been significantly influenced by what has become known loosely as revisionism.[32] Often vaguely referred to in the literature, 'revisionist' approaches to historical inquiry are frequently clustered and posited as a singular (i.e., 'the' revisionist approach) attempt at 'myth-busting' or re-writing the past, often from a 'colonial' perspective, and perhaps the work that suitably represents such an alleged agenda is Foster's *Modern Ireland*, published in 1989.[33] Acknowledging his debt to the pioneering work of Beckett,[34] Foster's intention is to "clarify some of the realities behind … [t]he tradition of writing the 'story of Ireland' as a morality tale, invented around the seventeenth century and retained (with the roles of hero and villain often reversed) until the twentieth century".[35] Revisionism has been conceptualised by Graham as a "fractured, and, as yet, inconclusive, attempt to reconstitute the idea of Irishness", with "little agreement on a new representation".[36] Indeed, a number of vitriolic disputes regarding the appropriateness of revisionism to Irish historical scholarship have been engaged.[37] As a disruptive influence, however, revisionism has been ultimately constructive in problematising dominant narratives and prompting reinterpretations of Ireland's past.[38]

One of the most significant impacts of works that could be considered 'revisionist' in nature for the writing of early modern Ireland has been a "growing awareness of the complexity of the relationship between natives and newcomers in the late sixteenth and early seventeenth centuries".[39] The concept of revisionism, however, is not necessary if one accepts the notion that historical scholarship can be transcended by myriad perspectives, interpretations and narratives, all situated in a wider historical discourse. Recent research in Irish historical geography has been inevitably implicated in the often simplified and unhelpful depiction of particular readings of Ireland's past as ostensibly either 'nationalist' or 'revisionist'.[40] The morass of the on-going revisionist 'controversy', which typically depicts a binary narrative tradition (nationalist versus revisionist), often fails of course to take into account the situated nuances of works at the scale below the 'national' or those that are engaged in broader theoretical debates. The controversy can be usefully transcended, however, by situating the debate in a broader discussion of theory, selectivity and subjectivity in historical inquiry, which enables a more fruitful engagement with the conflicting narratives that characterise cultural interaction in early modern Ireland.

The Kiowa poet and novelist, Momaday, in his personal reflections in Martin's *The American Indian and the Problem of History*, furnishes us with a compelling example of how the evidence of history can generate a multiplicity of facts, which can subsequently be utilised to write an array of legitimate narratives.[41]

In the case of Ireland, as Regan points out, "it is the interaction of these narratives which is likely to impede any easy or single notion of what constitutes [the] Irish experience".[42] In Brian Friel's play of nineteenth-century Irish society, *Translations*, it is submitted that "it is not the literal past, the "facts" of history, that shape us, but images of the past embodied in language".[43] Those 'facts', furthermore, as Wishart points out, "are determined as much by the narrative as the other way around".[44] He proceeds to underline the undeniable subjectivity of representation in the research and writing exercises, and argues "there is no objective way of judging the 'truth value' of a narrative".[45] Such a recognition, moreover, does not lead to a defeatist conception of historical inquiry but rather prompts an explicit theorising of one's subjectivity. As Hall and others have noted, "all discourse is 'placed'", and there is always a "politics of position" from which we "speak or write".[46] As my (re)presentation of Gaelic/English relations in early modern Ireland does not equate to a 'regularity of nature' but rather a "situated-geographic-imagination",[47] what follows below is essentially a theorising of that 'situated imagination' and further explication of what informs this work's interrogation of cultural interaction in early modern Ireland.

Theorising the Local

The barony of Kilnamanagh, the ancestral home of the Gaelic-Irish O'Dwyers, is illustrated in fig. 1.1.[48] Situated in west County Tipperary, it occupies a transitional location in Ireland between east and west in a region that has been described as "hybrid" in "physical, economic and cultural terms",[49] and as "an area of convergence where major strands in Ireland's history have met".[50] Kilnamanagh and its environs, as a 'contact zone' in early modern Ireland, were to embrace a host of intriguing and dynamic human geographies in the late sixteenth and early seventeenth centuries, which will be examined, in turn, through the course of this work. The question addressed initially here, however, is how the writing of this small, cohesive and little known area of south-western Ireland informs, and is itself informed by, wider perspectives on the nature of colonialism.

> Can we write local histories which acknowledge that places are not so much singular points as constellations – the product of all sorts of social relations which cut across particular locations in a multiplicity of ways?[51]

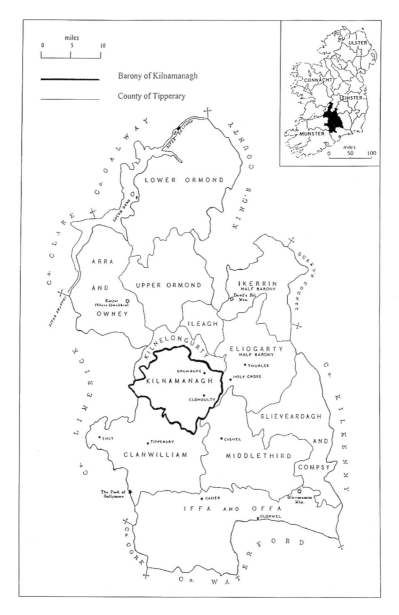

Fig. 1.1: **The Barony of Kilnamanagh, County Tipperary**. After Simington, *Civil Survey, County Tipperary, Vol. 2*, p. i

Driver and Samuel here ask the reader a key question. Many academics have noted the difficulties of theorising a sense of place and of generating a narrative to account for the complexities of the 'local'.[52] In the barony of Kilnamanagh, through the course of the early modern period, existing ecological and cultural settings were encountered and contested as part of the wider practices and imagination of English colonial expansion. As Said outlines in his seminal postcolonial work, *Orientalism*, the process of global 'visioning' or geographical 'imagining' played an integral part in the expansionist project.[53] He notes, elsewhere, how this was necessary for "the production, acquisition, subordination and settlement of space".[54] Clearly, however, practices of colonial visioning or imagining manifested themselves in varying and localised activities of occupation.[55]

Much recent work has underlined how the colonial project was both global in its scale and "messy in its local effects".[56] Emphasis has been increasingly lain upon localised analyses of colonial expansion as a departure from what Duncan and Cosgrove term the "monolithic totalities, explicated by global theories based on such concepts as Others, Orientalism, Imperialism".[57] They contend that the complexity of these global processes needs to be "unravelled through localised and historically specific accounts of colonial representations and practices".[58] Jacobs, too, argues that "through the local, rendered in detail, the complex variability of the colonial politics of identity and place can be known".[59] In addition to calls for attention to the local, recent works by Lester and others on the historical geographies of colonialism have emphasised the import of seeing the 'local' as constituted across broader geographical 'circuits' of knowledge and 'networks' of material practices.[60]

In this work, the principal concern has been the exploration of the localised, shared and contested spaces of a particular region of south-western Ireland, Kilnamanagh. The research involved an interrogation of the "inbetween space", or "spaces of betweenness", which have been examined increasingly in recent years in the context of the 'cultural turn'.[61] The geographical 'entity' of the barony of Kilnamanagh acts as a setting or context within which sites or spaces of 'betweenness' are interrogated. It is not envisaged here as a rigid, bounded locale but conversely as a fluid and interconnected space, unavoidably interlocking with, and transmuted by, developments elsewhere.[62] Its "meaning of place" is conceptualised as both "ephemeral and hybrid", and through the course of the work, its "constant renegotiation" over time is shown to "erode the polarities of Self and Other, creating 'inbetween space' invested with a variety of shared meanings".[63] The intention here is to explore the

> intersecting contact points between different facets of the colonial world, and the multiple constituents of the colonised world [which were] played out in a variety of ways and occupied different spaces, threaded into the fabric of everyday life.[64]

Underpinning such an approach to the study of the past are a variety of assumptions, however, regarding the signification of terms such as 'colonial', 'contact zone', 'culture' and 'landscape'. What follows below is a brief explication of their meanings in the context of this work. As Harris notes, to write the historical geography of an area nowadays "with any acuity is to take on not only [the particular] region and its landscapes and archives but also the main literatures on contact processes, colonialism, modernity and representation".[65]

(Re)presenting Gaelic Kilnamanagh

To begin with, the conceptual framework of this work is neither driven by a goal to orientate any one particular 'ism' nor indeed to pursue any explicit, rigid methodology to uncover and reveal what are often complex and intricate webs of meaning in the human action of the past. I recognise, however, the necessity of theorising the interpretive context of my research in order to accommodate an understanding of the situatedness of its findings, which is what this chapter, in part, concerns itself with. Therefore, following Cairns and Richards, this work takes as a starting point the problematised historic relationship of Ireland and England as one of the colonised and the coloniser.[66] As Said notes, "[b]eginnings have to made for each project in such a way as to *enable* what follows from them".[67] What follows from this beginning is, in essence, an interrogation of how the cultural geographies of early modern west Tipperary were inflected by this simplified and often contradictory 'colonial' relationship. It is essential, of course, to observe the fundamental complexities intersecting that simplified relationship. Ireland may well have been "positioned over many centuries as an Other against which a British state formulated itself",[68] but colonialism in Ireland, as elsewhere, was "a multifaceted phenomenon", for which there is "no agreement on how [it] should be defined". [69]

11

The discourse of colonialism, as Lester reminds us, has been dominated by the perspective of a Eurocentric world view, and, by extension, the coloniser.[70] Ireland's historical development, as paradoxically both a kingdom and a colony within Europe, presents an additional set of ambiguities and contradictions. Through the course of this work, the inconsistencies of the expansion of New English colonial activities in early modern west Tipperary have been utilised to ground an exploration of the intricacies and contestations inherent in the interaction of the "historical geographies of the colonised world" and the broader "historical geography of colonialism".[71] As Routledge argues, "practices of resistance cannot be separated from practices of domination, they are always entangled in some configuration".[72] Routledge's perspective typifies the postcolonial critique, which has problematised the categories of Self and Other as appropriate or useful conceptual tools in studying aspects of colonialism.[73] Pratt, for example, challenges the false rigidity of Self and Other by developing the notion of the 'contact zone' which

> emphasizes how subjects are constituted in and by their relations to each other ... not in terms of separateness or apartheid, but in terms of copresence, interaction, interlocking understandings and practices.[74]

The barony of Kilnamanagh is envisaged in this work as a contact zone of late medieval and early modern Irish society wherein an excellent opportunity is afforded to examine the "multiple 'historical geographies of the colonised world' ... in terms of contest and complicity, conflict and collusion, and to tackle the unwritten history of resistance".[75] The interaction of the Gaelic-Irish and New English is posited in the broader context of "the social spaces where disparate cultures meet, clash, and grapple with each other, often in highly asymmetrical relations of domination and subordination".[76] The intention is not, as Meinig stresses, "to gloss over the fact" that processes of colonialism were "painful experiences for the people caught up in them".[77] Rather, it is to adopt a position from which to explore those very experiences, their meanings and intrinsic ambiguities.

This work is also informed by some important recent developments in historical geography that have been "consonant with an interpretive turn in social science more generally, which has given credence to historiography and discourse as truths of a kind".[78] In historical geography, this has seen a widening of what constitutes the geographical 'field', recognition of the diversity of meaning within it and subsequently broader emphases of archival research and new questions being asked of the sources. Concepts such as culture and landscape – once signifying exclusively 'object' – have been retheorised to also signify a range of diverse, subjective meanings, and are no longer given ontological status or seen as explanatory variables.[79] As Henderson stresses, "[e]specially since the 1970s, it has been through these indeterminacies, not despite them, that [we] have divined cultural meanings and social processes".[80] In recent years, then, the ongoing reconfiguration and exploration of culture and colonialism and accompanying problematisation of dominant and often untheorised metanarratives have ultimately accommodated more nuanced and diverse understandings and concepts in historical geography. I conclude this chapter below by briefly assessing the challenges posed by the sources (or lack thereof) in examining the cultural geographies of early modern Ireland.

The Challenge of the Sources

> The whole landscape a manuscript we had lost the skill to read, a part of our past disinherited; but fumbled, like a blind man along the fingerprints of instinct.[81]

Looking out over the hills of his native County Tyrone, Montague eloquently observes above the difficulties of interpreting the geographical worlds of the past. In any investigation of the human geographies of history, the researcher encounters at once both the particular evidence itself and its accompanying difficulties of interpretation and representation. In relation to the O'Dwyers and the barony of Kilnamanagh, much of the interest of the early modern period lies in disentangling the endogenous from indigenous transformations, by working carefully with the source documents of a primarily colonial nature, including particularly the *State Papers*, *Patent Rolls*, *Fiants* and *Civil Survey*.[82] Throughout this rich and arealy comprehensive documentary material, there runs the prejudiced vein of an overwhelmingly political and administrative agenda, typical of any colonial administration. Duncan, in his examination of the Kandyan Kingdom in nineteenth-century Sri Lanka, notes the unavoidable interpretive difficulties of historical sources.[83] He outlines the problem of officialdom and power relations inherent in administrative sources, and highlights the need for awareness of the archive's empowerment of one and dispossession of another.[84]

Smyth, who has made excellent use of the central state administrative documents of early modern Ireland, has stressed the importance of the need for the careful applied use of archival sources for the purposes of historical geography.[85] Numerous others, such as Canny and Gillespie, join him in underlining the difficulties of interrogating and interpreting documentary source material of a colonial nature.[86] Thomas, in his thoughtful reassessment of "colonialism's culture", stresses that "colonialism has always been imagined and energised through signs, metaphors and narratives".[87] In the Irish experience of early modern colonialism, Daniels makes the point that in Tudor England the Irish were viewed as "the richest and most enduring source [of] demonology",[88] and as Aitken highlights, such "concerns for the political inscription of cultural texts and how they reflect dominant ideologies [has] turned geographers' attention to issues of resistance, contestation and subversion".[89] These considerations have also led to what Duncan and Ley underline as an "explicit recognition, problematisation and indeed theorisation of the varying relations between the empirical world and historically situated subjects".[90] In attempting, therefore, to (re)present the manner in which the O'Dwyers of Kilnamanagh encountered aspects of early modern English colonialism, clarifying the ideological context of the centralised state documents used has been a prominent feature of the research and writing exercises.[91]

Recovering the Gaelic-Irish 'voices' at the sites of interaction with the English colonial polity has proved to be an onerous task due essentially to the deficiencies of the evidence. The difficulties of examining the cultural production of those opposed to a dominant hegemony have been noted by Withers, who – by taking the example of the Scottish Highlands in his study of Gaelic reaction to cultural transformation – argues that the "relative paucity of historical documentation ... makes it difficult to understand the cultural productions *of* the Gaels as opposed to the cultural productions *imposed* on them".[92] He stresses, furthermore, that such a dearth in the historical record "raises historiographic issues", and cites the work of Richards on the Highland clearances to demonstrate how the problem of the "scantiness of historical material" has served to reinforce the idea that reaction was "undemonstrative and unresisting".[93] A further challenge lies in that "people at the lower levels of Gaelic society rarely appear in the surviving documentation".[94] O'Dowd underlines the broader historiographic challenge:

> there has been scarcely any detailed historical research into the nature and development of Gaelic society in the early modern

period. One reason for this is, of course, the unpromising nature of the sources. There are few Gaelic administrative records or chronicles which might permit an analysis of society from the native Irish viewpoint.[95]

Due largely, then, to the inauspicious extent and character of the sources, the research carried out for this work has been undertaken with reference to what is essentially an eclectic array of material. For the later sixteenth century, extensive use has been made of the diverse material contained within the *Carew Manuscripts*, *Ormond Deeds*, *Fiants* and *Annals of the Four Masters*, wherein valuable information regarding contemporary political, social and economic developments is recorded.[96] For the seventeenth century, the work focuses initially on interrogating the major central state documents preserved; namely the *State Papers*, *Patent Rolls* and *Civil Survey*.[97] By working with material such as the 'surrender and regrant' agreements recorded in the *Patent Rolls*, particular attention has been directed towards the manner in which the O'Dwyers attempted to redefine their localised, political, social and economic organisation in the context of an expanded English legal and socio-economic order.[98]

In exploring further questions concerning the fracture of the Gaelic-Irish polity and the (re)negotiation of identity in the context of aspects of colonialism, I have made particular use of two sources which in the extant literature have been seldom referred to; namely the *Egmont Manuscripts* and 1641 depositions.[99] Both reveal a series of crucial developments in the specific context of west Tipperary, which throw light on the impact of English legal, political and material practices on the region prior to the 1641 rebellion. Further material recorded points to the antithetical meanings inherent in the Gaelic-Irish response to both the changing proprietorial and ethnic make-up of the O'Dwyer lordship, and to the fracture of its traditional vertical alignments of social order. The origins and agendas of the insurrection of 1641, and the condition of Protestant settlers living in the environs of Cashel, and lands in neighbouring Kilnamanagh barony, are also indicated. Furthermore, in conjunction with both sources, the accounts of the Ormond biographer, Thomas Carte, pertaining to the outbreak of the 1641 rebellion in Tipperary, have been used to explore notions of English exclusivity and the perceivable reasons for the breakdown of social order.[100]

In attempting to recover the geographies of the colonised world of early modern west Tipperary, it is important to stress that the lack of evidence constitutes a recurring challenge. As Yeoh notes, "[i]t is often the case that simply not enough is known about colonised groups given the asymmetries in the historical record for anyone approaching the colonial period".[101] She argues that this does not prompt an atheoretical purging of existing empirical evidence but, rather, "a concerted effort to imaginatively mine the official archives and re-filter colonial discourse through 'other' lenses".[102] My own interrogation of the sources has especially involved an examination of their intrinsic 'contestation', which, in turn, has prompted new questions of the evidence. It is an approach which, as Yeoh observes, "takes seriously the hard work of rescuing the common people in colonised territories from the 'enormous condescension of posterity'", and "opens up the possibility of constructing [a variety of] historico-geographical accounts of the colonised world".[103] I have been particularly mindful of the pitfall of "overly ambitious theorizing", which, as Duncan points out, can serve to "obscure and bury even deeper indigenous knowledges and practices".[104]

A central concern throughout this work has been the recognition and interrogation of the diverse array of dominant and subaltern 'voices' of Gaelic-Irish accommodation and resistance that coexisted, interlocked and conflicted with each other in a multiplicity of ways through the course of early modern Ireland. Graham has argued convincingly that "recognition of heterogeneity is a precondition to any resolution of the contested nature of social understanding in Ireland".[105] In writing this work, it has become clear that even more challenging than the recognition of the heterogeneous nature of Irish society in the past for the historical geographer of the present is the conceptualisation of the emergence of that heterogeneity to reflect the contradictory essence of both the shared and bounded spaces of its peoples.

Notes

[1] Carte, *Ormond*, vol. 2, p. 267. Carte was the biographer of James Butler, first duke of Ormond, 1610-1688. The historic town of Cashel is situated in mid County Tipperary (see fig. 1.1, p. 9).

[2] The extent of surviving evidence is unusual for a Gaelic family and is discussed in more detail later in the chapter. It includes a notable number of revealing correspondences between the O'Dwyers and prominent New English individuals, as well as the state documentary remains of surrender and regrant agreements, rebel activities and pardons. The ancestral home of the O'Dwyers, Kilnamanagh, is also covered in the surviving remains of the official government surveys of the seventeenth century, the Civil Survey and Down Survey.

[3] *Civil Survey, County Tipperary*, vol. 2

[4] V.G. Kiernan, 1987, 'The Emergence of a Nation', in: C.H.E. Philpin (ed.), *Nationalism and Popular Protest in Ireland*, Past and Present Publications, Cambridge University Press, Cambridge, p. 18

[5] For a coherent review of the character of Irish historical geography, see B.J. Graham and L.J. Proudfoot, 1993, 'A Perspective on the Nature of Irish Historical Geography', in: *Idem.* (eds.), *An Historical Geography of Ireland*, Academic Press, London, pp. 1-18. Cf. W.J. Smyth, 1993, 'The Making of Ireland: Agendas and Perspectives in Cultural Geography', in: Graham and Proudfoot (eds.), *An Historical Geography of Ireland*, pp. 399-438

[6] A.R. Orme, 1970, *The World's Landscapes 4: Ireland*, Longman, London; F.H.A. Aalen, 1978, *Man and the Landscape in Ireland*, Academic Press, London. See also F. Mitchell, 1986, *The Shell Guide to Reading the Irish Landscape*, Country House, Dublin and F.H.A. Aalen, 1989, 'Imprints of the Past', in: D. Gillmor (ed.), *The Irish Countryside*, Wolfhound Press, Dublin, pp. 83-120. Cf. the recent work of J. Lydon, 1998, *The Making of Ireland: From Ancient Times to the Present*, Routledge, London

[7] Their works include: E. Estyn Evans, 1942, *Irish Heritage: The Landscape, the People and their Work*, Dundalgan Press, Dundalk; *Idem.*, 1981, *The Personality of Ireland: Habitat, Heritage and History* (Revised Edition), Blackstaff, Belfast; T. Jones Hughes, 1970, 'Town and Baile in Irish Place-Names', in: N. Stephens and R. Glasscock (eds.), *Irish Geographical Studies in honour of E. Estyn Evans*, Queen's University Belfast, Belfast, pp. 244-258; *Idem.*, 1984, 'Historical Geography of Ireland from *circa* 1700', *Irish Geography*, supplement to vol. 17, pp. 149-166; *Idem.*, 1985, 'Landholding and Settlement in County Tipperary in the Nineteenth Century', in: W. Nolan (ed.), *Tipperary: History and Society*, Geography Publications, Dublin, pp. 339-366. For commentary on these two prominent figures in Irish historical geography, see R.H. Buchanan, E. Jones and D. McCourt (eds.), 1971, *Man and his Habitat: Essays presented to Emryn Estyn Evans*, Routledge and K. Paul, London, and J.H. Andrews, 1988, 'Jones Hughes' Ireland: A Literary Quest', in: W.J. Smyth and K. Whelan (eds.), *Common Ground: Essays on the Historical Geography of Ireland presented to T. Jones Hughes*, Cork University Press, Cork, pp. 1-21

[8] Graham and Proudfoot, 'A Perspective on Irish historical geography', pp. 3-4

[9] See R.H. Buchanan, 1984, 'Historical Geography of Ireland Pre-1700', *Irish Geography*, supplement to vol. 17, pp. 129-148. Buchanan identifies the salient social and economic characteristics of Gaelic culture and the Ulster Plantation as the two central themes of

sixteenth and seventeenth-century Irish historical geography (see esp. pp. 138-140)

[10] W. Nolan (ed.), 1986, *The Shaping of Ireland: The Geographical Perspective*, Mercier Press, Cork; Smyth and Whelan (eds.), *Common Ground*

[11] W.J. Smyth, 1988, 'Society and Settlement in Seventeenth Century Ireland: The Evidence of the 1659 Census', in: *Idem.* and Whelan (eds.), *Common Ground*, pp. 55-83

[12] See, for example, W.J. Smyth, 1985, 'Property, Patronage and Population – Reconstructing the Human Geography of Mid-Seventeenth Century County Tipperary', in: Nolan (ed.), *Tipperary: History and Society*, pp. 104-138. My own undergraduate dissertation at Trinity College Dublin earlier built upon Smyth's work and was especially concerned with interrogating the socio-economic impacts of English colonialism in west Tipperary in the seventeenth century; see J. Morrissey, 1996, *Landscape and Society in Seventeenth Century West Tipperary*, Unpublished B.A. Thesis, Trinity College, University of Dublin

[13] P.J. Duffy, 1981 'The Territorial Organisation of Gaelic Landownership and its Transformation in County Monaghan, 1591-1640', *Irish Geography*, vol. 14, pp. 1-23; *Idem.*, 1988, 'The Evolution of Estate Properties in South Ulster, 1600-1800', in: Smyth and Whelan (eds.), *Common Ground*, pp. 110-123; W. Nolan, 1979, *Fassadinin: Land, Settlement and Society in South-East Ireland*, 1600-1850, Geography Publications, Dublin. See also A. Simms, 1988, 'Core and Periphery in Medieval Europe: The Irish Experience in a Wider Context', in: Smyth and Whelan (eds.), *Common Ground*, pp. 22-40; M. Hennessy, 1985, 'Parochial Organisation in Medieval Tipperary', in: Nolan (ed.), *Tipperary: History and Society*, pp. 60-70

[14] See, for example, M. McCarthy, 1999, 'Cross-Sectional Reconstructions of Historic Urban Landscapes: An Examination of the Nature and Comprehensiveness of a Mid-Seventeenth-Century Survey and Valuation", *Irish Archives*, 6 (1), pp. 3-13 or *Idem.*, 2000, 'Turning a World Upside Down: The Metamorphosis of Property, Settlement and Society in the City of Cork during the 1640s and 1650s', *Irish Geography*, 33 (1), pp. 37-55

[15] Graham and Proudfoot's edited work *An Historical Geography of Ireland* represented a notable departure from this in 1993.

[16] See, for example, the recent comments of M. McCarthy, 2002, 'Writing Ireland's Historical Geographies', *Journal of Historical Geography*, 28, 4, pp. 535-536

[17] On this point, see L.J. Proudfoot, 2000, 'Hybrid Space? Self and Other in Narratives of Landownership in Nineteenth-Century Ireland', *Journal of Historical Geography*, 26, 2, pp. 203-204. Proudfoot's approach serves to demonstrate the false rigidity of conventional readings of 'coloniser' and 'colonised' and accommodates an exploration of a hybrid and heterogeneous 'colonial' setting.

[18] L.J. Proudfoot, 1993, 'Regionalism and Localism: Religious Change and Social Protest, *c*.1700 to *c*.1900', in: Graham and Proudfoot (eds.), *An Historical Geography of Ireland*, p. 185

[19] See, for example, B. Graham, 1997, 'Ireland and Irishness: Place, Culture and Identity', in: *Idem.* (ed.), *In Search of Ireland: A Cultural Geography*, Routledge, London, pp. 1-15, Proudfoot, 'Hybrid Space', pp. 203-221 and W.J. Smyth, 1997, 'A Plurality of Irelands: Regions, Societies and Mentalities', in: Graham (ed.), *In Search of Ireland*, pp. 19-42

[20] The study of early modern Ireland received a comprehensive and rejuvenated treatment in the issue of the 'Early Modern Ireland' volume of The New History of Ireland series in 1976;

CULTURAL INTERACTION IN EARLY MODERN IRELAND

see T.W. Moody, F.X. Martin and F.J. Byrne (eds.), 1976, *A New History of Ireland III: Early Modern Ireland 1534-1691*, Clarendon Press, Oxford. Its publication was brought about in part to address the diminishing importance of work specifically concerned with Tudor and Stuart Ireland. Other important works in Irish history of the early modern period include Brady and Gillespie's edited collection of essays, *Natives and Newcomers*, a significant examination of Irish colonial society prior to the 1641 Rebellion; see C. Brady and R. Gillespie (eds.), 1986, *Natives and Newcomers: Essays on the Making of Irish Colonial Society, 1534-1641*, Irish Academic Press, Dublin. The works of Bradshaw, Brady, Caball, Canny, Ellis, Gillespie and many others all constitute noted contributions to early modern Irish history. See, for example: B. Bradshaw, 1998, 'The English Reformation and Identity Formation in Wales and Ireland', in: *Idem.* and P. Roberts (eds.), *British Consciousness and Identity: The Making of Britain 1533-1707*, Cambridge University Press, Cambridge, pp. 43-111; C. Brady, 1996, 'England's Defence and Ireland's Reform: The Dilemma of the Irish Viceroys, 1541-1641', in: B. Bradshaw and J. Morrill (eds.), *The British Problem, c.1534-1707: State Formation in the Atlantic Archipelago*, MacMillan Press Ltd., Basingstoke, pp. 89-117; M. Caball, 1994, 'Providence and Exile in Early Seventeenth-Century Ireland', *Irish Historical Studies*, vol. 29, no. 114, pp. 174-188; N. Canny, 1995, 'What Really Happened in Ireland in 1641?', in: J.H. Ohlmeyer (ed.), *Ireland from Independence to Occupation 1641-1660*, Cambridge University Press, Cambridge, pp. 24-42; S.G. Ellis, 1998, *Ireland in the Age of the Tudors, 1447-1603: English Expansion and the End of Gaelic Rule*, Longman, London; and R. Gillespie, 1993, 'Explorers, Exploiters and Entrepreneurs: Early Modern Ireland and its Context, 1500-1700', in: Graham and Proudfoot (eds.), *An Historical Geography of Ireland*, pp. 123-157

[21] See, for example, P.J. Duffy, D. Edwards and E. FitzPatrick (eds.), 2001, *Gaelic Ireland c.1250-c.1650: Land, Lordship and Settlement*, Four Courts Press, Dublin

[22] M. Heffernan, 1997, 'Editorial. The Future of Historical Geography', *Journal of Historical Geography*, 23, 1, p. 2

[23] McCarthy, 'Writing Ireland's Historical Geographies', pp. 545-546. Nash and Graham have alerted us to the danger of defining "the limits of historical geography against the encroachments of other areas of research", and have pointed out conversely that historical geography has always been hybrid, interdisciplinary and eclectic; see C. Nash and B. Graham, 2000, 'The Making of Modern Historical Geographies', in: B. Graham and C. Nash (eds.), *Modern Historical Geographies*, Prentice Hall, Harlow, p. 4

[24] D. Wishart, 1997, 'The Selectivity of Historical Representation', *Journal of Historical Geography*, 23, 2, p. 111

[25] *Ibid.*, p. 117

[26] For commentary on the polemical nature of narratives written often exclusively from the perspective of 'native' or 'planter', see N. Canny, 1988, *Kingdom and Colony: Ireland in the Atlantic World 1560-1800*, John Hopkins University Press, Baltimore, pp. 135-141. See also S. Regan, 1992, 'Ireland's Field Day', *History Workshop Journal*, 33, pp. 25-37, esp. pp. 28-30

[27] Quoted in: S. Hutton and P. Stewart, 1991, 'Introduction. Perspectives on Irish History and Social Studies', in: *Idem.* (eds.), *Ireland's Histories: Aspects of State, Society and Ideology*, Routledge, London, p. 1

[28] There is a large body of material that deals with the subject of the place of the metanarrative in the representation of Ireland's past. See, for example, Graham and Proudfoot, 'A Perspective on the Nature of Irish Historical Geography', pp. 4-8; Smyth, 'The Making of Ireland', pp. 427-433; S. Richards, 1991, 'Polemics on the Irish Past: The 'Return to the Source' in Irish Literary Revivals', *History Workshop Journal*, 31, pp. 120-135; and Hutton and Stewart, 'Perspectives on Irish History', pp. 1-10

[29] B.J. Graham, 1994, 'No Place of the Mind: Contested Protestant Representations of Ulster', *Ecumene*, 1 (3), pp. 257-281; see esp. pp. 259-260, 266-267, 272-276. A number of works implicitly display a select empathy with either a native, or planter, viewpoint. For contrasting analyses of the contribution of the Protestant settler population in Ireland's historical development, for example, cf. the nationalist perspective of W.F.T. Butler, 1917, *Confiscations in Irish History*, Talbot Press, Dublin or *Idem.*, 1925, *Gleanings from Irish History*, Longmans, Green, London, and Beckett's avowed attempt to emphasise the progress of their enterprise: J.C. Beckett, 1976, *The Anglo-Irish Tradition*, Faber and Faber, London

[30] Hutton and Stewart, 'Perspectives on Irish History', p. 1

[31] D.W. Meinig, 1982, 'Geographical Analysis of Imperial Expansion', in: A.R.H. Baker and M. Billinge (eds.), *Period and Place: Research Methods in Historical Geography*, Cambridge University Press, Cambridge, p. 71

[32] For a coherent analysis of the impact of revisionism on Irish historical scholarship, see H. Kearney, 1991, 'The Irish and Their History', *History Workshop Journal*, 31, pp. 149-155. Cf. D. Cairns, 1991, 'Recent Irish Histories', *History Workshop Journal*, 31, pp. 156-162

[33] R.F. Foster, 1989, *Modern Ireland 1600-1972*, Penguin, London

[34] J.C. Beckett's *The Making of Modern Ireland 1603-1923* (Faber and Faber, London, 1981 – first pub. 1966) represents an earlier, equally comprehensive and useful reference work.

[35] Foster, *Modern Ireland*, p. 1. Cf. the recent British context of historical developments in Ireland in M. Nicholls, 1999, *A History of the Modern British Isles, 1529-1603: The Two Kingdoms*, Blackwell, Oxford

[36] Graham, 'No Place of the Mind', p. 260

[37] See, for example, the debate between Bradshaw and Ellis: S.G. Ellis, 1986, 'Nationalist Historiography and the English and Gaelic Worlds in the Late Middle Ages', *Irish Historical Studies*, vol. 25, no. 97, pp. 1-18; B. Bradshaw, 1989, 'Nationalism and Historical Scholarship in Modern Ireland', *Irish Historical Studies*, vol. 26, no. 104, pp. 329-351; S.G. Ellis, 1991, 'Historiographical Debate. Representations of the Past in Ireland: Whose Past and Whose Present?', *Irish Historical Studies*, vol. 27, no. 108, pp. 289-308. See also R.F. Foster, 1986, 'We are all Revisionists Now', *Irish Review*, 1, pp. 1-5 and T.J. Dunne, 1992, 'New Histories: Beyond "Revisionism"', *Irish Review*, 12, pp. 1-12

[38] See, for example, the comments of Cairns, 'Recent Irish Histories', pp. 156-162. Cf. S.G. Ellis, 1996, 'Writing Irish History: Revisionism, Colonialism, and the British Isles', *Irish Review*, 19, pp. 1-21, D.G. Boyce and A. O'Day (eds.), 1996, *Modern Irish History: Revisionism and the Revisionist Controversy*, Routledge, London and McCarthy, 'Writing Ireland's Historical Geographies', pp. 538-541

[39] B. Cunningham and R. Gillespie, 1990, 'Englishmen in Sixteenth-Century Irish Annals', *Irish Economic and Social History*, XVII, p. 5

[40] This binary conceptualisation, for example, is writ large in McCarthy's recent review of the evolving sub-discipline of historical geography in Ireland. See McCarthy, 'Writing Ireland's Historical Geographies', esp. pp. 535-538

[41] N.S. Momaday, 1987, 'Personal Reflections', in: C. Martin (ed.), *The American Indian and the Problem of History*, Oxford University Press, New York, pp. 156-161

[42] Regan, 'Ireland's Field Day', p. 36

[43] Quoted in: *ibid.*, p. 25

[44] Wishart, 'The Selectivity of Historical Representation', p. 114

[45] *Ibid.*, p. 116. For further comment on this point, cf. D. Demeritt, 1994, 'Ecology, Objectivity and Critique in Writings on Nature and Human Societies', *Journal of Historical Geography*, 20, 1, pp. 22-37 and W. Cronon, 1994, 'Comment. Cutting Loose or Running Around', *Journal of Historical Geography*, 20, 1, pp. 38-43

[46] S. Hall, 1997, 'Cultural Identity and Diaspora', excerpts reprint. in: L. MacDowell (ed.), *Undoing Place? A Geographical Reader*, Routledge, London, pp. 231-232, 234. Jacobs, too, notes that in writing the cultural geographies of the past one is not "outside an unavoidable politics of power"; see J.M. Jacobs, 1996, *Edge of Empire: Postcolonialism and the City*, Routledge, London, p. 8

[47] J. Duncan and D. Ley, 1993, 'Representing the Place of Culture', in: *Idem* (eds.), *Place/Culture/Representation*, Routledge, London p. 13. On this point, cf. S. Daniels, 1989, 'Marxism, Culture and the Duplicity of Landscape', in: R. Peet and N. Thrift (eds.), *New Models in Geography, Vol. 2*, Unwin Hyman, London, pp. 196-220 and M. Ogborn, 1996, 'History, Memory and the Politics of Landscape and Space: Work in Historical Geography from Autumn '94 to Autumn '95', *Progress in Human Geography*, vol. 20, no. 2, pp. 222-229

[48] The early modern barony boundary of Kilnamanagh is divided into upper and lower sections today.

[49] W.J. Smyth, 1983, 'Landholding Changes, Kinship Networks and Class Transformation in Rural Ireland: A Case-Study from County Tipperary', *Irish Geography*, vol. 16, p. 16

[50] Jones Hughes, 'Landholding and Settlement in County Tipperary', p. 339. There have been a number of localised historical studies of Tipperary at the county, barony and parish levels; the prevalence of which prompted the establishment of the *Tipperary Historical Journal* in 1988. See, for example: D.G. Marnane, 1997, 'Writing the Past: Tipperary History and Historians', *Tipperary Historical Journal*, 10, pp. 1-41; T.P. Power, 1993, *Land, Politics and Society in 18th Century Tipperary*, Clarendon Press, Oxford; M. Hallinan (ed.), 1993, *Tipperary County: People and Places*, Kincora Press, Dublin; W.G. Skehan, 1993, *Cashel and Emly Heritage*, Abbey Books, Portlaoise, Co. Laois; P.C. Power, 1989, *History of South Tipperary*, Mercier Press, Cork; Nolan (ed.), *Tipperary: History and Society*; D.G. Marnane, 1985, *Land and Violence: A History of West Tipperary from 1660*, Fitzpatrick Bros., Tipperary; M. Callanan, 1938, *Records of Four Tipperary Septs*, O'Gorman Ltd., Galway; and, in the context of Kilnamanagh, M. O'Dwyer, 1933, *The O'Dwyers of Kilnamanagh: The History of an Irish Sept*, John Murray, London

[51] F. Driver and R. Samuel, 1995, 'Editorial. Rethinking the Idea of Place', *History Workshop Journal*, 39, p. vi

[52] For further exploration of the multiple meanings of 'place', see for example: D. Massey,

1997, 'A Global Sense of Place', reprint. in: T. Barnes and D. Gregory (eds.), *Reading Human Geography: The Poetics and Politics of Inquiry*, Arnold, London, pp. 322-323; Duncan and Ley, 'Representing the Place of Culture', p. 12; and T. Cresswell, 1996, *In Place/Out of Place: Geography, Ideology and Transgression*, University of Minnesota Press, Minneapolis. For wider comment, see: G. Bridge, 1997, 'Guest Editorial. Towards a Situated Universalism: On Strategic Rationality and 'Local Theory'', *Environment and Planning D: Society and Space*, 15, pp. 633-639; *Idem.*, 2000, 'Rationality, Ethics, and Space: On Situated Universalism and the Self-Interested Acknowledgement of 'Difference', *Environment and Planning D: Society and Space*, 18, pp. 519-535; G. Henderson, 1998, 'Review Article. "Landscape is Dead, Long Live Landscape": A Handbook for Sceptics', *Journal of Historical Geography*, 24, 1, pp. 94-100; A. Sayer and M. Storper, 1997, 'Guest Editorial. Ethics Unbound: For a Normative Turn in Social Theory', *Environment and Planning D: Society and Space*, 15, pp. 1-17; and C. Katz, 1996, 'Towards Minor Theory', *Environment and Planning D: Society and Space*, 14, pp. 487-499

[53] E. Said, 1979, *Orientalism: Western Conceptions of the Orient*, Vintage, New York; see esp. chap. 1

[54] *Idem.*, 1989, 'Representing the Colonised: Anthropology's Interlocutors', *Critical Inquiry*, 15, p. 218

[55] On this point, see the recent comments of A. Lester, 2000, 'Historical Geographies of Imperialism', in: Graham and Nash (eds.), *Modern Historical Geographies*, pp. 102-103

[56] Jacobs, *Edge of Empire*, p. 5

[57] J. Duncan and D. Cosgrove, 1995, 'Editorial. Colonialism and Postcolonialism in the Former British Empire', *Ecumene*, 2 (2), p. 127

[58] *Ibid.*

[59] Jacobs, *Edge of Empire*, p. 6

[60] In this sense, Massey's concept of the dualism of the 'specificity' and 'global sense' of place (see Massey, 'A Global Sense of Place', p. 322) has been transcended by the notion of networks/routes and fluidity/inter-connectivity of place and the local. See, for example, A. Lester, 2002, 'British Settler Discourse and the Circuits of Empire', *History Workshop Journal*, 51 (1), pp. 24-48. Cf. C. Nash, 2002, 'Genealogical Identities', *Environment and Planning D: Society and Space*, 20, pp. 27-52

[61] For a useful collection of essays concerning the intricate, fluid spaces of colonialism, see the special issue 'Colonial Geographies: Accommodation and Resistance', in *Historical Geography*, vol. 27. Cf. A. McClintock, 1995, *Imperial Leather: Race, Gender and Sexuality in the Colonial Contest*, Routledge, London, Proudfoot, 'Hybrid Space?', pp. 203-221 and Katz, 'Towards Minor Theory', pp. 487-499

[62] For example, through the course of the work, the experiences of neighbouring baronies throughout County Tipperary and beyond are shown to be inextricably linked to developments 'within' Kilnamanagh, and are accordingly posited as integral parts of developments therein.

[63] Proudfoot, 'Hybrid Space?', p. 204

[64] B.S.A. Yeoh, 2000, 'Historical Geographies of the Colonised World', in: Graham and Nash (eds.), *Modern Historical Geographies*, p. 162

[65] R.C. Harris, 1996, 'Classics in Human Geography Revisited. R.C. Harris, 1971, 'Theory and Synthesis in Historical Geography', *Canadian Geographer*, 15, pp. 157-172: Author's

Response', *Progress in Human Geography*, vol. 20, no. 2, p. 200

[66] D. Cairns and S. Richards, 1988, *Writing Ireland: Colonialism, Nationalism and Culture*, Manchester University Press, Manchester, p. 1. This working elementary relationship is, of course, problematic. A recurring theme of this work is a problematisation and retheorisation of the inadequacies and complexities of this simplified coloniser/colonised relationship. For some of the shortcomings of viewing early modern Ireland in a strictly colonial context, see: D. Kiberd, 1997, 'Modern Ireland: Postcolonial or European?', in: S. Murray (ed.), *Not on any Map: Essays on Postcoloniality and Cultural Nationalism*, University of Exeter Press, Exeter, pp. 81-100; Ellis, 'Writing Irish History', pp. 1-21; Foster, *Modern Ireland*, esp. chap. 1; and K.S. Bottigheimer, 1978, 'Kingdom and Colony: Ireland in the Westward Enterprise 1536-1660', in: K.R. Andrews, N.P. Canny and P.E.H. Hair (eds.), *The Westward Enterprise: English Activities in Ireland, The Atlantic and America, 1480-1650*, Liverpool University Press, Liverpool, pp. 45-64

[67] Quoted in: Cairns and Richards, *Writing Ireland*, p. 1

[68] S. Sharkey, 1997, 'Irish Cultural Studies and the Politics of Irish Studies', in: J. McGuigan (ed.), *Cultural Methodologies*, Sage, London, p. 172

[69] J. Ruane, 1992, 'Colonialism and the Interpretation of Irish Historical Development', in: M. Silverman and P.H. Gulliver (eds.), *Approaching the Past: Historical Anthropology through Irish Case Studies*, Columbia University Press, New York, pp. 294, 319

[70] Lester, 'Historical Geographies of Imperialism', pp. 100-103. See also *Idem.*, 1998, *Colonial Discourse and the Colonisation of Queen Adelaide Province, South Africa*, Historical Geography Research Series, 34, HGRG, London, pp. 94-100

[71] Yeoh, 'Historical Geographies of the Colonised World', p. 146

[72] P. Routledge, 1997, 'A Spatiality of Resistances: Theory and Practice in Nepal's Revolution of 1990', in: S. Pile and M. Keith (eds.), *Geographies of Resistance*, Routledge, London, p. 70

[73] For a useful introduction to postcolonial theory, see R.J.C. Young, 2001, *Postcolonialism: An Historical Introduction*, Blackwell, Oxford, esp. chaps. 1, 5, 24-28. For its inherent tensions and shortcomings, see the comments of J. Crush, 1994, 'Post-Colonialism, De-Colonisation and Geography', in: A. Godlewska and N. Smith (eds.), *Geography and Empire*, Blackwell, Oxford, pp. 333-350, D. Kennedy, 1996, 'Imperial History and Post-Colonial Theory', *Journal of Imperial and Commonwealth History*, 24, pp. 345-363 and A. Lester, 1998, ''Otherness' and the Frontiers of Empire: The Eastern Cape Colony, 1806-c.1850', *Journal of Historical Geography*, 24, 1, pp. 2-19. For an excellent engagement with the connections between postcolonialism as a discourse and geographical analysis, see A. Blunt and C. McEwan (eds.), 2002, *Postcolonial Geographies*, Continuum, London

[74] M.L. Pratt, 1992, *Imperial Eyes: Travel Writing and Transculturation*, Routledge, London, p. 7

[75] Yeoh, 'Historical Geographies of the Colonised World', p. 149; see also pp. 150-152, 162-165

[76] Pratt, *Imperial Eyes*, p. 7

[77] Meinig, 'Geographical Analysis of Imperial Expansion', p. 71

[78] Henderson, 'Landscape is Dead, Long Live Landscape', p. 94

[79] This notion has been prevalent since the mid-1970s. See, for example: D. Lowenthal, 1975,

'Past Time, Present Place: Landscape and Memory', *The Geographical Review*, 65, pp. 1-36; *Idem.*, 1979, 'Age and Artifact: Dilemmas and Appreciation', in: D.W. Meinig (ed.), *The Interpretation of Ordinary Landscapes*, Oxford University Press, New York, pp. 103-128; J. Appleton, 1975, *The Experience of Landscape*, John Wiley and Sons, New York; Y.-F. Tuan, 1977, *Space and Place: The Perspective of Experience*, University of Minnesota Press, Minneapolis; and *Idem.*, 1979, 'Thought and Landscape', in: Meinig (ed.), *Interpretation of Ordinary Landscapes*, pp. 89-102. See also: C.W.J. Withers, 1988, *Gaelic Scotland: The Transformation of a Culture Region*, Routledge, London, esp. chap. 1; F. Fanon, 1967, *The Wretched of the Earth*, trans. C. Farrington, Penguin, Harmondsworth; C. Geertz, 1973, *The Interpretation of Cultures*, Basic Books, New York; J. Duncan, 1980, 'The Superorganic in American Cultural Geography', *Annals, Association of American Geography*, 70 (2), pp. 181-198; and E. Said, 1993, *Culture and Imperialism*, Routledge, London

[80] Henderson, 'Landscape is Dead, Long Live Landscape', p. 94

[81] Quoted in: J.W. Foster, 1991, *Colonial Consequences: Essays in Irish Literature and Culture*, Lilliput Press, Dublin, p. 152

[82] *Cal. S.P. Ire.*, 24 vols.; *Cal. pat. rolls Ire., Hen. VIII-Chas. I*, 3 vols.; *Cal. pat. rolls, Jas. I*; *Fiants Ire.*, 3 vols.; *Civil Survey, County Tipperary*, vol. 2

[83] J. Duncan, 1990, *The City as Text: The Politics of Landscape Interpretation*, Cambridge University Press, Cambridge, chap. 1

[84] *Ibid.*, pp. 18-19

[85] See, for example, W.J. Smyth, 1992, 'Making the Documents of Conquest Speak: The Transformation of Property, Society and Settlement in 17th Century Counties Tipperary and Kilkenny', in: Silverman and Gulliver (eds.), *Approaching the Past*, pp. 236-237

[86] N. Canny, *Kingdom and Colony: Ireland in the Atlantic World*, p. 141; R. Gillespie, 1991, *The Transformation of the Irish Economy 1550-1700*, Studies in Irish Economic and Social History 6, The Economic and Social History Society of Ireland, p. 3

[87] N. Thomas, 1994, *Colonialism's Culture: Anthropology, Travel and Government*, Polity Press, Cambridge, p. 2

[88] S. Daniels, 1993, *Fields of Vision: Landscape Imagery and National Identity in England and the U.S.*, Polity Press, Cambridge, p. 6

[89] S.C. Aitken, 1997, 'Analysis of Texts: Armchair Theory and Couch-Potato Geography', in: Flowerdew and Martin (eds.), *Methods in Human Geography*, p. 200

[90] Duncan and Ley, 'Representing the Place of Culture', p. 8

[91] Issues of authenticity, symbolism and meaning in the sources are discussed at relevant points in the text.

[92] Withers, *Gaelic Scotland*, p. 327

[93] *Ibid.*; E. Richards, 1985, *A History of the Highland Clearances Volume 2: Emigration, Protest, Reasons*, Beckenham, p. 389

[94] M. O'Dowd, 1986, 'Gaelic Economy and Society', in: C. Brady and R. Gillespie (eds.), *Natives and Newcomers: Essays on the Making of Irish Colonial Society, 1534-1641*, Irish Academic Press, Dublin, p. 129

[95] *Ibid.*, p. 120. For further commentary on the surviving evidence, see: R.W. Dudley Edwards and M. O'Dowd, 1985, *Sources for Early Modern Irish History, 1534-1641*, Cambridge University Press, Cambridge; W. Nolan, 1982, *Tracing the Past: Sources for*

CULTURAL INTERACTION IN EARLY MODERN IRELAND

Local Studies in the Republic of Ireland, Geography Publications, Dublin; H. Wood, 1919, *A Guide to the Public Records Deposited in the P.R.O. of Ireland*, I.M.C., Dublin; and *Idem.*, 1938, 'The Tragedy of the Irish Public Records', *Irish Genealogist*, vol. 1, no. 3, pp. 67-71. For a selection of some of the sources, see J. Carty (ed.), 1951, *Ireland from the Flight of the Earls to Grattan's Parliament 1607-1782: A Documentary Record*, C.J. Fallon Ltd., Dublin
[96] *Cal. Carew MSS*, 6 vols.; *Cal. Ormond Deeds*, 6 vols.; *Fiants Ire.*, 3 vols.; *A.F.M.*, 7 vols.. The *Carew MSS* (1515-1624) and *Ormond Deeds* (1172-1603) comprise a series of documents respecting assorted and unconnected events in late medieval and early modern Ireland. In the context of this work, both volumes nevertheless serve to furnish occasional papers relating to the O'Dwyers and west Tipperary. The *Fiants* record a series of pardons administered in the Tudor period (1521-1603) to various individuals throughout Ireland for a variety of transgressions against the crown. They have been utilised in this work to explore the internal structure of the O'Dwyer lordship of Kilnamanagh and the various dynamics and forms of resistance transcending it in the late sixteenth century. The *Annals*, written by early seventeenth-century Franciscan monks, constitute a chronology of Ireland, from earliest times to 1616, produced under the auspices of the Counter-Reformation, and as part of Catholic Ireland's attempt to underline its historical legitimacy. They are used here to outline how the O'Dwyers were influenced by aspects of an emerging Catholic nationality; particularly the impact of the Ulster confederacy in the late sixteenth and early seventeenth centuries.
[97] *Cal. S.P. Ire.*, 24 vols.; *Cal. pat. rolls Ire., Hen. VIII-Chas. I*, 3 vols.; *Cal. pat. rolls, Jas. I*; *Civil Survey, County Tipperary*, vol. 2. All three sources have served in this work to provide valuable information regarding specific political, economic and social developments in early modern west Tipperary. The wealth of material recorded has also furnished crucial evidence of the ideological visioning of colonial practices in contemporary Ireland; particularly the reading of the cultural Other and the construction of New English exclusivism. Other sources consulted include: *Cal. Clarendon Papers*, vol. 1; *Census Ire., 1659*; *Hastings MSS*, vol. iv; *Hearth Money Records 1665-1666/7*; and *Mansfield Papers*. Again, the information contained in these diverse collections of documents, lists and surveys relate to a number of different themes, which will be explored in due course in relevant chapters.
[98] Throughout the work, reference is also made to a diverse collection of documents housed in the National Library of Ireland (N.L.I.) and National Archives of Ireland (N.A.I.), recording numerous national and localised proceedings of the early modern period. See the 'manuscript sources' section of the bibliography below, for a brief description of the relevant material to this work housed in both repositories.
[99] *Egmont MSS*, 2 vols.; T.C.D., MS 821
[100] Carte, *Ormond*, vol. 2. The political and social commentaries of prominent contemporaries such as Edmund Spenser, Sir John Davies, Geoffrey Keating and Richard Hadsor, and anonymous works such as *Pairlement Chloinne Tomáis* and 'The Supplication', have also been referred to and cited at various junctures of the text: E. Spenser, *A View of the Present State of Ireland* (*c*.1596), ed. W.L. Renwick, Clarendon Press, Oxford, 1970; *Idem.*, 'A Brief Note of Ireland' (*c*.1598), reprint. E.A. Greenlaw *et al.* (eds.), *The Works of Edmund Spenser: A Variorum Edition*, vol. 10, pp. 233-245, 11 vols., John Hopkins University Press, Baltimore, 1932-1949; J. Davies, *A Discovery of the True Causes Why Ireland was Never*

Entirely Subdued and Brought Under Obedience of the Crown of England until the Beginning of His Majesty's Happy Reign (1612), reprint. J.G. Barry, Irish University Press, Shannon, 1969; G. Keating, *Foras Feasa ar Éirinn: The History of Ireland (c.*1633), ed. D. Comyn and P.S. Dineen, 4 vols., Irish Texts Society, London, 1902-1914; V. Treadwell, 1997, 'New Light on Richard Hadsor, I: Richard Hadsor and the Authorship of 'Advertisements for Ireland', 1622/3', *Irish Historical Studies*, vol. 30, no. 119, pp. 305-336; J. McLaughlin, 1997, 'New Light on Richard Hadsor, II: Richard Hadsor's 'Discourse' on the Irish State, 1604', *Irish Historical Studies*, vol. 30, no. 119, pp. 337-353; *Pairlement Chloinne Tomáis*, ed. N.J.A. Williams, Dublin Institute for Advanced Studies, Dublin, 1981; 'The Supplication of the Blood of the English Most Lamentably Murdered in Ireland, Cryeng Out of the Yearth for Revenge (1598)', intro. W. Maley, 1995, *Analecta Hibernica*, 36, pp. 1-77

[101] Yeoh, 'Historical Geographies of the Colonised World', p. 149

[102] *Ibid.*

[103] *Ibid.*, pp. 149, 162. On this point, cf. T. Ploszajska, 2000, 'Historiographies of Geography and Empire', in: Graham and Nash (eds.), *Modern Historical Geographies*, pp. 121-126

[104] J. Duncan, 1999, 'Complicity and Resistance in the Colonial Archive: Some Issues of Method and Theory in Historical Geography', *Historical Geography*, 27, p. 127

[105] Graham, 'No Place of the Mind', p. 260

Chapter 2

Kilnamanagh and the Advent of
New English Order

Other Irishmen's countries ... as O'Kenedy and O'Dwyre and the
Carrowlles, doth bear galloglasses [hired soldiers] to his Majesty
without contradiction, which were wont to be mortal enemies to the
English pale. So as in all the circuit before mentioned is contained
half the realm, which with small charge will be brought to civil
obedience; and if all the countries were made counties that the law
might have his course, then they would prosper; for the sheriffs
would put back their Irish laws and election of captains – *Sir Thomas
Cusake, Lord Chancellor of Ireland, 1553* 1

Sir Thomas Cusake alludes above to one of the central agendas of Tudor
expansion in Ireland, that of reforming the Gaelic lordships such as the
O'Dwyers of Kilnamanagh. The process was to become a long and conflicting
one as the New English of the sixteenth century embarked on an often
inconsistent campaign to establish crown control in an island characterised by
a patchwork of self-governing Gaelic-Irish and Old English lordships. The
political and military efforts of successive New English administrations in
Ireland sought to bring about reform through the systematic extension of the
common law and English political and material practices. They were faced,
however, with the challenge of extending political control beyond the frontiers
left as a legacy of the earlier Anglo-Norman (later known as the Old English)
conquest; frontiers that had retreated eastwards towards the Pale from the mid-
fourteenth century as the Gaelic-Irish reasserted and consolidated territorial
and political control. This chapter initially presents the barony of Kilnamanagh
as one such frontier of Gaelic-Irish and Old English worlds in late medieval
Ireland. Subsequently the region's human geographies as a contact zone of
early modern New English colonialism are explored, particularly the manner
in which the Gaelic O'Dwyers endeavoured to simultaneously both resist and
situate themselves in the new political, economic and social context of English
authority in the late sixteenth century.

Kilnamanagh and the Frontier in Medieval Ireland

In the aftermath of the coming of the Anglo-Normans to Ireland in 1169, the colonisers, having establishing themselves primarily in the south and east of the country, attempted to consolidate and extend their territory in the thirteenth and early fourteenth centuries. In County Tipperary, the Slieve Phelim mountains and Kilnamanagh hills had formed a natural physical barrier to their advance, and Kilnamanagh barony can be visualised as a microcosm of the frontier of their territorial and political extent and influence throughout Ireland at this point.[2] North-westwards, beyond this frontier, Gaelic-Irish autonomy prevailed, and indeed a brief inspection of the proprietorial geography of later mid-seventeenth century Tipperary highlights the enduring significance of this contact zone as a hybrid area separating the south and east of the county – dominated by the Anglo-Normans (or more specifically Old English at this point) – from the north and west – largely controlled by the Gaelic-Irish.[3]

Despite the physical barrier of the Slieve Phelim mountains, the Anglo-Normans attempted to strengthen their territorial and political realm in Tipperary in the late thirteenth century by extending their influence and control to the lowland regions of Kilnamanagh. Between c.1280 and 1317, the Augustinian Priory and Hospital of St. John the Baptist outside the New Gate, Dublin, had established a holding of 148 acres in the parish of Clogher, in the south-east of Kilnamanagh.[4] Such monastic houses as St. John the Baptist played an essential role in the colonisation process of the Anglo-Normans in that they facilitated the crystallisation of the parish network as the primary basis of political order and administration, especially in those areas like Kilnamanagh which remained controlled by the Gaelic-Irish.[5] At this site, too, a mill controlled by the Priory of St. John the Baptist had been set up by 1321, which would have constituted another influential component in the dissemination of Anglo-Norman material practices and arable-based economy in an area dominated by the pastoral farming characteristic of the Gaelic-Irish.[6] By the early fourteenth century, too, another Anglo-Norman monastic house of the Order of Knights Templars had been established in Clonoulty parish, again in the south-eastern lowlands of the barony.[7] Despite, then, the limited proprietorial penetration of the Anglo-Normans to Kilnamanagh, the religious houses guaranteed their influence and impact, and the church – particularly in later centuries – became an important point of contact between the two cultures.[8]

In the lowland areas to the south and east of Kilnamanagh, the powerful Anglo-Norman family, the Butlers – from their base in the geographically contiguous lordship of Ormond – began to effect a noted and significant impact from the thirteenth century.[9] By c.1290, they had gained control of important tracts of land in the lowland regions of Clogher and Ballintemple parishes to the southeast of the barony, and had begun to set up 'rents' to 'Irish tenants'.[10] In 1303, they had also established themselves in Moyaliff parish (to the east of the barony), and by 1307 they had founded a manor and borough there.[11] From the 1307 manorial extent of Moyaliff, it is seen that at this point a thriving manor and market borough had been set up that included a manor house, parish centre, borough court and bailiff, and fifty-six burgesses, together with major free tenants, farmers and knights paying rents and services to the lord of the manor.[12] The manorial extent also points to the manner in which links were being forged with surrounding areas through trade; evidenced by the directive to burgesses to carry corn and iron to the neighbouring market town of Cashel approximately ten miles due south.[13] The manor and borough were situated on the east bank of the Clodiagh river, which facilitated the establishment of burgesses, mills and small boat transport, but lay vulnerably at the base of the Kilnamanagh hills, contiguous to the O'Dwyer strongholds to the west, which was to prove disastrous as the fourteenth century progressed.

Subsequent to the combined difficulties of war, plague and famine affecting the Anglo-Norman colonies in Ireland in the early fourteenth century, the 1338 manorial extent of Moyaliff reflects the degree to which the manor and borough had failed to withstand these pressures and the degree to which the Gaelic-Irish had conversely absorbed them and set about reasserting territorial control.[14] By 1338, the demesne lands of the manor had been granted to the O'Dwyers "to keep the peace"; the meadow lands – once mowed – were now used only for pasture; the woodland area of the manor had also reverted to the Gaelic-Irish; while the manor and borough legal and economic functions had all been discontinued.[15] These developments signified a reassertion of territorial control by the O'Dwyers in the barony and correspondingly involved the rejuvenation of their associated material practices such as pastoral farming and woodkern (or bandit) activity. Such developments, too, marked the boundary of the frontier in Kilnamanagh and distinguished the O'Dwyers and their associated cultural production from their Anglo-Norman neighbours. A contact zone, brought about by geographical contiguity to the Anglo-Norman settlements, did facilitate a level of interaction between the O'Dwyers and Anglo-Norman material practices. However, it is important to emphasise that the existence of the frontier differentiated the O'Dwyers and their followers in political, economic and legal terms. They did not, for example, come under the jurisdiction of the common law, and, therefore, designating certain of them as 'felons' in the 1338 manorial extent did not, in effect, have any tangible or consequential meaning. Furthermore, the extent to which an actual physical frontier existed – possessing both symbolic and psychological manifestations – is indicated by the declaration that no English would "dare to hold or let the said land".[16] The rejuvenation of Gaelic-Irish autonomy in Kilnamanagh continued in the later fourteenth century when in 1377 an inquisition post-mortem into the manor of Clogher[17] reveals that it "is worth nothing, because it is wasted by the O'Duyres [O'Dwyers] and O'Mobrions [O'Mulryans or Ryans], the King's Irish enemies".[18]

Gaelic-Irish territorial reassertion in Kilnamanagh was neither a continuous nor consistent feature of the late medieval period, however; James Butler, the first earl of Ormond, for example, continued to have landholdings in the barony as evidenced by the affirmation in 1337 of his tenure of lands in Ballintemple parish.[19] The manor of Clogher soon reverted to James Butler, second earl of Ormond, after the 1377 inquisition post-mortem mentioned above.[20] Such developments problematise, to a significant degree, the notion of an unrelenting Gaelic revival, and conversely substantiate Graham's visualisation of the relationship between the two medieval cultures as being "complex, ambiguous and dynamic".[21] The dynamic and interconnected nature of Gaelic-Irish/ Anglo-Norman relations in Kilnamanagh is best indicated by the continued involvement of the earls of Ormond in the area – in the factional, political context – throughout the later medieval period. Allegiances, for example, forged between successive earls and the O'Dwyers, coupled with the jurisdiction that they increasingly had over the Kilnamanagh lordship, represented a very important component to events unfolding within the lordship and its connection to the outside English political world. In this context, the grant of Moyaliff to the O'Dwyers in 1338 can also be interpreted as an attempt by the then earl of Ormond to forge factional links with neighbouring Gaelic-Irish lords, consonant with the political realities of the turbulent aftermath of earlier fourteenth-century socio-economic disasters. This contention relates closely to the idea that the notion of Gaelic revival in the late medieval period is an over-simplified one, imbued within a nationalist tradition of narrating medieval Ireland.

The event which has been posited as symbolic of the Gaelic revival, particularly in the nationalist historiography of the period, is that of the Leinster Irish coming together in 1327 and making Donal, son of Art MacMurrough, their king. His intention was to place his banner within two miles of Dublin and "afterwards to travel throughout all the lands of Ireland", and although he did not succeed (he was in fact captured and imprisoned in Dublin castle) the developments were nonetheless important because, as Lydon points out, "[t]his was the first inauguration of its kind in Leinster since the twelfth century and it marks a significant advance in the revival of old Irish institutions".[22] Cosgrove has highlighted that during the same period O'Brien had styled himself king of Munster from his lordship in Thomond in County Clare.[23] Indeed, the process of Gaelic revival manifested itself throughout much of Ireland in the later Middle Ages in the form of a rejuvenation of Gaelic-Irish institutions and a reassertion of territorial control, particularly in border regions with both a Gaelic and Anglo-Norman presence such as Kilnamanagh. However, in Kilnamanagh and elsewhere, the course of events was wholly more complex, contradictory and localised than that portrayed by a traditional Hiberno-centric perspective.

The question of Gaelic-Irish revival has, in recent years, been strongly contested. Barry asserts that "our attitudes to the period are deeply imbued with the notion" and that

> we are loath to see explanations of political or even settlement phenomena within either the wider context of general European decline and subsequent revival during the fourteenth century, or of structural transformation.[24]

This he attributes to an orthodox nationalist historiography, which dismisses outside influences as "deleterious".[25] It is a view that had earlier been expounded by Ellis who considered the concept of Gaelic revival pivotal to the Irish Free State of the 1920s in terms of the provision of medieval antecedents to the emerging nationalist polity.[26] The contextualisation of the late medieval Gaelic revival to incorporate a wider geographical context (for example, the general decline of medieval feudalism in contemporary Europe[27]) and also to consider more universally applicable conceptual ideas (for example, the intrinsic selectivity and subjectivity of historical enquiry in general[28]) is a very useful way of steering clear of the rather simplified nationalist versus revisionist debate and instead situating the mode of explanation in a broader context. It could be argued, for example, that the process of Gaelic revival was simultaneously one of a Gaelicisation of Anglo-Norman elites, and that seeing it as solely a revival of an 'ancient' Gaelic order there is the danger of seeing Gaelic-Irish society as being static, leading to an exaggeration of its stability and isolation.[29]

The idea of Gaelic revival in Kilnamanagh also needs to be seen in the wider context of the fragmentation of government control and influence across the country in the late medieval period. The contraction of the King's writ was increasingly a feature of the late medieval period: all of Connacht was lost by 1347; the border areas of Westmeath in Leinster passed out of crown control by the late fourteenth century; the occupation by the MacMurroughs of the Kilkenny/Carlow border region precipitated the loss of strategic government influence in the south; and, by 1399, the royal justices had ceased to sit in Munster where jurisdiction was abandoned to local lords.[30] In east Munster and Kilkenny, at this point, the social structure and law were overseen by a mixture of English and Gaelic principles, of which "the former was gradually and insidiously being replaced by the latter".[31] Despite the fact that the 'English' element of society remained comparatively strong in the Ormond territories of Kilkenny and Tipperary, the fragmentation of authority persisted. Evidence from the ordinances of the Butler lordships of the early fifteenth century, for example, reveal a society in which a fusion of Anglo-Norman and Gaelic-Irish traditions of law and government was necessitated by the inadequacy of centralised administration.[32]

Nicholls connects the idea of fragmentation of authority in the period to the notion of Gaelic revival by stressing that throughout the fourteenth and fifteenth centuries the marcher areas (such as Kilnamanagh) "saw a gradual replacement of Gaelic for English institutions"; a pattern that continued until the mid-sixteenth century.[33] He proceeds to underline how in the relevant areas of the country to which Gaelic reconquest extended, the Anglo-Norman manorial and economic systems were "swept away, along with numerous village settlements and boroughs.[34] This pattern has been shown to have taken place in Kilnamanagh also in the overrunning of Moyaliff manor and borough as early as 1338. However, it is important to emphasise that the various 'Gaelic' human geographies of Kilnamanagh were far from static. Despite their territorial gains, the various political, socio-economic and cultural worlds of Kilnamanagh were inevitably transmuted by, and interlocked with, Anglo-Norman ones throughout the late medieval period by geographical contiguity to lordships such as the Butlers of Ormond. Furthermore, the persistence of their autonomy in the region was not solely due to their fourteenth-century territorial reconquests. They had to sustain their standing in society as the late medieval period unfolded, and one pivotal means of achieving this was to situate themselves in the intricate political and factional order of the time.

Throughout the later medieval period, the O'Dwyers sought to maintain their position in County Tipperary by forging strategic alliances with both neighbouring Gaelic-Irish and Anglo-Norman lords. From a brief inspection of the genealogy of the O'Dwyers it is clear that from as early as *c.*1100 they had begun to secure links with important families throughout Tipperary and neighbouring counties through intermarriage.[35] In the high Middle Ages, they connected themselves to many powerful Gaelic-Irish lordships such as the O'Briens of Thomond in Clare, the O'Carrolls of Ely in north Tipperary and south King's County, and the O'Kennedys of Ormond in north Tipperary. These allegiances were frequently calculated to effect new networks of alliance that cut across the vertical links between overlords, lords and vassals. They also reflected the intermittent conflicts between the Gaelic-Irish concerning land, tribute and cattle-raiding.[36] The later Middle Ages saw the O'Dwyers draw increasingly into closer relations with geographically contiguous Anglo-Norman (known as the Old English at this point) families such as the Burkes of Clanwilliam barony to the south of Kilnamanagh, the Burkes of Clanrickard in south Galway, and perhaps, most significantly, to the different houses of Dunboyne and Ormond, which was concomitant with the closer political alliances forged between the Butlers and the O'Dwyers in the later medieval and early modern period.

The closer relations engendered between the Butlers and O'Dwyers reflect the degree to which the Anglo-Normans/Old English and Gaelic-Irish, in the wider context, were increasingly intertwined by ties of marriage, fosterage, political alliance and service in late medieval Ireland.[37] Nicholls believes that the extent to which the Old English adapted the concept of the 'clan' – particularly evident in the extended, kin-related, family network of the Butlers in Tipperary and Kilkenny – constitutes "the most outstanding feature" in their Gaelicisation.[38] Concomitant with this, there developed what Graham sees as the inevitable alteration of Gaelic-Irish society by the Old English presence and material practices.[39] Watt, furthermore, points to a protracted succession of indentures and compositions that testify to acculturation being "an ordinary feature of Irish social and political life" throughout the later Middle Ages.[40] In late medieval Kilnamanagh, geographical contiguity to Ormond and the perennial necessity of political alliances, service and intermarriage had collectively combined to compel the O'Dwyers to become acquainted with, interconnected to, and inevitably modified by, English political, economic and legal practices.

Finally, the idea of interconnectivity and co-existence of Gaelic-Irish and Old English worlds is intimately linked to the consideration of nomenclature used to delineate the often-simple dichotomy of native and foreigner in the medieval and later periods. The system of names used has significant relevance to the politics of the twentieth century,[41] and can also be intrinsically linked to the notion of the origin-legend of Ireland and a distinctive nationalist perspective.[42] Of most importance, however, is that the debate ensuing from the nomenclature used in this period can assist the broader exploration of the complicated and localised nature of medieval Irish society. Frame points out the problem of dividing Irish society in the medieval period into the simple categories of Gaelic and English,[43] by underlining that "[t]he dichotomy was real enough; but it may be regarded as representing two poles, between which large elements of the population oscillated".[44] Cosgrove, too, has argued that in late medieval Ireland there was no consistent antagonism between the different groups.[45] This, of course, had the effect of rendering the mosaic of autonomous and semi-autonomous lordships even more complex without a national or simple ethnic dimension to the various battles for advantage, political influence and territorial control. In essence, then, the complexity of the situation on the ground defied a reduction to such fundamental groupings as Gaelic and English.[46] In Kilnamanagh and elsewhere, as we have seen above, intermarriage and a prolonged series of compositions and indentures testify to co-existence and interconnectivity being commonplace from the very beginning.[47]

A New Contact Zone / A New English World

By the late medieval period, the barony can be best visualised as a 'contact zone' of interconnected and amalgamated Gaelic-Irish and Anglo-Norman worlds. As the New English expanded their territorial and administrative control in the sixteenth century, they re-encountered this contact zone and others throughout the country. At the local level, these 'contact zones' were known as the marches, or 'lands of war' – tracts of land held and contested through the course of the earlier medieval period by both the Anglo-Normans and the Gaelic-Irish.[48] These 'contested lands' in the early modern period are visually recognisable in the landscape by the prevalence of tower houses, or castles.[49] As Barry notes, each tower house represented the "frontier-like existence in microcosm", and that "as Ireland was covered by a 'patchwork' of lordships ... there were also a multiplicity of regional frontiers".[50] The frequency of tower houses in the lowland regions of Kilnamanagh – seen in the Down Survey map of the barony presented in fig. 2.1 – is typical of the numerous frontiers throughout Ireland at this juncture.[51] Indeed the extent to which sixteenth century Ireland, or Hibernia, was envisioned and posited as a western frontier of Britain, ripe for settlement and colonisation is wonderfully captured in Abraham Ortelius' map of Ireland, seen in fig. 2.2, which first appeared in his popular atlas *Theatrum Orbis Terrarum* in 1573. The 'east to west' orientation brings into sharp relief the real and imagined frontiers within.

These various frontiers of early modern Ireland manifested themselves politically, socially and culturally in the landscape as well as physically.[52] Moreover, the idea of the frontier – that needed and thereby justified 'civilising' – was a common conviction of the contemporary New English administration. Seen in the wonderfully vivid drawings of John Derricke's *The Image of Irelande* (1581) are depictions of the usual themes underpinning the legitimisation of 'taming the frontier'.[53] They include: the demonisation of the Gaelic-Irish (fig. 2.3); the civilised order of Dublin and the English Pale (fig. 2.4); marching gloriously to the frontier (fig. 2.5); the rout of the Irish (fig. 2.6); and the anticipated endpoint of English colonialism in Ireland – submission of the Gaelic chiefs (fig. 2.7). However, it is more useful, conceptually, to visualise the 'frontier' in early modern Ireland as a 'contact zone' (as discussed in chapter one). Gaelic areas such as Kilnamanagh were neither static, uniform nor bereft of contradiction in the early modern period, and are perhaps best envisaged as fluid and intersecting locales that enable an interrogation of the complex and contested spaces of contemporary Ireland.[54]

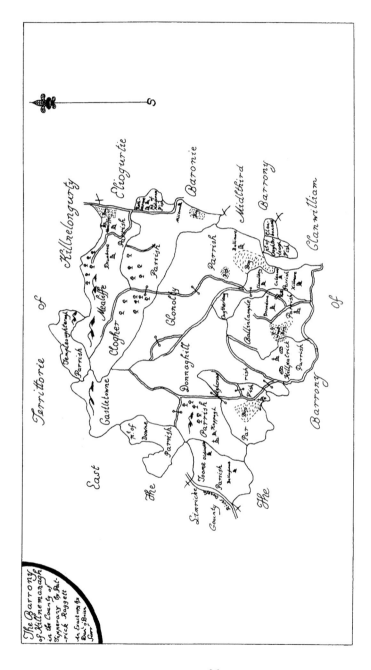

Fig. 2.1: **The Down Survey Barony Map of Kilnamanagh, c.1654.** Copied from source: N.L.I., MFIC Pos. 7384 b.

Fig. 2.2 : **Hibernia, 1573**. Source : A. Ortelius, *Theatrum Orbis Terrarum* (additamentum), Neptune Gallery, Dublin

A Here creepes out of Sainct Filchers denne, a parke of prowling mates,
  Most hurtfull to the Englishe pale, and noysome to the States:
  Whiche space no more their countrey byrth, then those of thy englishe race,
  But yeld to each a like good turne, when as they come in place.
B They spoyle, and burne, and beare away, as fitte occasions serue,
  And thinke the greater ill they doe, the greater prayse deserue:

2 They passe not for the poore mans cry, nor yet respect his teares,
  But rather ioy to see the fire, to flash about his eares.
  To see both flame, and smoulding smoke, to burst the christall skyes,
  Seen to their pray, therein I say, their second glory lyeß.
C And thus bereauing him of houße, of cattell and of those:
  They do returne backe to the wood, from whence they came before.

Fig. 2.3: **The Demonisation of the Gaelic-Irish.** From John Derricke's *Image of Irelande, 1581*

38

Fig. 2.4: **The Civilised Order of the English Pale.** From John Derricke's *Image of Irelande, 1581*

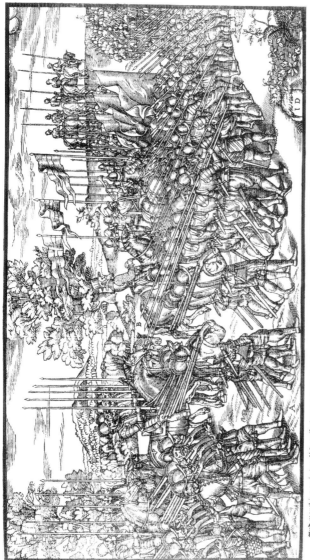

8

And marching on in warlicke wise, set out in battaple ray,
We doth pronounce by heavy doome: the enemies paye to lay,
And all the rable of the foes, by bloudy blade to quell
O barsting shall afflict the foxe, which trayterously rebell.
Durst be nurt to approche the fielde, to try it by the marshall la wes,
Not one of this rebelling sout, that thinkes himselfe most fure
Is able to abide the knight or patient his endure.

For why it is to of all the Karne, that may withstand her power,
Oyet terrif so great a Iustice, one minute of an houre,
If he of they both ragge and ragge, for maynteaunce of their cause,
Delivering them to open spoyle, from most unto the leade,
And byd them welcome harte to unto that golden feast.

Fig. 2.5: **Marching to the Frontier.** From John Derricke's *Image of Irelande, 1581*

40

Fig. 2.6: **The Defeat of the Gaels.** From John Derricke's *Image of Irelande, 1581*

Fig. 2.7: **The Submission of the Gaelic Chiefs.** From John Derricke's *Image of Irelande, 1581*

By the mid-sixteenth century, Kilnamanagh was effectively a frontier that had not yet been closed. The Gaelic-Irish in the barony at this point found themselves at the contact zone of New English colonialism, having earlier been transmuted but ultimately withstood the advance of Anglo-Norman colonisation. Like many Gaelic-Irish families finding themselves at the contact zone of an ever-strengthening New English presence, the O'Dwyers of Kilnamanagh sought to maintain their position in County Tipperary by forging strategic alliances with neighbouring Gaelic-Irish and Old English lords.[55] Typical of many Gaelic families in the later sixteenth century, the O'Dwyers continued the medieval system of political faction by establish marriage ties with prominent neighbouring Gaelic and Old English families.[56] They were situated within a system of faction in County Tipperary – localised in its extent – that characterised the disjointed political order of the country,[57] and which was consonant with the fragmented nature of the lordships of Ireland, c.1534.[58] The enterprise of the O'Dwyers in maintaining their territorial and societal positions typify the extent to which, as Watt observes in the broader context, "the urge of Gaelic Ireland to preserve its own culture and freedom was inevitably curbed by realistic appreciation of the perennial necessity to achieve coexistence".[59]

From the mid-sixteenth century onwards, there began a sustained, albeit inconsistent, attempt to rejuvenate English government in Ireland.[60] In early 1540, an indenture between "the King and Conohour O'Dowir [of] Kilnemanagh, captain of his nation", reveals a covenant whereby the chief of the O'Dwyers agreed to pay a certain sum of money "out of every "carue" of land, and find 40 galloglas for a month" for the New English administration in Tipperary.[61] Similar covenants were made to the king at this time from O'Brien of Arra and O'Mulryan of Owny, to the north-west of Kilnamanagh, reflecting the degree to which the King's writ was being extended in the region.[62] This process, whereby the government made agreements with individual lords, formed part of what Brady sees as the initial phase of Tudor reform, characterised by a programme of general political assimilation; facilitated in County Tipperary largely by the earls of Ormond.[63]

The first Butler earl of Ormond had been granted palatinate powers in the newly-created liberty of Tipperary (coterminous with the then county of Tipperary) by Letters Patent from Edward III in 1328; these palatinate powers continued to be held by successive heirs of the Butlers by various regrants and confirmations from the crown until 1621.[64] The palatinate, jurisdictional privileges enjoyed by the earls of Ormond in the liberty of Tipperary were quite considerable. They included the appointment of a sheriff and sub-sheriff and "the holding of courts, the appointment of justices and other court officers, coroners and other county officials, and the power of granting pardon for transgressions of the law".[65] The practice of these instruments of English law and administration gradually induced elements of Gaelic-Irish participation. The majority of appointed seneschals and sheriffs of the liberty in the period up to c.1515 were of Anglo-Norman (Old English) origin; many being members of the extended Butler family.[66] However, in the later sixteenth and early seventeenth centuries, though the Old English were still dominant, the Gaelic-Irish played a more active part in local administration; members of the O'Dwyers, for example serving as sheriffs in the early seventeenth century.[67]

The influence of the earls of Ormond in the region, then, served to interconnect the barony of Kilnamanagh to wider political and socio-economic developments in contemporary Ireland and prompt recognition from the O'Dwyers and others of the necessity to come to terms with the New English administration.[68] Accordingly, they sought to consolidate their position in what was an increasingly centralised and integrated political world. They were beginning to situate themselves in the new political context in an outward-looking and progressive manner, which reflected, for example, how many smaller lords "saw the wisdom of holding their lands from the crown in order to remove themselves from the grip of overlords".[69] At this juncture, then, there is a clear inconsistency of antagonism between the Gaelic-Irish, Old English and New English; power struggles taking place at the local level, without a national or simple ethnic dimension to the various battles for political advantage and territorial control.[70]

The factional nature of the lordships in mid-sixteenth century Tipperary, however, served to inhibit the effectiveness of government reform. The New English administration in the county, for example, sustained an annual monetary tribute to the influential O'Carroll lordship of Ely by 1549.[71] In this sense, the chief of the O'Dwyers' indenture with the king in 1540 represented an integral part of the reforming agenda of successive New English administrations, which attempted to address the problem of allegiances and powerful independent magnates by seeking covenants with individual lords.[72] Efforts to centralise control, however, continued to be impeded by the intricate system of faction.[73] The O'Dwyers, for example – despite their indenture with the king – continued to come under the respective prerogatives as magnates of royal authority in the region from the thirteenth century, enabled the dissemination of English political and socio-economic ideologies and heightened the awareness of

English material practices and institutions. The local government system was being rejuvenated and intensified in the county as early as 1551, when the then sheriff summoned jurors "for enquiring into the operation of the Statutes of Labourers and the presentment of felonies".[76] As quoted at the beginning of this chapter, the participation of the O'Dwyers in the civilising and reforming objectives of the New English saw them upholding galloglasses in the king's forces by 1553. In 1564, injunctions to apprehend and punish any rebels were issued to the O'Dwyers and others in Tipperary.[77] By 1569, the O'Dwyer lordship's standing forces were 12 horsemen and 120 footmen; these forces serving with those of the tenth earl of Ormond in suppressing the second Desmond rebellion in Munster of the late 1570s and early 1580s.[78]

The process of reform in the liberty of Tipperary did not constitute direct central government administration, however, and had one central dependency: reliance on the earl of Ormond. Elsewhere, in Tudor Britain, the establishment of regional organs of government administration, such as the council of the north in England and the council of the marches in Wales, had effectively facilitated the consolidation of centralised control. However, no effective appointments were made in Munster until 1571 when Sir John Perrot took up office as president of the province, but as his governmental directives for reform greatly surpassed the resources available to him, effectual administration was again compromised.[79] Furthermore, as Hayes-McCoy outlines,

> the local lords, great and small, opposed the presidents, and since the
> state was not yet strong enough to dispense with whatever assistance
> the lords were willing to give, the presidencies suffered, in their early
> years, from the extemporaneous nature of government policy.[80]

The rejuvenation of English institutions in Munster, then, relied considerably on the influence of powerful Old English magnates, chiefly the earl of Desmond (in north Kerry and west Limerick, where the Fitzgerald dynasty had been established in the thirteenth century) and the earl of Ormond. The earls of Desmond and their extensive network of subordinate lordships throughout Munster had consistently resisted the New English presence from the mid-sixteenth century and were progressively mistrusted to oversee government reforms; a process which saw them revolt against crown control, initially in the late 1560s and early 1570s and again in the late 1570s and early 1580s.[81] There was, however, a substantial conflict of interests, too, between the New English administration and the tenth earl of Ormond, Thomas Butler.

From the 1550s, it was felt by the New English government, in Munster and Dublin, that Ormond's continued royal jurisdiction and powers in the palatinate liberty of Tipperary served to inhibit the effectual execution of government reform. Lord Deputy of Ireland, Sir Henry Sidney, wrote to Queen Elizabeth in 1567 reporting that the earl of Ormond's palatinate privileges were "productive of much mischief through the incompetency of his officers".[82] Sidney made known his plans to dismantle Ormond's jurisdictional liberty in Tipperary and consolidate strong government control in Munster by setting up a presidential system. He informed the Privy Council in 1576 that the Queen's writ was not allowed currency in the liberty of Tipperary and conjectured that "as long as any subject has any jurisdiction palatine ... there will be no perfect reformation in Munster".[83] Critically, however, the ineptitude of the New English administration in dealing with the two Desmond rebellions of the 1570s and 1580s – which Ormond was ultimately required to suppress – confirmed the earl "as the most effective defender of the Crown's interests in Ireland".[84] All government efforts, thereafter, to abolish the liberty of Tipperary, in the later sixteenth century, were frustrated by the realisation of Ormond's necessity and by the royal favour he enjoyed with Elizabeth who, in fact, called him her faithful Lucas.[85]

The prolonged conflict between the earls of Ormond and Desmond, in essence, constituted a struggle between those who sought to actively participate in government reform and those who forcefully strove to resist it. The discord mirrored closely the intricate dynamics of change throughout the country, where Old English and Gaelic-Irish attempts to fashion a new political awareness and redefinition – in the context of the New English presence – in turn precipitated varying and contradictory recurrences in society. With Ormond's position assured, he continued to exert substantial influence in the lordship of Kilnamanagh, where it has been shown the O'Dwyers were incorporated into wider political and socio-economic developments but, nevertheless, inconsistencies in what was effectively a piecemeal reform process in the liberty of Tipperary remained. The jurors, for example, summoned by the sheriff of the liberty of Tipperary in 1551 – of which there were 138 collectively in the towns of Cashel, Fethard, Clonmel and elsewhere in Tipperary – were mostly from the south and east of the county and of Anglo-Norman origin.[86] This was clearly a reflection of the degree to which English institutional practices were preserved in the Old English areas, but was an illustration, too, of the slow, cautious involvement of the Gaelic-Irish in what was considered to be a mistrusted and external administration. The participation of some members of the O'Dwyers, for example, in the first Desmond rebellion against the New English in Munster is suggested for the year 1568, which illustrates the inconsistency of the reform process in Kilnamanagh.[87]

Resistance and Conformity in the Late Sixteenth Century

A substantial level of resistance to New English reforms was a continued feature of society in the lordship of Kilnamanagh from the mid-sixteenth century. The Irish Fiants of the Tudor sovereigns reveal a consistent series of pardons to prominent O'Dwyers from the late 1540s to the early 1600s.[88] The fiants are an important collection of documents that uncover the extent to which strong residual elements of the old world persisted in Kilnamanagh; a world that was distinctly Gaelic-Irish in character and at odds with the new one being devised and effected by the New English. Resistance, then, was an inevitable and constituent part of the reform process, and pardons to the O'Dwyers were granted for such transgressions against New English authority as "trading in horses, victuals, and arms, with the Irish enemy".[89] The recorded pardons do not usually specify as to what offence was committed but they do, importantly, point to deviations from the New English social norms that were being externally imposed on the O'Dwyer lordship in the later sixteenth century. Pardons and fines were issued successively to foremost members of the O'Dwyers in the 1570s and 1580s.[90]

The series of pardons impart, too, information regarding the internal structure of the O'Dwyer lordship; the evidence of which, although notably scant, illustrates the fundamental incompatibility of Gaelic-Irish social and economic order and that which was externally imposed by the New English administration. Moreover, it provides an important context to the forms of resistance occurring in the late sixteenth century. In 1578, for example, a pardon and fine issued to leading members of the extended O'Dwyer lordship, reveals a society in which a sophisticated order emerges, where individuals of a 'husbandman', 'yeoman' and 'freeholder' status existed alongside those of a 'gentleman' or land-owning delineation.[91] This is significant in that it highlights a system of landholding and associated social structure that was clearly in conflict with the English institutions of single ownership, primogeniture and the common law. In

Kilnamanagh, the evidence highlights a fragmented and intricate Gaelic-Irish freehold system, and points to the subsequent difficulty of its assimilation into English legal, social and economic norms.[92]

The O'Dwyers, through their practice of arbitrary exactions within the lordship, partnership farming and pastoral husbandry, simultaneously resisted the implementation of English material practices such as the establishment of a rent-based economy. This form of resistance was witnessed in Clonoulty parish, for example, in 1582, when it is seen that the commandry of Clonoulty, which had passed into crown control in the aftermath of the dissolution of monastic lands begun in the mid-1530s, "remained waste above three years, in consequence of the troubles there by undutiful subjects".[93] Furthermore, it is seen that the rents initiated in Clonoulty had been lost and that the lands had been "burned, and other ways spoiled".[94] A later pardon issued to members of the O'Dwyers in 1586 also reveals the extent to which the Kilnamanagh lordship was militarised, where galloglasses (hired soldiers) and kerns (foot soldiers or bandits) are evident.[95] These groups – operative throughout the country in the late sixteenth century – posed a substantial threat to the peace and order of the New English administration through their mercenary activities such as cattle-raiding, and via the manner in which they arbitrarily demanded lodging and protection within the lordships.[96]

The Gaelic-Irish world of Kilnamanagh, then, and throughout Ireland constituted a sensitive and frequently intractable impediment to government reforms. Edmund Spenser and Sir John Davies – two of the most distinguished commentators and writers on early modern Irish society – documented the unruly and ungovernable nature of the Gaelic-Irish lordships in the late sixteenth and early seventeenth centuries.[97] Spenser's *View* and Davies' *Discovery*, however, formed merely a fragment of a long-established series of colonial pamphlets and propaganda situated in the context of a justified 'reforming' and 'civil' mission of the New English regime in early modern Ireland.[98] Numerous New English writers and travellers of the late sixteenth century condemned the material practices associated with the Gaelic-Irish system of landholding and social order, such as tanistry, gavelkind, coign and livery.[99] Sir John Davies, for example, in his denunciation of the practice of tanistry and gavelkind, declared that

> [t]hese two Irish customs made all [the Gaelic-Irish] possessions uncertain, being shuffled and changed so often by new elections and

partitions ... [and are] the true cause of such desolation and barbarism in this land.[100]

These writings and intellectual currents provided the legitimisation of the agenda of reform set out by New English officials throughout the Tudor period, which included, particularly, the extirpation of Gaelic-Irish customs and material practices deemed detrimental to the effectual centralised government of the lordships. Sir John Perrot, Lord Deputy of Ireland, 1584-1588, for example, outlined the necessity of

> [cutting] away the Captainries and Tanisthips used among the mere[101] Irishry, to the end that the seignories of the Irish lords should descend from father to son, according to the common laws of England.[102]

He believed, moreover, that "the surrendering of their land, and taking the same back again, must breed quietness, obedience and profit".[103] Perrot belonged to the 'reform tradition' of government officials and writers that advocated correction through education and assimilation, as referred to by Hadfield and McVeagh, which included such individuals as Edmund Campion, Sir William Gerard and Sir William Herbert; whose works collectively illustrate "a confidence that the spread of the English legal system to Ireland would achieve the desired effect [of reform]".[104]

Accordingly, from the mid-sixteenth century, the New English administration had sought to effect reform in west Tipperary by extending the jurisdiction of the common law and disseminating English institutional practices. The successive confirmations of the town charters of Cashel in 1554, 1557, 1584 and 1592 convey a pronounced opposition to Gaelic-Irish customs, and a determination to uphold English economic institutions and the common law.[105] Furthermore, the Irish Fiants highlight the extent to which attempts to bring the O'Dwyers into line with English norms had been occurring since the early 1550s, when pardons incorporated the condition that 'security' be given.[106] Successive pardons in the 1570s and 1580s reveal the manner in which New English attempts to secure its jurisdiction over the lordship in Kilnamanagh resulted in yet more stringent security provisions being stipulated with each pardon, whereby acquittals occurred

[p]rovided that within six months [the various members of the
O'Dwyers] appear before commissioners in their county, and give
security to keep the peace and answer at sessions when called
upon.[107]

The fines attached to specific pardons were also becoming increasingly more
severe. A fine of £20, for example, was issued to Philip O'Dwyer, the then chief
of Kilnamanagh, in 1572 for an undisclosed transgression;[108] and, later in 1587,
a pardon administered to leading members of the O'Dwyers included the
proviso that

[t]hey are to abide any order by the lord deputy affecting their lands,
and any who have been in actual rebellion to find £200 English,
security, to obey such orders.[109]

Clearly, however, such rigorous and uncompromising government directives
may merely suggest the ineffectiveness of their administration, given the dearth
of evidence of compliance with these orders. Notwithstanding this, the 1587
pardon was notably the last substantial pardon given to prominent members of
the O'Dwyer lordship until 1600, which may suggest that the repercussions of
offences against the crown deterred subsequent violations. In any case, however,
the mere existence of the pardons points to the manner in which the New
English administration in Tipperary had increasingly attempted to superimpose
their jurisdiction over the authority of the chief in Kilnamanagh; the success of
which becomes more apparent in the early seventeenth century.

In the later sixteenth century, the O'Dwyers increasingly participated in the
new order. In 1575, for example, "Philip O'Duire, captain of his nation and the
country of Kellnemannagh" oversaw and guaranteed the grant of "the castle,
lordship and town of Grantestown with all the messuages, lands, tenements,
etc." between members of the Burkes of Clanwilliam, immediately south of
Kilnamanagh.[110] This is significant in that it reveals the degree to which the
O'Dwyers, in an effort to safeguard their position, identified the importance of
law and order in the vicinity of Kilnamanagh and were, in effect, seeking to
redefine and present themselves as subjects capable of progressive involvement
in the new society. As highlighted earlier, they had recognised the exigency of
situating themselves in the new political composition from the mid-sixteenth
century. However, in attempting to answer why there was such a simultaneously
prolonged and inconsistent course of reform in Kilnamanagh in succeeding

decades, it is important to recognise that the enduring resistance of Gaelic-Irish order and material practices ensured the intricate and contradictory dynamics affecting the O'Dwyer lordship.

Change in early modern Kilnamanagh, therefore, was a complicated affair; inherently constituting the reluctance, resistance and fears of a society attempting to reconcile itself to demanding political realities. The imperative of the O'Dwyers, however, to come to terms with the New English presence was accentuated by the manifest power of the new administration to appropriate their lands. In the aftermath of the dissolution of the Catholic monastic houses in the 1530s, landed estates throughout Kilnamanagh were transferred to crown control and, moreover, were increasingly leased to New English settlers through the course of the later sixteenth century.[111] In addition, as MacCurtain argues, the process inaugurated the channel of legal inquiry into landownership which underpinned later government plantation schemes.[112] The extent of the Munster plantation, too, in the aftermath of the second Desmond rebellion in the mid-1580s [113] – which affected large tracts of lands in neighbouring Clanwilliam barony to the south of Kilnamanagh – had further illustrated to the O'Dwyers the powers of confiscation of the New English administration, and the necessity of fashioning an effective response to the emerging context of New English rule.

The Exclusiveness of New English Government

Later sixteenth-century government administration in Ireland was becoming progressively more centralised and effectual but simultaneously grew increasingly more intolerant of the Gaelic-Irish population.[114] The plans for the Munster plantation, for example, explicitly illustrate the exclusive ethnicity of the New English, wherein it is revealed that the grantees were expressly directed

> not to marry with any but with some person born of English parents, or of such as shall descend from the first patentees [and] [t]he patentees and English people now newly to be planted there, not to set their estates to any Irish.[115]

The 'reform tradition' of assimilation, therefore, was but one of two distinct and opposing ideological influences on government policy in the Tudor period; the other being one of 'exclusiveness' and primarily advancing the notion that reform ultimately demanded reconquest and plantation. Reform thought progressively yielded to an exclusivist and racialist rhetoric in the later sixteenth and early seventeenth centuries, when writers such as Fynes Moryson, Barnaby Rich, Sir John Davies and, most notably, Edmund Spenser, advocated the necessity of a complete reconquest of Ireland.[116]

In relation to the above notion, Brady postulates that it was

> the last flowering of renaissance humanism that underlay the brave attempt to assimilate Ireland's different ethnic groups into one civic culture; and it was the first appearance of a pessimistic and exclusive Calvinism, coupled with a new elitist ethnology that gave rise to the policy of conquest.[117]

There are difficulties with the concept of a shift in the ideological underpinnings of the Tudor administration in Ireland, given the recurrence of inconsistencies in government policy. Brady, for example, also stresses that recognition of the idea of two disparate phases of government generates an overstated sense of a "simple division" of the sixteenth century into "soft and tough phases of policy", which ignores the "periodic oscillations and simultaneous inconsistencies which were a feature of Tudor government in practice".[118] He goes on to question the "propriety of applying such general conceptual categories as 'humanism', 'Calvinism', or colonial thought as direct influences in the formulation of particular Irish policies".[119] Bradshaw, too, casts doubt upon "the existence of a colonial consensus among the New English of Elizabethan Ireland", and argues that it is more appropriate to "explore the tensions within the colonial ethos rather than search for a dubious consensus".[120]

Notwithstanding these important assertions, a continuum of exclusivist ideological thought can be traced back to the twelfth century, when the works of Giraldus Cambrensis (Gerald of Wales) comprehensively established the notion of 'English' superiority and 'Celtic' barbarity.[121] His *Topographia Hibernica* and *Expugnatio Hibernica*, both written in the late 1180s, were to prove the benchmarks of later English colonial thought and writing in the context of Britain and Ireland. Canny remarks that "no sixteenth-century Englishman surpassed Gerald in his vituperative dismissal of Gaelic culture";[122] and, furthermore, as Gillingham points out, "English writers of the sixteenth and seventeenth centuries were to do little more than play variations on themes already well and truly established in Gerald's Irish writings".[123] It is important to underline, then, that the exclusiveness of the Tudor administration was not a 'New' English phenomenon but was, in fact, fundamental to English government in Ireland from the twelfth century. In addition, as Gillingham notes, "the subsequent history of centuries of half-completed conquest meant that the new attitude of superiority, hostility and alienation was to remain deeply entrenched".[124]

The exclusivist and racialist rhetoric intensified in government circles in the late sixteenth century. As early as the late 1570s, "it was being stated openly by English Protestant officials in Ireland that the presumed loyal population was neither English nor loyal".[125] As Canny points out, such theses – advancing the idea that the "only true subjects of the Crown" were those who were committed Protestants, and that all others were "a threat to the security of the English Crown and its position in Ireland because of their persistent attachment to Catholicism" – were being increasingly designed by "English-born officials and soldiers in Ireland to discredit their principal critics and rivals for patronage"; arguments that he asserts "received a sympathetic hearing form senior officials in London".[126] The New English most palpably demonstrated this fundamental exclusiveness of their agenda when their administration was strong enough to do so. However, given the piecemeal nature of Tudor government in Ireland – which reflected both its logistical inability to carry out its programme of reform, and its reliance on some level of cooperation from the existing population – complexities and contradictions in early modern Irish society were inevitable. Less than three years after the plan for the Munster plantation was originally drawn up, for example, it is seen that its implementation had degenerated into indiscriminate expropriation and extortion of profit, with little apparent government control. Sir William Herbert, for example, writes, in 1588, that

> [o]ur pretence in the enterprise of plantation was to establish in these parts piety, justice, inhabitation and civility, with comfort and good example to the parts adjacent. Our drift now is, being here possessed of land, to extort, make the state of things turbulent, and live by prey and pay.[127]

In a related manner, the corruption of local government in Tipperary is evident in 1591, when Sir Richard Shea, governor and sheriff of Counties Tipperary and Kilkenny, was accused of the "taking of black rents and other extortions and abuses".[128] The then chief of Kilnamanagh, Philip O'Dwyer, had paid him for three year's surety in the liberty of Tipperary in the late 1580s.[129]

Developing the above point, it is clear that the enterprise of the O'Dwyers and others in Tipperary – in reconciling their lordships to the new order – encountered a level of malpractice in government administration that inevitably generated a level of distrust of the New English presence. The controversy in the 1590s over the payment of 'cess' (or purveyance) to government administrators for the maintenance of crown troops throughout the country, for example, illustrates the antagonism of both the Old English and Gaelic-Irish communities to the "single-minded and exclusive administrative style" of contemporary New English government.[130] In County Tipperary, for instance, subsequent to "a composition in lieu of cess" being imposed in 1592, when 100 footmen were "to be victualled in the said county", Lord Deputy, Sir William Fitzwilliam, informed the Privy Council that attempts to "assemble all the gentlemen, freeholders, and tenants in the said county" – to bring about their reform in relation to their opposition to the composition – were met with "dissent and disagreement to yield to Her Highness".[131] The earl of Ormond had attempted to use his influence with Elizabeth to secure leniency regarding the controversy but, by 1595, the queen had directed Tipperary "to be joined in the composition for cess" and had issued a commission to the vice-president of Munster for the enlargement of the composition in Munster.[132]

In Kilnamanagh and throughout Tipperary, too, further unease was inevitably engendered by the manner in which the New English planters who effected the Munster plantation were perceived to have gained ownership of land through the unscrupulous use of the common law; which was comprehended by the Gaelic-Irish and Old English to be in favour of the New English minority.[133] The perceived grievances of the Gaelic-Irish and Old English– concomitant with the sustained exclusive style of Tudor government – had the effect of increasingly alienating both communities, who began to collectively oppose what they discerned as the injustices of an external regime. As Hayes-McCoy points out, although the surviving evidence "permits but slight insight into any Gaelic Irishman's mind" in the late sixteenth century, the "outlook was certainly unpromising enough to provoke an increasingly hostile reaction to what must have been recognised as the settled methods of the government".[134]

Accordingly, a sense of unease had formed throughout the province of Munster in the mid-1590s that was exacerbated by the rising in Ulster of Hugh O'Neill, earl of Tyrone, and the advent of the Nine Years War. O'Neill, along with Hugh O'Donnell, earl of Tyrconnell (in County Donegal), and fellow dissidents of the newly-formed Ulster confederacy, attempted to nationalise the struggle to safeguard the existing political and landholding order, within Ulster, by championing himself as the defender of "Christ's catholic religion".[135] He correspondingly entreated "the gentlemen of Munster" to "make war" with him, and, as Hayes-McCoy observes, "the commencement of attacks on the Munster settlers showed that the call was heard" when rebellion broke out in the province in late 1598.[136] A letter from the Privy Council to Sir George Carew, President of Munster, confirmed, furthermore, that by 1600 many settlers and their tenants "had fled for fear of the rebels".[137] The earl of Tyrone had also invoked Spanish assistance, offering King Philip II the crown of Ireland "if he would deliver them from their English oppressors";[138] and subsequently, as the president of Munster feared, the "expectation of Spaniards" lifted up "the spirits of the Irishry" and caused further stirring in Tipperary.[139]

In late 1599 and early 1600, Tyrone (who the English referred to as the 'Archtraitor' at this point) marched through west Tipperary en route to the south coast of Ireland, where he would rendezvous with a Spanish expeditionary force and eventually meet an English army under the command of the new Irish viceroy, Charles Blount, Lord Mountjoy, at the Battle of Kinsale in December 1601.[140] That the English did effectively complete the Tudor conquest of Ireland, in the wider context, by their victory at Kinsale is commonly attested. However, prior to Kinsale, Tyrone's march through County Tipperary and the ensuing exacerbation of revolt provides us with an excellent opportunity of interpreting the complex and contradictory process of resistance and simultaneous compliance with crown administration, which characterised the attempts of Gaelic-Irish lords such as the O'Dwyers to survive in age of upheaval. Many of the O'Dwyers' Gaelic-Irish and Old English neighbours in Tipperary, such as the O'Mulryans of Owny and the O'Kennedys of Ormond to the north-west, and the Purcells of Loughmoe in Eliogarty barony to the east, were in revolt by 1599;[141] by which time the town of Cashel was "standing in great fear and danger, and intended by the rebels to be surprised and betrayed".[142] However, the O'Dwyers were to take a more complicated path, by essentially playing the roles of both recusants and loyal subjects.

Hayes-McCoy points out that Tyrone's activities in Munster, prior to the Battle of Kinsale, involved "the practice of chastisement of those who were unwilling to join the Ulster confederacy".[143] The O'Dwyers, then, were faced with the challenge of effecting a response to the presence of the northern forces. Accordingly, the *Annals of the Four Masters* record that

> although these chieftains [the O'Dwyers] had for some time stood by their Sovereign, they were glad to obtain terms of peace from those strange warriors, who were traversing every territory.[144]

The *Annals* proceed to refer to the cautious allegiance of the O'Dwyers to these Ulstermen; forming "a confederacy and friendship with O'Neill's people [who had] induced every territory ... to join them", and who had for some time remained in the vicinity of Kilnamanagh.[145] Further to this, by 1599, it is seen that the chief of Kilnamanagh, "having delivered his son in pledge for his loyalty, began to revolt".[146] Later that year, Queen Elizabeth wrote to Ormond requesting him to take order with the chief regarding his appropriation of lands and goods belonging to the Anglican archbishop of Cashel.[147] The archbishop, Miler Magrath, complained that O'Dwyer had broken his castle and burned and spoiled the town of Ballymore, in Clonoulty parish, Kilnamanagh, and had pillaged the dioceses of Emly (in west Tipperary) "to the number of eleven towns and villages".[148]

Faced with escalating tension and resistance, a common tactic of successive New English administrations in the late sixteenth century was to actively seek the loyalty of Gaelic-Irish and Old English noblemen formerly in arms against the crown. This mirrored the extent to which the government throughout the country was not capable, as yet, of defending itself without the support of the existing lords. The president of Munster and the earl of Ormond, for instance, continued to take pledges of loyalty in the late 1590s and early 1600s.[149] This specific process crucially reflected a broader design whereby

> many of the meaner sort in action should be bought over by protections and pardons, so that the enemy might be weakened and the pardoned men used for further service.[150]

Accordingly, the chief of Kilnamanagh and other leading members of the O'Dwyers were pardoned successively in 1600 and 1601;[151] a comprehensive pardon also being issued to the foremost members of the O'Dwyer lordship in May 1601.[152] The O'Dwyers' loyalty to the crown was required and they subsequently duly took the opportunity of proving their conformity in an effort to safeguard their position within the new order.

In early 1600, Ormond reported to the Privy Council that Dermot O'Dwyer, the chief of Kilnamanagh, was "a martial man (under correction) not meet to be urged for further surety of the peace";[153] and testament to the O'Dwyers' loyalty to the crown, their chief had become sheriff of the liberty of Tipperary for the years 1599-1600. Furthermore, it is seen that the new sheriff "manifested his duty by killing and apprehending some of Tyrone's men, standing constantly with Her Majesty's service in all this time of rebellion".[154] In addition, throughout 1600 and 1601, O'Dwyer was commended for his service against the rebels in Tipperary;[155] an unforeseen eventuality one year previously, at which time he was in open rebellion against the crown. The partially colonised world of sixteenth-century Kilnamanagh, therefore, cannot, ultimately, be depicted as "a passive flattened out world, stamped upon by more powerful others, and fashioned solely in the image of colonialism".[156] The loyalty of the O'Dwyers and the involvement of their chief in government demonstrates how aspects of an English colonial polity predicated on exclusivist grounds, and characterised by notions of Self and Other, were transcended by a series of fluid and contradictory power relations in practice.[157] This illustrates, furthermore, one of the principal recurring themes of this work; namely the calculated expediency of both the New English administration and the Gaelic-Irish lords at the contact zone of a frontier that had not yet closed.[158]

The above contention implores one further notable question of the evidence: how had O'Dwyer situated himself within the new order to such an extent that he had managed to transform himself from dissident insubordinate to sheriff in such a short space of time? The simplest answer, of course, is that he had not really transformed himself, but had merely acted as opportunely as the administration had when they needed him. There is, however, a more fundamental and subtle explanation. A concise examination of an important letter he wrote to Ormond in 1600, concerning his dispute over land with the archbishop of Cashel, reveals how he had proved flexible enough to construct an effective response to the strengthening crown authority and New English government in the localities.[159] He informed Ormond, for example, that he had

> … attended at the last assizes holden at Clonmell within the liberty, with [his] learned counsel, expecting the Lord Archbishop coming hither touching these causes [of dispute] whereby they might be

determined according the course of Her Majesty's laws; where the Lord Archbishop came not in person, nor by attorney, so as (by means of his absence) nothing could be done.[160]

O'Dwyer had evidently acquired an acute knowledge of both the New English legal and local government system and, moreover, the means to access it. He had comprehended the identifiable benefits to his lordship of situating himself within the new order and, accordingly, in later years, acted with similar prudence and progressiveness.

Conclusion

In bringing this chapter to a close, it is important to underline that the upheavals descending upon the O'Dwyer lordship in the turbulent late medieval and Tudor periods were situated within the wider context of the contradictory struggle of the Gaelic-Irish and Old English lords to resist, come to terms with, and position themselves within the new order. The inconsistencies of successive English administrative and coercive attempts to extend English rule further engendered the fundamental complexity characterising late sixteenth-century Irish society. This intricacy needs to be explicitly recognised in order to elucidate the essential contradictory meanings inherent in the sites of cultural interaction in early modern Ireland.

The Tudor reconquest established the exclusive sovereignty of the English crown in Ireland, which meant that, for the first time, all the inhabitants of the island were subject to the authority of a centralised government. In Kilnamanagh and elsewhere, however, the frontier had not been effectively closed, which ensured the continued contestation of political, economic and social spaces in early seventeenth-century Ireland. This subsequently forms the initial subject of exploration in chapter three, wherein the continued determined efforts of the O'Dwyers to safeguard their respective positions in Tipperary, as part of a broader attempt of Gaelic Ireland to redefine itself and survive the upheavals of the early modern period, are examined.

Notes

[1] *Cal. Carew MSS, 1515-1574*, p. 237

[2] See W.J. Smyth, 1992, 'Making the Documents of Conquest Speak: The Transformation of Property, Society and Settlement in: M. Silverman and P.H. Gulliver (eds.), *Approaching the Past: Historical Anthropology through Irish Case Studies*, Columbia University Press, New York, pp. 236-290

[3] *Civil Survey, County Tipperary*, vol. 2, pp. 71-112

[4] M. Hennessy, 1988, 'The Priory and Hospital of New Gate: The Evolution and Decline of a Medieval Monastic Estate', in: W.J. Smyth and K. Whelan (eds.), *Common Ground: Essays on the Historical Geography of Ireland*, Cork University Press, Cork, p. 44

[5] *Ibid.*, p. 47. See also *Idem.*, 1985, 'Parochial Organisation in Medieval Tipperary', in: W. Nolan (ed.), *Tipperary: History and Society*, Geography Publications, Dublin, pp. 60-70

[6] N.L.I., D. 658

[7] *Atlas of the Parishes of Cashel and Emly*, Thurles, Co. Tipperary, 1970, pp. iii, xiv

[8] See J.A. Watt, 1987, 'Gaelic Polity and Cultural Identity' in: A. Cosgrove (ed.), *A New History of Ireland, II, Medieval Ireland, 1169-1534*, Clarendon Press, Oxford, pp. 344-345

[9] See C.A. Empey, 1985, 'The Norman Period: 1185-1500', in: Nolan (ed.), *Tipperary: History and Society*, pp. 71-91 for the extent of the Anglo-Norman advance in County Tipperary.

[10] N.L.I., D. 370-372

[11] N.L.I., D. 458; *Red Bk. Ormond*, pp. 64-67

[12] *Red Bk. Ormond*, pp. 64-67

[13] *Ibid.*, p. 66. Other Anglo-Norman boroughs had also been established at Ardmayle, Athassel and Kilfeakle in Middlethird and Clanwilliam baronies, to the south of Kilnamanagh, at this point.

[14] P.R.O., London, c. 135, 55, m. 5

[15] *Ibid.*

[16] *Ibid.*

[17] There is no surviving documentation concerning the manor; it most likely being established on the lands granted to Edmund Butler c.1290 referred to above (N.L.I., D. 370-372).

[18] *Cal. Carew MSS, Bks. Howth, Misc.*, p. 444

[19] N.L.I., D. 794. The Butlers had earlier gained control of these lands by c.1290; see N.L.I., D.370-372

[20] *Cal. Carew MSS, Bks. Howth, Misc.*, p. 444

[21] B.J. Graham, 1993, 'The High Middle Ages: c.1100 to c.1350', in: *Idem.* and L.J. Proudfoot (eds.), *An Historical Geography of Ireland*, Academic Press, London, p. 65

[22] J. Lydon, 1987, 'The Impact of the Bruce Invasion, 1315-27', in: Cosgrove (ed.), *A New History of Ireland II*, p. 302. See also J.A. Watt, 1987, 'The Anglo-Irish Colony under Strain, 1327-99', in: Cosgrove (ed.), *A New History of Ireland II*, pp. 352-396

[23] A. Cosgrove, 1981, *Late Medieval Ireland, 1370-1541*, Helicon, Dublin, p. 9

[24] T.B. Barry, 1993, 'Late Medieval Ireland: The Debate on Social and Economic Transformation, 1350-1550', in: Graham and Proudfoot (eds.), *An Historical Geography of Ireland*, p. 101

[25] *Ibid.*

[26] S.G. Ellis, 1986, 'Nationalist Historiography and the English and Gaelic Worlds in the Late Middle Ages', *Irish Historical Studies*, vol. 25, no. 97, pp. 2-3

[27] See, for example, V.G. Kiernan, 1993, 'The British Isles: Celt and Saxon', in M. Teich and R. Porter (eds.), *The National Question in Europe in Historical Context*, Cambridge University Press, Cambridge, pp. 1-34 and *Idem.*, 1980, *State and Society in Europe, 1550-1660*, Basil Blackwell, Oxford

[28] On this point, see the comments of D. Wishart, 1997, 'The Selectivity of Historical Representation', *Journal of Historical Geography*, 23, 2, pp. 111-118 and G. Bridge, 1997, 'Guest Editorial. Towards a Situated Universalism: On Strategic Rationality and 'Local Theory'', *Environment and Planning D: Society and Space*, 15, pp. 633-639

[29] On this point, see K.W. Nicholls, 1982, 'Anglo-French Ireland and After', *Pertia*, 1, p. 392

[30] *Idem.*, 1972, *Gaelic and Gaelicised Ireland in the Middle Ages*, Gill and MacMillan, Dublin, pp. 18-19

[31] *Ibid.*, p. 19

[32] C.A. Empey and K. Simms, 1975, 'The Ordinances of the White Earl and the Problem of Coign and Livery in the Later Middle Ages', *Proceedings of the Royal Irish Academy*, vol. 75, sec. C, pp. 161-188

[33] Nicholls, *Gaelic and Gaelicised Ireland*, p. 4

[34] *Ibid.*, p. 17

[35] N.L.I., MFIC Pos. 8302

[36] *A.F.M.*, vol. 4, p. 1085

[37] See A. Nic Ghiollamhaith, 1995, 'Kings and Vassals in Later Medieval Ireland', in: T.B. Barry, R. Frame and K. Simms (eds.), *Colony and Frontier in Medieval Ireland*, Hambledon Press, London, pp. 201-216

[38] Nicholls, *Gaelic and Gaelicised Ireland*, p. 8

[39] Graham, 'The High Middle Ages', p. 65

[40] Watt, 'Gaelic Polity and Cultural Identity', p. 317

[41] See F.X. Martin, 1987, 'Introduction: Medieval Ireland', in: Cosgrove (ed.), *A New History of Ireland II*, pp. xlix-lxii

[42] On this point, see Graham, 'The High Middle Ages', pp. 60-63

[43] The question of when the Anglo-Normans can be referred to as Anglo-Irish has been examined by Martin (above p. liii). He attributes Anglo-Irish to the period after 1216. However, as this term is quite ambiguous and misleading in the light of later historical developments, it is not one that is used here in a medieval context. Hereafter the term Anglo-Norman is used expediently to refer to the descendants of the Anglo-Normans who were later to become known as the Old English, and, when quoted, the term Anglo-Irish refers to the same.

[44] R. Frame, 1990, *The Political Development of the British Isles 1100-1400*, Clarendon Press, Oxford, pp. 203-204

[45] Cosgrove, *Late Medieval Ireland*, pp. 79-81

[46] The idea that the Anglo-Norman colony was substantially transformed through contact with, and adoption of, Gaelic-Irish practices has been well documented; see, for example, J.A. Watt, 1987, 'Approaches to the History of Fourteenth-Century Ireland', in: Cosgrove (ed.), *A New History of Ireland II*, p. 310. There has been notably less exploration of the

impact of the Anglo-Norman world on the Gaelic-Irish one until recently. Some of the reasons for this would appear to be the lack of specific documentary evidence and the prevalence of a traditional nationalist perspective on the cohesion and continuity of Gaelic society. Nonetheless, Nic Ghiollamhaith has importantly drawn attention to the fact that the expansion of the Anglo-Norman colony had the general effect of fragmenting the Gaelic polity, in a geographical and political sense, with the emergence of frontiers. She points to the fewer Gaelic-Irish dynastic marriages and inter-provincial alliances, the lesser involvement by Gaelic-Irish kings in one another's kingdoms, and the creation of a new network of alliances (that significantly also cut across hierarchical links between overlords and their vassals) as substantial evidence of the impact of fragmentation brought about by the Anglo-Norman colonisation; see Nic Ghiollamhaith, 'Kings and Vassals in Later Medieval Ireland', pp. 201-216. Graham, too, has highlighted that "Gaelic-Irish society was inevitably altered by the Anglo-Norman presence" by the most usual form of contact through warfare and by the intermittent adoption of feudal practices; see Graham, 'The High Middle Ages', p. 65

[47] Another aspect of 'co-existence' was "the mutual adjustment of [the] two legal systems, Irish brehon law and English common law"; see Watt, 'Gaelic Polity and Cultural Identity', p. 317

[48] B. Smith, 1988, 'The Concept of the March in Medieval Ireland: The Case of Uriel', *Proceedings of the Royal Irish Academy*, vol. 88, sec. C, pp. 257-269. The retreat of centralised administrative authority in the later Middle Ages in Ireland was also situated within the wider shrinkage of political control from periphery to core in late fourteenth-century England and in the pan-European context of the transition within late medieval feudalism; see B.N.S. Campbell, 1990, 'People and Land in the Middle Ages, 1066-1500', in: R.A. Dodgshon and R.A. Butlin (eds.), *An Historical Geography of England and Wales*, Second Edition, Academic Press, London, p. 102. Cf. A. Simms, 1988, 'Core and Periphery in Medieval Europe: The Irish Experience in a Wider Context', in: Smyth and Whelan (eds.), *Common Ground*, pp. 22-40

[49] Subsequent to recovery and the shift towards regionalised power bases in the later Middle Ages, the tower house has been interpreted as having had a role of nucleating settlement and providing security at the local level. See: Barry, 'Late Medieval Ireland', pp. 108-110, 119; M. MacCurtain, 1988, 'A Lost Landscape: The Geraldine Castles and Tower Houses of the Shannon Estuary', in: J. Bradley (ed.), *Society and Settlement in Medieval Ireland*, Boethius Press, Kilkenny, pp. 429-444; M. O'Dowd, 1986, 'Gaelic Economy and Society', in: C. Brady and R. Gillespie (eds.), *Natives and Newcomers: Essays on the Making of Irish Colonial Society, 1534-1641*, Irish Academic Press, Dublin, pp. 127-128; and W.J. Smyth, 1985, 'Property, Patronage and Population – Reconstructing the Human Geography of Mid-Seventeenth Century County Tipperary', in: Nolan (ed.), *Tipperary: History and Society*, pp. 125-130

[50] T.B. Barry, 1995, 'The Last Frontier: Defence and Settlement in Late Medieval Ireland', in: *Idem. et al* (eds.), *Colony and Frontier*, pp. 217, 227

[51] For a useful map of the distribution of tower houses in County Tipperary, see C.T. Cairns, 1987, *Irish Tower Houses: A County Tipperary Case Study*, Athlone, Co. Westmeath, p. 3. Cf. C. O'Danachair, 1977-1979, 'Irish Tower Houses and their Regional Distribution', *Béaloideas*, 45-47, pp. 158-163

[52] See, for example, C. Parker, 1995, 'The Internal Frontier: The Irish in County Waterford

in the Later Middle Ages', in: Barry *et al* (eds.), *Colony and Frontier*, pp. 139-154 and K. Simms, 1995, 'Frontiers in the Irish Church - Regional and Cultural', in: Barry *et al* (eds.), *Colony and Frontier*, pp. 177-200
[53] J. Derricke, *The Image of Irelande* (1581), reprint. J. Small, Adam and Charles Black, Edinburgh, 1883
[54] See M.L. Pratt, 1992, *Imperial Eyes: Travel Writing and Transculturation*, Routledge, London. Cf. P. Routledge, 1997, 'A Spatiality of Resistances: Theory and Practice in Nepal's Revolution of 1990', in: S. Pile and M. Keith (eds.), *Geographies of Resistance*, Routledge, London, pp. 68-86
[55] I have discussed this notion in detail elsewhere; see J. Morrissey, 2000, *Encountering Colonialism: Gaelic-Irish Responses to New English Expansion in Early Modern West Tipperary, c.1541-1641*, Unpublished Ph.D. Thesis, University of Exeter, esp. pp. 74-86
[56] N.L.I., MFIC Pos. 8302
[57] On this point, see Nic Ghiollamhaith, 'Kings and Vassals in Later Medieval Ireland', pp. 201-216
[58] See D.B. Quinn and K.W. Nicholls, 1976, 'Ireland in 1534', in: T.W. Moody, F.X. Martin and F.J. Byrne (eds.), *A New History of Ireland III: Early Modern Ireland 1534-1691*, Clarendon Press, Oxford, pp. 1-38. See esp. the map of the numerous and fragmented lordships of Ireland, *c.*1534, on pp. 2-3.
[59] Watt, 'Gaelic Polity and Cultural Identity', p. 350. Cf. K.W. Nicholls, 1987, 'Gaelic Society and Economy in the High Middle Ages', in: Cosgrove (ed.), *A New History of Ireland II*, pp. 397-438
[60] There have been a number of reasons put forward to explain the extension of English administrative and military control of Ireland in the sixteenth century: McGurk, for example, points out that the expansion of crown central policy was facilitated by the centralisation of Elizabethan government in contemporary England during the Nine Years' War from 1594 to 1603. This, he argues, accommodated a sustained effort to effect a reconsolidated English administration in Ireland, which was no longer a low priority as it had earlier been; see J. McGurk, 1997, *The Elizabethan Conquest of Ireland (The 1590s Crisis)*, Manchester University Press, Manchester, pp. 262, 265. Morgan asserts, too, that if there was a common, though not axiomatic, 'British' policy being pursued by English statesmen during the sixteenth century, it was "to keep foreign powers out of the periphery"; see H. Morgan, 1996, 'British Policies before the British State', in: B. Bradshaw and J. Morrill (eds.), *The British Problem, c.1534-1707: State Formation in the Atlantic Archipelago*, MacMillan Press Ltd., Basingstoke, p. 66. Furthermore, as Bottigheimer argues, "the late medieval decline of effective English influence in Ireland intersected calamitously with the growing need of the early modern monarchy for strategic support in the western island"; see K.S. Bottigheimer, 1978, 'Kingdom and Colony: Ireland in the Westward Enterprise 1536-1660', in: K.R. Andrews, N.P. Canny and P.E.H. Hair (eds.), *The Westward Enterprise: English Activities in Ireland, The Atlantic and America, 1480-1650*, Liverpool University Press, Liverpool, p. 48
[61] *Cal. Carew MSS, 1515-1574*, p. 158
[62] C. Brady, 1986, 'Court, Castle and Country: The Framework of Government in Tudor Ireland', in: *Idem.* and Gillespie (eds.), *Natives and Newcomers*, pp. 25-26
[63] *Ibid.*, pp. 22-23. The second phase identified generally by Brady, which dominated during

the reign of Elizabeth, was typified by "the enforcement of royal authority through systematic coercion and dispossession"; see *ibid.*, p. 22

[64] H. Wood, 1919, *A Guide to the Public Records Deposited in the P.R.O. of Ireland*, I.M.C., Dublin, p. 261

[65] D.A. Murphy, 1994, *The Two Tipperarys*, Regional Studies in Political and Administrative History, no. 1, Relay, Nenagh, Co. Tipperary, pp. 2, 4

[66] See T. Blake Butler, 1953, 'Seneschals of the Liberty of Tipperary', *Irish Genealogist*, vol. 2, no. 10, pp. 297-298 and *Idem.*, 1959, 'The Sheriffs of the Liberty of The County Tipperary', *Irish Genealogist*, vol. 3, no. 4, pp. 120-123

[67] *Idem.*, 1960, 'The Sheriffs of the Liberty of The County Tipperary', *Irish Genealogist*, vol. 3, no. 5, pp. 158-161

[68] Ormond's lease of Miltown in Clogher parish, to the south-east of Kilnamanagh in 1544, further facilitated his influence in the barony; see *Cal. Ormond Deeds, 1509-1547*, p. 265

[69] O'Dowd, 'Gaelic Economy and Society', p. 134

[70] See Cosgrove, *Late Medieval Ireland*, p. 81

[71] *Cal. Carew MSS, Bks. Howth, Misc.*, p. 257

[72] *Ibid.*, pp. 255-256

[73] Factionalism, as Brady outlines, was "intense and pervasive" and profoundly influential throughout all four provinces in Ireland in "structuring social and political relations"; see Brady, 'Court, Castle and Country', p. 29. Brady argues that by 1541 "such authority as the king of Ireland [Henry VIII] might have claimed had already been substantially pre-empted by an alternative and highly sophisticated political system which had established itself long before the Tudors came to power: the political system of faction"; see *ibid.*

[74] See also *Cal. S.P. Ire., 1509-1573*, p. 78, where tributes of horses and men paid by the O'Dwyers to the Butlers are recorded for 1547.

[75] A. McClintock, 1988, 'The Earls of Ormond and Tipperary's Role in the Governing of Ireland (1603-1641)', *Tipperary Historical Journal*, 1, pp. 159-172

[76] *Cal. Ormond Deeds, 1547-1584*, p. 62

[77] *Cal. S.P. Ire., 1509-1573*, p. 243

[78] *Cal. Carew MSS, 1515-1574*, p. 394. The O'Dwyers had defeated William Grane McBryan (one of the principal protagonists of the second Desmond uprising) and 20 of his men in 1583; see *Cal. S.P. Ire., 1574-1585*, pp. cx, 437

[79] G.A. Hayes-McCoy, 1976, 'Conciliation, Coercion and the Protestant Reformation, 1547-71' in: Moody *et al* (eds.), *A New History of Ireland III*, pp. 91-92

[80] *Idem.*, 1976, 'The Completion of the Tudor Conquest and the Advance of the Counter-Reformation, 1571-1603', in: Moody *et al* (eds.), *A New History of Ireland III*, p. 99. The difficulties and failings of the Tudor administration in Ireland are also outlined and explored in C. Brady, 1996, 'England's Defence and Ireland's Reform: The Dilemma of the Irish Viceroys, 1541-1641', in: Bradshaw and Morrill (eds.), *The British Problem*, pp. 89-117 and S.G. Ellis, 1985, *Tudor Ireland: Crown, Community and the Conflict of Cultures 1470-1603*, Longman, London, pp. 315-316

[81] See C. Brady, 1994, *The Chief Governors: The Rise and Fall of Reform Government in Tudor Ireland 1536-1588*, Cambridge University Press, Cambridge, chapters 4-5

[82] *Cal. S.P. Ire., 1509-1573*, p. 330

[83] *Cal. Carew MSS, 1575-1588*, p. 41

[84] C. Brady, 1989, 'Thomas Butler, Earl of Ormond (1531-1614) and Reform in Tudor Ireland', in: *Idem.*, (ed.), *Worsted in the Game: Losers in Irish History*, Lilliput Press, Dublin, p. 56

[85] *Ibid.*, p. 54

[86] *Cal. Ormond Deeds, 1547-1584*, pp. 60-62

[87] *A.F.M.*, vol. 5, p. 1629

[88] The earliest pardons appear for the years 1549 and 1550; see *Fiants Ire., Hen. VIII-Eliz., 1521-1558*, nos. 363, 434. Foremost members of the O'Dwyers continued to be pardoned for various offences against crown administration in Tipperary until 1602; see *Fiants Ire., Hen. VIII-Eliz., 1586-1603*, nos. 6706-6707

[89] Pardon to John O'Dwyer of Donohill, Kilnamanagh, 1552; see *Fiants Ire., Hen. VIII-Eliz., 1521-1558*, no. 966

[90] *Fiants Ire., Hen. VIII-Eliz., 1558-1586*, nos. 1964, 2024, 2082, 3102, 3364, 4371, 4907; *Fiants Ire., Hen. VIII-Eliz., 1586-1603*, nos. 4937, 5085

[91] *Fiants Ire., Hen. VIII-Eliz., 1558-1586*, no. 3364

[92] The diverse artisan composition of the O'Dwyer lordship, which included horsemen, clerks, priests, tailors and harpers, is also revealed in various pardons; see, for example, *Fiants Ire., Hen. VIII-Eliz., 1558-1586*, nos. 1964, 3102

[93] *Cal. pat. rolls Ire., Eliz.*, pp. 48-49

[94] *Ibid.*

[95] *Fiants Ire., Hen. VIII-Eliz., 1558-1586*, no. 4907. See also *ibid.*, no. 2082, where it is seen that in 1572 galloglasses, kerns and footmen were again operative within the O'Dwyer lordship.

[96] See, for example, John Derricke's contemporary accounts in *The Image of Irelande*. Cf. J.H. Ohlmeyer, 1998, ''Civilizinge of those Rude Partes': Colonization within Britain and Ireland, 1580-1640s', in: N. Canny (ed.), *The Origins of Empire: British Overseas Enterprise to the Close of the 17th Century*, The Oxford History of the British Empire, vol. 1, Oxford University Press, Oxford, pp. 124-147, esp. pp. 127-130

[97] E. Spenser, *A View of the Present State of Ireland* (*c.*1596), ed. W.L. Renwick, Clarendon Press, Oxford, 1970; *Idem.*, 'A Brief Note of Ireland' (*c.*1598), reprint. E.A. Greenlaw *et al.* (eds.), *The Works of Edmund Spenser: A Variorum Edition*, vol. 10, pp. 233-245, 11 vols., John Hopkins University Press, Baltimore, 1932-1949; J. Davies, *A Discovery of the True Causes Why Ireland was Never Entirely Subdued and Brought Under Obedience of the Crown of England until the Beginning of His Majesty's Happy Reign* (*c.*1612), reprint. J.G. Barry, Irish University Press, Shannon, 1969

[98] There is a large body of material that deals with the subject of the legitimisation of English activities in Ireland. See, for example, the works of: A. Hadfield, 1998, *Literature, Travel and Colonial Writing in the English Renaissance 1545-1625*, Clarendon Press, Oxford; *Idem.*, 1997, *Edmund Spenser's Irish Experience: Wild Fruit and Salvage Soyl*, Clarendon Press, Oxford; P. Neville-Sington, 1997, ''A Very Good Trumpet': Richard Hakluyt and the Politics of Overseas Expansion', in: C.C. Brown and A.F. Marotti (eds.), *Texts and Cultural Change in Early Modern England*, MacMillan Press Ltd., Houndmills, Basingstoke, pp. 66-81; A. Hadfield, 1993, 'Briton and Scythian: Tudor Representations of Irish Origins', *Irish Historical Studies*, vol. 28, no. 112, pp. 390-408; D.J. Baker, 1993, 'Off the Map: Charting Uncertainty in Renaissance Ireland', in: B. Bradshaw, A. Hadfield and W. Maley (eds.),

Representing Ireland: Literature and the Origins of Conflict, 1534-1660, Cambridge University Press, Cambridge, pp. 76-92; S.T. Cavanagh, 1993, "The fatal destiny of that land': Elizabethan Views of Ireland', in: Bradshaw *et al* (eds.), *Representing Ireland*, pp. 116-131; L. Jardine, 1993, 'Encountering Ireland: Gabriel Harvey, Edmund Spenser, and English Colonial Ventures', in: Bradshaw *et al* (eds.), *Representing Ireland*, pp. 60-75; W. Maley, 1993, 'How Milton and Some Contemporaries Read Spenser's *View*', in: Bradshaw *et al* (eds.), *Representing Ireland*, pp. 191-208; J. Reinhard Lupton, 1993, 'Mapping Mutability: or, Spenser's Irish Plot', in: Bradshaw *et al* (eds.), *Representing Ireland*, pp. 93-115; B. Bradshaw, 1988, 'Robe and Sword in the Conquest of Ireland', in: C. Cross, D. Loades and J.J. Scarisbrick (eds.), *Law and Government under the Tudors*, Cambridge University Press, Cambridge, pp. 139-162; and the earlier comprehensive work of D.B. Quinn, 1966, *The Elizabethans and the Irish*, Cornell University Press, Ithaca

[99] 'Tanistry' refers to the Gaelic-Irish system of the succession of the chief or lord where descent took place not by primogeniture but by an intricate selection of the most able in the lordship; 'gavelkind' involved the equal inheritance of land by each landowner's sons; and 'coign and livery' entailed the feudal practices of billeting and extortion by kerns, galloglasses and others within the lordship.

[100] Davies, *Discovery*, p. 164

[101] This was not a derogatory term; its contemporary meaning being 'pure' or 'unmixed'.

[102] *Cal. Carew MSS, 1589-1600*, p. 27

[103] *Ibid.*, p. 28. This legitimised conviction underpinned the government programme of 'surrender and regrant' agreements, which were to be increasingly utilised in the early seventeenth century; a substantial point which will be returned to in chapter three below.

[104] A. Hadfield and J. McVeagh (eds.), 1994, *Strangers to that Land: British Perceptions of Ireland from the Reformation to the Famine*, Colin Smythe, Gerard's Cross, Bucks., p. 39; see also pp. 37-41, 47-49

[105] *Cal. pat. rolls Ire., Hen. VIII-Eliz.*, pp. 340-341; *Cal. pat. rolls Ire., Eliz.*, pp. 236-240

[106] See, for example, the pardon to John O'Dwyer in 1552 recorded in *Fiants Ire., Hen. VIII-Eliz., 1521-1558*, no. 966

[107] Pardon to leading O'Dwyers, 1578: *Fiants Ire., Hen. VIII-Eliz., 1558-1586*, no. 3364. Similar stipulated requirements were incorporated into pardons given in 1577, 1584, 1586 and 1587; see *ibid.*, nos. 3102, 4371, 4907 and *Fiants Ire., Hen. VIII-Eliz., 1586-1603*, nos. 4937, 5085

[108] *Fiants Ire., Hen. VIII-Eliz., 1558-1586*, no. 2024

[109] *Ibid.*, no. 5085

[110] *Cal. Ormond Deeds, 1547-1584*, p. 262

[111] The rectory and affiliated lands of Clogher were leased as early as 1543, and were renewed in 1561 and 1569; see *Fiants Ire., Hen. VIII-Eliz., 1521-1558*, no. 374 and *Fiants Ire., Hen. VIII-Eliz., 1558-1586*, nos. 322, 1250. The parsonage and estate of Ballintemple were also leased in 1570 and renewed in 1582; see *Fiants Ire., Hen. VIII-Eliz., 1558-1586*, nos. 1643, 4013

[112] M. MacCurtain, 1972, *Tudor and Stuart Ireland*, The Gill History of Ireland 7, Gill and MacMillan, Dublin, p. 89

[113] Hayes-McCoy highlights that as many as 12,000 colonists may have been in Munster by 1598; see Hayes-McCoy, 'The Completion of the Tudor Conquest', p. 114

[114] The Old English, too, were increasingly viewed as having degenerated from civility and become Gaelicised; see, for example, the comments N. Canny, 1993, 'The Attempted Anglicization of Ireland in the Seventeenth Century: An Exemplar of "British History"', in: R.G. Asch (ed.), *Three Nations – A Common History: England, Scotland, Ireland and British History c.1600-1920*, Universitatsverlag Dr. Brockmeyer, Bochum, p. 56

[115] *Cal. Carew MSS, 1575-1588*, p. 419

[116] See Hadfield and McVeagh, *Strangers to that Land*, chap. 6, esp. pp. 73-80, 83-87 and C. Brady, 1989, 'The Road to the View: On the Decline of Reform Thought in Tudor Ireland', in: P. Coughlin (ed.), *Spenser and Ireland: An Interdisciplinary Perspective*, Cork University Press, Cork, pp. 25-45. Residual elements of reform thought were discernible in later English colonial discourse but these came to be superseded ultimately by more radical objectives; cf., for example, C. Durston, 1986, '"Let Ireland Be Quiet": Opposition in England to the Cromwellian Conquest in Ireland', *History Workshop Journal*, 21, pp. 105-112 and N. Carlin, 1993, 'Extreme or Mainstream? The English Independents and the Cromwellian Reconquest of Ireland, 1649-1651', in: Bradshaw *et al* (eds.), *Representing Ireland*, pp. 209-226

[117] Brady, 'Court, Castle and Country', p. 22-23

[118] *Ibid.*, p. 23

[119] *Ibid.*

[120] B. Bradshaw, 1988, 'Robe and Sword in the Conquest of Ireland', in: C. Cross, D. Loades and J.J. Scarisbrick (eds.), *Law and Government under the Tudors*, Cambridge University Press, Cambridge, p. 162. In a related manner, Morgan's recent edited work extends the exploration of the English colonial polity in Ireland beyond the appraisal of the more commonly-cited treatises of Spenser, Herbert and Beacon to include an examination of the contemporary works of, for example, O'Sullivan Beare, Rothe, Usher and Rich; see H. Morgan (ed.), 1999, *Political Ideology in Ireland, 1541-1641*, Four Courts Press, Dublin

[121] Giraldus Cambrensis (Gerald of Wales), *Topographia Hibernica (The History and Topography of Ireland)* (1188-1189), trans. J.J. O'Meara, Penguin, Harmondsworth, 1982; *Idem.*, *Expugnatio Hibernica (The Conquest of Ireland)* (1188-1189), ed. and trans. A.B. Scott and F.X. Martin, Royal Irish Academy, Dublin, 1978

[122] N. Canny, 1988, *Kingdom and Colony: Ireland in the Atlantic World 1560-1800*, John Hopkins University Press, Baltimore, p. 3

[123] J. Gillingham, 1993, 'The English Invasion of Ireland', in: Bradshaw *et al* (eds.), *Representing Ireland*, p. 24

[124] *Ibid.*

[125] Canny, 'The Attempted Anglicization of Ireland, p. 56

[126] *Ibid.*

[127] *Cal. S.P. Ire., 1588-1592*, p. 62

[128] *Ibid.*, p. 425

[129] *Ibid.*, p. 426

[130] Brady, *The Chief Governors*, p. 89; see also chap. 6 for a more detailed discussion of purveyance and the opposition to cess (most vocally by the Old English within the Pale) in the late sixteenth century.

[131] *Cal. S.P. Ire., 1592-1596*, p. 7

[132] *Ibid.*, p. 326. The county of Tipperary was also compelled to contribute money for the English invasion of Ulster in 1595; see *ibid.*, p. 361

[133] See D.B. Quinn, 1966, 'The Munster Plantation: Problems and Opportunities', *Cork Historical Society Journal*, LXXI, pp. 19-40, esp. p. 33 and A.J. Sheehan, 1983, 'Official Reaction to Native Land Claims in the Plantation of Munster', *Irish Historical Studies*, vol. 23, no. 92, pp. 297-318, esp. pp. 313-317. For west Tipperary, it is seen that one New English adventurer, George Sherlocke, had acquired holdings of land in Clonoulty and Ballintemple parishes in Kilnamanagh and other lands in Clanwilliam barony by 1591; see *Cal. Ormond Deeds, 1584-1603*, pp. 106-109

[134] Hayes-McCoy, 'The Completion of the Tudor Conquest', p. 116

[135] *Cal. Carew MSS, 1589-1600*, p. 179

[136] Hayes-McCoy, 'The Completion of the Tudor Conquest', p. 123

[137] *Cal. Carew MSS, 1589-1600*, p. 457

[138] Hayes-McCoy, 'The Completion of the Tudor Conquest', p. 122

[139] *Cal. Carew MSS, 1601-1603*, p. 103. See also *Cal. S.P. Ire., 1600-1601*, pp. 425, 444

[140] Regarding Tyrone's march through Tipperary and his activities there in late 1599 and early 1600, see *Cal. S.P. Ire., 1599-1600*, pp. 425-430, 460, 473, 489-492. See Hayes-McCoy, 'The Completion of the Tudor Conquest', pp. 115-137 and J.C. Beckett, 1981, *The Making of Modern Ireland 1603-1923*, Faber and Faber, London (first pub. 1966), pp. 21-24 for detailed and cogent accounts of the Nine Years, the failure of Spanish assistance and the ultimate collapse of the Ulster confederacy after the defeat at Kinsale.

[141] *Cal. Carew MSS, 1589-1600*, p. 299

[142] *Cal. S.P. Ire., 1598-1599*, pp. 453-454

[143] Hayes-McCoy, 'The Completion of the Tudor Conquest', p. 131

[144] *A.F.M.*, vol. 6, pp. 2077-2079

[145] *Ibid.*, pp. 2079, 2149. Interestingly, the later Irish translation for 'Clonoulty', the largest parish in the barony, became 'Cluain an Ultaigh', which means 'meadow of the Ulstermen'.

[146] *Cal. S.P. Ire., 1599-1600*, p. 45

[147] *Ibid.*, p. 297

[148] *Ibid.*, p. 471. Much of Magrath's accusations can be considered exaggerated propaganda given the fact that he was later discredited, though treated mercifully, by James I, who did not want to publicly draw attention to the corruption of his Protestant church activities in west Tipperary (see the letter from King Jas. I to Lord Deputy, Sir Arthur Chichester, 1609: *Cal. S.P. Ire., 1601-1603*, Addenda, pp. 655-656). However, the important consideration is that O'Dwyer had effected a level of activity deemed rebellious to the crown.

[149] *Cal. S.P. Ire., 1598-1599*, p. 454

[150] *Cal. S.P. Ire., 1601-1603*, p. 32

[151] *Fiants Ire., Hen. VIII-Eliz., 1586-1603*, nos. 6441, 6522

[152] *Ibid.*, no. 6531

[153] *Cal. S.P. Ire., 1600*, p. 11

[154] *Ibid.*

[155] *Cal. S.P. Ire., 1599-1600*, p. 428, *Cal. S.P. Ire., 1600*, pp. 165, 233; *Cal. S.P. Ire., 1601-1603*, p. 33

[156] B.S.A. Yeoh, 2000, '*Historical Geographies of the Colonised World*', in B. Graham and

C. Nash (eds.), *Modern Historical Geographies,* Prentice Hall, Harlow, p. 162

[157] For a broader examination of the contradictory nature of the interaction of spaces of domination and resistance in the colonial context, see the comments of Routledge, 'A Spatiality of Resistances', pp. 68-86

[158] Similar themes of accommodation and expediency have been identified for frontier societies in Connacht and Ulster in the later sixteenth century; see B. Cunningham and R. Gillespie, 1990, 'Englishmen in Sixteenth-Century Irish Annals', *Irish Economic and Social History*, XVII, pp. 5-21, esp. pp. 14-20, H. Morgan, 1988, 'The End of Gaelic Ulster: A Thematic Interpretation of Events between 1534 and 1610', *Irish Historical Studies*, vol. 26, no. 101, pp. 8-32, esp. pp. 8-9, 32, and T. Bartlett, 1982, 'The O'Haras of Annaghmore *c.*1600-*c.*1800: Survival and Revival', *Irish Economic and Social History*, IX, pp. 34-52, esp. pp. 34-37

[159] *Cal. S.P. Ire., 1600*, pp. 378-379

[160] *Ibid.*, p. 378

Chapter 3

The Quest for Survival in the
Early Seventeenth Century

Many things want reformation … but if a Parliament were soon
holden, the churches re-edified, a learned ministry planted, more
judges sitting in the courts of justice, and the laws roundly executed
but for one year … this nation would be … as willing to be ruled as
the people of England – *Sir John Davies, 1604* [1]

Request to surrender to his Majesty all his lands and seignories and
to have the same regranted to him to hold of his majesty by English
tenure, and thereby to reduce his country, being all Irish, to civility,
and forasmuch as the best means thereto is to have the true use and
the execution of the common law which is wanting there – *Petition
of Dermot O'Dwyer, chief lord of the country of Kilnemanagh, to Sir
Arthur Chichester, lord deputy of Ireland, 1607* [2]

A growing confidence in the execution of government administration – evident
above in the beliefs of Sir John Davies – emerged in the aftermath of the
Elizabethan conquest. The flight of the Ulster earls of Tyrone and Tyrconnell
in 1607, subsequent to their defeat in the Nine Years War, opened the way for
the establishment of a comprehensive plantation in the province, while the
reinvigoration of the Munster plantation began to attract large numbers of
colonists from South-West England. The consolidation, too, of political
structures modelled closely on those of England had facilitated for the first time
the effectual implementation of English rule throughout the island. Accordingly,
leading members of the O'Dwyers – such as the chief quoted above – sought
to redefine their political, economic and social organisation in the context of the
common law and a stronger government authority. This chapter, by focusing
specifically on landholding, aims to explore the impact of New English legal
and material practices in Kilnamanagh prior to the 1641 rebellion and to
elucidate the manner in which foremost members of the O'Dwyer lordship
attempted to adapt themselves to the new order.

Securing Landownership in the Early 1600s

Numerous writers on early modern Ireland have ascribed critical importance to landholding as the fundamental organising principle and dynamic in society.[3] Smyth, for example, observes that the "ownership and control of land was the central fulcrum of economic and political power ... shaping the location and character of most human activities".[4] Gillespie, too, stresses that early modern Irish society "passed from a medieval world into a modern social order by means of a revolution in landownership and in its social, economic and political structures".[5] Furthermore, land was the principal basis of *localised* power – particularly important in such a yet factional world as early seventeenth-century Ireland – and subsequent to the establishment of centralised crown authority in the later Tudor period, there emerged in the early years of James I's reign an acute necessity to adjust claims to landownership in the context of the common law and English tenurial, inheritance and land management practices.

The New English administration in the wake of the Nine Years War had begun to seize lands of the Ryans, O'Kennedys and others throughout Tipperary relinquished by those slain or active in the rebellion, and had also set about reasserting their rights to premises that had earlier passed into crown control following the dissolution of monastic lands in the mid-sixteenth century.[6] The extension of English legal practices, furthermore, had come to indirectly affect the landholding structure of the O'Dwyer lordship given that the lands therein – although not confiscated – were not held in accordance with the common law. In this context, further pressures on land claims came from within the lordship itself, where a series of disputes over ownership of particular holdings between members of the O'Dwyers and others reflected the degree to which the nature of property rights was in a state of transition.[7] A litigation from 1605, for example, reveals a disagreement concerning the Gaelic-Irish custom of gavelkind (division of property equally amongst the owner's sons) as an appropriate means of inheritance of specific lands in the barony.[8] The case stated that 'gavelkind' constituted the tradition of descent "used and continued time beyond man's memory in the manor and lordship of Kylnemanagh", but the dispute over its continued practice underlines the extent to which the older Gaelic-Irish order was being challenged from within via the English court system.[9] Cunningham and Gillespie have argued that a similar pattern is evident for Connacht in the later sixteenth century, from which time "the native

Irish were eager to use the machinery of the common law to resolve disputes among themselves".[10]

Further to the above, the 'Commission for the Remedy of Defective Titles', established in 1606, required landowners to prove their right of title or forfeit their possessions to the crown. Many landowners were to fail in their attempts to confirm their legal rights to holdings at court, which resulted in the redistribution of lands in the midlands and elsewhere in the early decades of the century.[11] The imperative of the O'Dwyers, therefore, to verify the legality of their landholdings became increasingly critical to their survival. Equally important was the necessity of the leading landowners in the barony to demonstrate their capacity to redefine and present themselves as *de facto* landlords, in the English tradition, given the increased external pressures of a stronger and more centralised government authority. In 1602, for example, the lord deputy, Lord Mountjoy, had written to the president of Munster, Sir George Carew, concerning his doubts over the "honest disposition" of Dermot O'Dwyer, the chief of Kilnamanagh, and had requested him to send for O'Dwyer to put him "upon good assurance for [his] future subjection".[12] O'Dwyer, who had so effectively situated himself in the new order at the turn of the century, as outlined in chapter two, was being impelled to continue to present himself as a willing and progressive subject during the early years of the Stuart administration.

O'Dwyer's recognition of the necessity to reconstitute existing landholding and social structures in Kilnamanagh in the context of accepted 'English' norms induced him to signal his intention to participate in the 'surrender and regrant' agreements, which had become an essential mechanism of reform government in the early Stuart period. This form of 'reducing' the country was not unique to Ireland. As Kiernan notes, a similar process of crown control was evident in contemporary Scotland and elsewhere.[13] The 'Commission for Surrenders' was set up in 1605 for the purpose of extending the operation of the policy,[14] and in 1607, as quoted at the beginning of this chapter, O'Dwyer forwarded a petition to Lord Deputy Chichester requesting the legal, economic and administrative arrangements of the surrender and regrant programme, in order to "reduce his country" to "civility".[15] O'Dwyer's appreciation of the agenda of the new order is indicated by his emphasis of the urgency of having the "true use" and "execution of the common law" in his lordship because "there [was] neither court leet nor court baron nor any fair or market".[16]

Accordingly, he further petitioned the inclusion of the following important components in his regrant:

> that he may hold a court leet in and throughout the said country of Kilnemanagh and have the profits and perquisites thereof, together with another court there in the nature of a court baron, and also two yearly fairs upon St. Mark's day (April 25) and St. Bartholomew's day (Aug. 24) respectively, each to continue for two days, and a weekly market in the town of Kilshenan with the profits of the same.[17]

O'Dwyer's petition of the above privileges demonstrates simultaneously an informed appreciation of the government agenda of reform and the extent to which he desired to present himself to the Stuart administration as an 'improving' landlord.[18] It reveals, particularly, his knowledge of the essential constituents of the legal and economic framework of the common-law system, which enabled him to adjust progressively to the new order. O'Dwyer's political awareness and competence subsequently brought about the inclusion of all his requests in his surrender and regrant of June 1607; the content of which is examined below.[19]

Redefining Landholdings in the Context of the Crown

The initial important consideration of Dermot O'Dwyer's surrender and regrant agreement is that it is seen to have instituted in the lordship of Kilnamanagh the commutation of arbitrary exactions to an annual fixed rent, whereby the Gaelic-Irish redistributive customs of service, therein stated as "cuttings, cuddye, cesse, presse, cosherie, and bonnagh", and hitherto paid to the "captains or thanists", were replaced by "chief rents" payable by the "several tenants" of the delineated lands.[20] Such a directive to standardise the rents and services within the O'Dwyer lordship reflected the broader design of government to bring about the abolition of the Gaelic-Irish material practices deemed deleterious to authoritative centralised administration and order. The agreement's inclusion of the rights to hold a court leet and baron, and the licence to hold two fairs each year and a weekly market (all of which O'Dwyer had requested) reflected the extent of his desire to meet the legal and economic requirements of the English common-law system and associated material practices. Evident, too, is the degree to which the Gaelic-Irish traditions of society and economy were being regulated and transformed.

Elsewhere in Ireland, in the early seventeenth century, the process of standardised commutation of rents has been associated with the consolidation of English commercialised order and the simultaneous collapse of the Gaelic-Irish landholding superstructure of society. Duffy, for example, attributes the "commercial forces" of the capitalist early modern economy as crucial in "bringing about an insidious transformation in social and landholding structures in parts of Ireland".[21] The evidence from the regrant of the O'Dwyers' chief substantiates, moreover, Ohlmeyer's contention that

> in order to survive and succeed in this 'civilising' English world and
> to be considered 'worthy subjects', [the Gaelic-Irish chieftains] had
> no alternative but to exploit the economic advantages of the English
> system of landlord-tenant relations and of a commercial economy.[22]

A further notable feature of the surrender and regrant of Dermot O'Dwyer was the distinction drawn between holdings held by the chief as his 'demesne' lands and those listed as 'rent' lands elsewhere throughout the barony.[23] The lands marked out as subject to rent included the articulation of the rights and services due to other landholders in the lordship. It is seen, for example, that the rights of other leading O'Dwyer landowners were carefully delineated and preserved, whereby those in possession, partly or wholly, of their own lands, were "freed from the said chief rent for ever".[24] The rents and services due to the earl of Ormond and "divers others" in Kilnamanagh were also upheld.[25] This points to a substantial level of continuity in the landholding structure of the barony, and illustrates, moreover, the limited capacity of the surrender and regrant policy as a mechanism of reform.[26]

O'Dwyer's surrender and regrant agreement reveals that, despite a substantial superimposition of 'English' economic and social order in Kilnamanagh, the government administration was also attempting to secure peace by expediently maintaining strong residual elements of the old order.[27] In Kilnamanagh, this was clearly a necessary constituent of the regrant process given the complicated delineation of the landholdings, which prevailed to the mid-seventeenth century, as evidenced by the *Civil Survey*.[28] As Gillespie notes, County Tipperary in the 1640s had "a bewildering complexity of different types of tenures operating side by side".[29] Similarly, in County Sligo, in the north-west of the country, numerous landholding arrangements were "adopted by families living in a society where observance of a uniform land law was only slowly being introduced".[30] It is therefore important, at this juncture, to note that the *legal* redefinition of Gaelic-Irish order in accordance with the common law and associated social norms did not necessarily involve the reconstitution of Gaelic-Irish *tenurial* arrangements and, accordingly, the ensuing complicated landholding superstructure of society needs to be seen in this context. In essence, the convoluted landholding structure of Kilnamanagh was rendered even more intricate by the incomplete manner in which English legal and socio-economic order was introduced, which subsequently contributed to conflicting ideologies and developments in the barony in succeeding decades.

The evidence from the early seventeenth century suggests then that the New English administration sought actively to bring about order in the Gaelic-Irish lordships by an inconsistent adoption of numerous existing material practices. MacCarthy-Morrogh reminds us, for instance, that "it was not until 1606 that inheritance by tanistry was declared illegal".[31] Even more important was the manner in which the administration upheld the factional nature of the lordships by maintaining the intricate ownership and co-ownership patterns of landholding and associated rights and services due. The prominent government arbiter and author, Sir John Davies, for example, "dealt a friendly part" in the protection of the earl of Ormond's "rights and services due on the cantred of Kilnemanagh", whose landed and other interests therein were subsequently included in the chief's regrant.[32] The inclusion, too, of a weekly market and two yearly fairs in the regrant can be interpreted as a form of commercialisation in the O'Dwyer lordship that was adapted to reflect the dominance of a pre-existing Gaelic-Irish pastoral economy. In this context, the evidence from Kilnamanagh points to the notion that the early Stuart administration required the most expedient means to ensure order in the Gaelic-Irish lordships and were prepared to achieve this in a piecemeal fashion.

One of the most striking features of early seventeenth-century Ireland is the transitional and inconsistent nature of society emerging from the upheavals of war and New English conquest. Clarke expresses the intricacy of the picture by asserting that "the lines of division in early Stuart Ireland were less clear and less rigid than an unqualified emphasis upon political and religious alignments might indicate".[33] Bottigheimer develops this point by underlining Ireland's ambiguous nature as a colony in comparison to colonial America:

[i]n the reign of James I Ireland and America were linked in colonial propaganda as fertile areas for investment and adventure; but the proximity of Ireland to England was more balanced by the ambiguity of its frontier, the cloudy and changeable status of its natives, and the numerous impediments created by generations of prior claimants to the land.[34]

Bottigheimer's last point is particularly relevant to the frontier, or contact zone, of Kilnamanagh, where such 'impediments' to New English settlement in the early Stuart period did inhibit an effectual implementation of a coherent plantation project.

These 'impediments' included the high level of political awareness of the existing Gaelic-Irish landowners. The chief of the O'Dwyers, for example, ably requested the various articles and franchises he wished to have included in his surrender and regrant agreement; the negotiation of which involved foremost government officials such as the lord deputy of Ireland, Sir Arthur Chicester, and the influential writer and public commentator, Sir John Davies. O'Dowd cites, too, other examples to illustrate the competency of many Gaelic-Irish lords in their respective negotiations with the crown.[35] In this context, she asserts that the surrender and regrant agreements "should not, therefore, be seen as being arranged between an aggressive and aggrandising state and politically naive native chiefs", and argues conversely that "[m]any native lords were well aware of the implications and welcomed the support which the crown could offer them".[36] Gillespie also points out that chieftains frequently used the surrender and regrant technique to "reduce the status of their freeholders to tenants" and thereby "increase the duties received from them".[37] Although Dermot O'Dwyer's surrender and regrant did evidently guarantee the landholding rights of the *major* freeholders within his lordship, it, nevertheless, constituted a clear and comprehensive reassertion of his powerful political and social position in the barony in the context of his tenants and smaller landholders.

The question of how the 'lesser' landed interests in the Gaelic-Irish lordships of contemporary Ireland reacted to the changed political and legal contexts of the early seventeenth century is worth considering briefly at this point as it adds another important layer to the dynamic nature of contemporary Gaelic-Irish society – a dimension often overlooked due to the dearth of evidence. Many smaller landowners throughout the island recognised "the wisdom of holding their lands from the crown in order to remove themselves from the grip of overlords".[38] This was also an integral constituent of the government programme of reform in the Gaelic-Irish lordships. Treadwell notes, for example, how the contemporary crown counsel to Irish affairs in London, Richard Hadsor, in his 'Discourse' presented to King James I, in 1604, advocated the

> extension of the policy of 'surrender and regrant' to break the dependence of Irish landholders on their traditional leaders and to bring them into a direct tenurial relationship with the crown.[39]

Accordingly, throughout Gaelic Ireland in the early seventeenth century, many smaller landholders, subordinate to their respective chiefs, began to secure legal title to their lands individually with the crown.

In Kilnamanagh, the two foremost lesser landholders, Connor O'Dwyer and John O'Dwyer, were granted their individual lands in the barony directly from King James I in 1609 and 1611 respectively.[40] Connor O'Dwyer is seen to have taken advantage of the 'Commission for the Remedy of Defective Titles' and secured his holdings in this context for a specified fine,[41] while John O'Dwyer's grant also incurred a fine for the specification of his new legal entitlement to properties in relation to the crown.[42] Evident in both grants is the extent again to which other landholders' rights were preserved, such as Dermot O'Dwyer's rents out of the two premises, guaranteed in the context of that previously delineated in his surrender and regrant.[43] However, in both grants, the landholding rights of others were declared without either a specific delineation of where the respective tracts of separate landholdings overlapped or a clear stipulation concerning the associated privileges involved. This points to the localised and non-standardised nature of the agreed arrangements. Thus, as with the surrender and regrant of Dermot O'Dwyer, further evidence from the grants of his two principal subordinate landowners suggests the emergence of a complicated and localised landholding structure which was in essence a 'hybrid' one – incorporating a framework of the common-law system, whilst simultaneously retaining strong residual elements of the traditional Gaelic-Irish co-ownership pattern. Comparable currents to the hybrid nature of the landed and socio-economic system of Kilnamanagh are evident elsewhere in contemporary Ireland. Gillespie, for example, notes that Counties Antrim and Down in the opening decades of the century were

characterised by the consolidation of landed, political and economic
interests as both settler and native adjusted to the political situation
created by the English subjugation of Ireland in 1603.[44]

He proceeds to argue that this "process of consolidation was initially supported
by the central administration in an effort to enforce stability quickly and
cheaply".[45]

Notwithstanding the notable level of contradictory and hybrid social, economic
and political arrangements in the O'Dwyer lordship in the early seventeenth
century, the expansion of a common-law system of property rights had initiated
changes that were to have a considerable impact on the stability of Gaelic-Irish
economic and social order. The inclusion of licences "to hold a court baron" in
the grants to Connor and John O'Dwyer is indicative of the expansion of the
common-law local court system, which had been extended throughout Ireland
in the opening decade of the seventeenth century.[46] O'Dowd points out that
"the establishment of local courts to which all had access" reflected the
government proclamation of 1605, which declared that

> all tenants and inhabitants were to be the 'free, natural and immediate
> subjects of the king' and were no longer to be 'reputed or called
> natives or natural followers' of any lord or chieftain.[47]

Due to a lack of evidence, it is not possible to assess the extent to which such
a proclamation affected the O'Dwyer lordship or, indeed, how it, or the local
court system, altered the relationship between the chief and his traditional
followers. In addition, there is a manifest absence of records relating to the
function and status of the lesser freeholders and sub-tenants within the lordship
at this juncture (the primary surviving documentation typically concerning the
land-owning elites). It does become apparent from the evidence emerging in
succeeding decades, however, that the traditional power of the landholding
classes over their respective patrons fragmented and weakened with the
consolidation of English legal and socio-economic order. By 1641, a court
baron, for example, appears to be fully functional in Ballintemple parish to the
south of Kilnamanagh.[48]

The consolidation of English legal and political order gained further momentum
in the later years of James I's reign. In 1608, the customs of tanistry and

gavelkind, which Beckett notes as "essential parts of the Gaelic social and political system", were declared by the courts to be "void in law".[49] By the 1620s, there had developed a strong desire of the central administration to "exercise more control in the localities, mainly [as] a result of administrative reforms in central government".[50] In this context, the grants from the king to the leading O'Dwyer landholders in the opening decades of the century were, of course, part of an on-going attempt of government to strengthen and compound its jurisdiction and control over the Gaelic-Irish lordships. By making agreements with landowners such as the O'Dwyers, the crown also built up its revenue in Ireland and consequently became more powerful. All three grants to the O'Dwyers, for example, resulted in the accumulation of rents to the crown, which were secured by the king's commissioners in virtue of the 1605 'Commission of Surrenders' and 1606 'Commission for the Remedy of Defective Titles'.[51]

The consolidation of New English administration in the localities in Tipperary was further demonstrated in the second decade of the seventeenth century by the diminishing power of the earl of Ormond. Thomas Butler, the tenth earl,[52] had died in 1614 and, as a result, the eleventh earl, Walter Butler, petitioned the king for a full regrant of the palatinate privileges of the liberty of Tipperary, which his ancestors had enjoyed since the early fourteenth century.[53] The king's response reflected the perpetual desires of the New English government in Ireland, as outlined in chapter two, to rebuke the powers of the earls of Ormond and subsequently take direct and centralised control of the existing administration of the county. With the death of the tenth earl, the lord deputy, Sir Arthur Chichester, expeditiously advised King James I of the liberty's "offence and grievance [to] most of the inhabitants of that county and of neighbouring counties adjoining".[54] The ensuing court inquiry ordered by the king into the continuation of the authority of the county palatine recommended the termination of all privileges involved, and the liberty was subsequently forfeited in 1620.[55] The fate of the liberty of Tipperary mirrored the contemporary expansion of the Stuart administration throughout the country, which exerted further pressures on the Gaelic-Irish landholding and associated social systems, which were already in a diminished and disjointed state.[56]

The Opening of a Market in Land

The expansion of a common-law system of property rights had a number of important consequences in relation to the superstructure of early seventeenth-century Irish society. Gillespie stresses that one of the most striking repercussions of the emerging social structure – "based on grants from the king and leases to tenants rather than on Gaelic social conventions" – was the resulting "creation of a standard system of landholding throughout the whole island".[57] This, he argues, "played a vitally important part in opening Ireland up to greater trading activity".[58] The spread of standardised landholding rights also brought about "a more careful definition of private property",[59] safeguarded new-found property rights "through statute law", and ultimately had the effect of successfully attracting British settlers to Ireland.[60] Canny points out that the number of British settlers migrating to Ireland during the first half of the seventeenth century

> is likely to have been greater than that of the total movement to North America over the same period, and the number of skilled manufacturing and agricultural workers included was also probably greater in the case of Ireland.[61]

His suggestion that approximately 100,000 British settlers migrated to Ireland during the years 1603-1641 has won general academic favour, and of these he asserts that as many as 70,000 English and Welsh settled in the south and east, particularly during the 1610s and early 1620s.[62] MacCarthy-Morrogh, too, submits that the growth of English settlers in the province of Munster is likely to have risen to 22,000 in the 1630s, many of whom "provided the personnel which staffed central and local government".[63]

Arguably, the most important consequence of the delimiting of property rights in early seventeenth-century Ireland was the opening up of a market in land. A stimulated land market resulted in what Duffy observes as "the general adoption of individualistic mercenary attitudes to landownership and the gradual infiltration of opportunistic colonial investors".[64] This, he suggests, meant correspondingly that "the *raison d'etre* of the Gaelic territorial organisation was fast disappearing".[65] Gillespie, too, points out that various different groups exploited the expanding property market in the opening decades of the seventeenth century.[66] He outlines, for example, how the rising merchant class of the principal port towns, such as Galway and Dublin, sought increasingly "to become landowners as part of their ascent on the social scale", and that the Old English gentry also began to secure ownership of large tracts of land throughout Ireland.[67] Exploiting the new land market also became a central concern of the Gaelic-Irish.

A series of land transactions in west Tipperary prior to 1641 reflect the noted extension of standardised property rights and emerging dynamic land market of the period. Disputes within the O'Dwyer lordship over landownership, and other rights such as church dues, continued throughout the first half of the century.[68] A succession of government inquisitions from 1617 to 1637 into numerous smaller landowners' rights of title to specific lands throughout the barony exerted further pressures on various members of the O'Dwyers to secure their respective possessions individually.[69] Disagreements over inheritance rights – subsequent to the death of a landowner – also persisted, which mirrored both the extent of the increasingly fluid land market and the degree of existing complex Gaelic-Irish landholding arrangements.[70] Furthermore, land purchases, leases and mortgages[71] became increasingly commonplace as the O'Dwyers and their Gaelic-Irish neighbours adjusted to the emerging commercialised economic structure. Kiernan has pointed out a similar picture for contemporary Gaelic Scotland.[72]

In Kilnamanagh, the fluctuating landholding arrangement became progressively characterised by individualistic concerns and was exploited accordingly by numerous Gaelic-Irish landowners. Dermot O'Dwyer, the chief, for example, appropriated control of lands throughout west Tipperary and elsewhere in the 1620s.[73] Philip O'Dwyer, who succeeded him as chief in 1629,[74] also acquired possession of substantial properties in Kilnamanagh in the 1620s and 1630s by recent mortgage or purchase, and had gained many of his additional properties at the expense of lesser landholders.[75] Smyth has pointed out a similar trend for Arra, in Owney and Arra barony in north County Tipperary, where the chief of the O'Briens and his foremost kinsmen were similarly active in land purchases and mortgages, prior to the 1641 rebellion, which resulted in the reduction of landholdings of lesser O'Briens and others.[76] A more complicated trend, however, in the landholding transfers of 1620s and 1630s is evident for Kilnamanagh, where it emerges that the other principal landholder of the barony, Anthony O'Dwyer (son to the former chief Dermot), was conversely mortgaging much of his properties and was subsequently in possession of considerably less than he legally owned.

Anthony O'Dwyer was actively mortgaging substantial tracts of land throughout the barony in the decades preceding the 1641 rebellion, which suggests that he may have been experiencing a measure of financial difficulty.[77] Interestingly, however, he did not mortgage his lands solely to substantial landholders such as Philip O'Dwyer, his chief, but did so also to less prominent O'Dwyers and others throughout the Kilnamanagh lordship and elsewhere, as evidenced by the *Civil Survey*.[78] The evidence from Kilnamanagh, then, suggests that a considerable number of hitherto smaller and less powerful landholders within the lordship were also consolidating and extending their properties prior to the outbreak of rebellion in 1641. Other minor Gaelic-Irish and Old English property-owners within, and adjacent to, the O'Dwyer lordship had also acquired possession of considerable portions of his properties via the mortgage device.[79] In addition, many of the smaller landholders of the O'Dwyers were availing of the opportunity to purchase and, more frequently obtain mortgages of, substantial tracts of land in Clanwilliam barony to the south of Kilnamanagh.[80] A useful example of the process of smaller landholders capitalising on changing circumstances and acquiring possession of lands *individually* (and independently from their chief) was seen in 1621 when a lesser member of the O'Dwyers leased lands from the king subsequent to another O'Dwyer being attainted for high treason.[81] Crucially, therefore, this suggests that the land market had significantly fragmented vertical alignments of social order within the O'Dwyer lordship. Despite, then, the fact that Gaelic-Irish landownership and associated features such as joint possession of holdings persisted in Kilnamanagh and elsewhere to *c.*1640, the landholding superstructure had been substantially altered and rendered more individualistic by the extension of property rights modelled on the common-law system of single ownership.

A complicated picture, therefore, emerges of the landholding structure of Kilnamanagh for the early seventeenth century; the order of which is perhaps best visualised as hybrid. This 'hybridity' mirrored, as Clarke observes, how "[b]oth traditional native and authentic feudal arrangements survived in many places in varying stages of modification", and how the surrender and regrant agreements often served merely to complicate the position further, where the result was "perhaps more often to put a veneer on Irish arrangements than to replace them".[82] Most importantly, however, the evidence from Kilnamanagh presented above suggests that this 'hybrid' nature of landholding existing in Ireland by the mid-seventeenth century embodied an inherent dynamic character distinguished by individualistic concerns. With the onset of a common-law system of property rights in the opening decade of the century, and subsequent to the redefinition of individual holdings in the context of the crown, land appears to be no longer viewed in terms of the Gaelic-Irish freehold system but rather as an essential means to secure individual survival. The quest, furthermore, to guarantee this survival became even more critical with the arrival on the property scene of moneyed New English entrepreneurs.

The Entry of the New English Adventurer Class

The influential New English government officials and landowners in Ireland in the early seventeenth century, known as the 'adventurers', possessed the wealth and access to power to build up substantial holdings throughout the country.[83] In the decades preceding the outbreak of the 1641 rebellion, they zealously demonstrated their capacity to exploit the newly-established free market in land, and in Kilnamanagh, which had not been hitherto directly affected by government plantation efforts, their impact was considerable. The barony, as argued above, witnessed a partial re-ordering of the landholding and related social structures since the mid-sixteenth century. It had not, however, been included in the Munster plantation plans following the defeat of the Desmonds in the 1580s or in the aftermath of the Elizabethan conquest in 1603, and accordingly had not yet experienced a direct engagement with New English settlers or landowners. Victory in the Nine Years War and the subsequent reassertion of crown control, however, facilitated the assiduous rise of New English entrepreneurs and property speculators, who in Kilnamanagh and throughout Ireland were to have a marked impact on the political, economic and social arenas of the early decades of the seventeenth century.

The passage of the adventurer class to the forefront of Irish society in the mid-seventeenth century was an insidious one and is sometimes understated in the historiography of the period, thereby placing too much emphasis on the effectiveness of government plantation efforts in 'transforming' the localities.[84] The influence of the adventurers throughout the country, however, was considerable, especially in those areas unaffected by direct plantation and, therefore, warrants specific attention. Accordingly, their distinct impact in relation to Kilnamanagh is examined below, which has been accommodated by the survival in the *Egmont Manuscripts* of the family records of one of the most prominent and powerful contemporary New English entrepreneurs in Ireland, Sir Philip Percivall.[85] Percivall's recorded correspondences reveal the process whereby the adventurer class comprehensively infiltrated the Irish landholding scene prior to the 1641 rebellion, particularly in the 1620s and 1630s. Crucially, too, his chronicled activities indicate the level of interaction and cooperation reached between him and the Gaelic-Irish, and more specifically in the context of this work, the O'Dwyers.

Hayes-McCoy points out that the "system whereby land, the source of wealth, was owned and used in the Irish and gaelicised areas formed the basis of local independence".[86] The localised landholding arrangements of west Tipperary have been shown above to have been substantially altered within the O'Dwyer lordship in the early part of the seventeenth century by the redefinition of holdings in accordance with an individualistic-style, common-law system of property rights. Despite the fact, however, that the constitution of landholdings and related social structure had been substantially modified, land confiscations had not occurred, and the dominance of Gaelic-Irish landowners persisted. What, then, were the means by which the New English adventurer class gained access to the property market there, and, more importantly, what does the process reveal about the nature of interaction between 'natives' and 'newcomers' in contemporary society?

In respect of the rise of the adventurer class, Ranger argues that the process of their consolidation is "concealed rather than illuminated" by the surviving documentary evidence.[87] He argues that the patent rolls of James I, for example, seem to record a

> series of grants to courtiers and their clients of vast estates in Ireland, when in most cases little of the land mentioned went to the grantee and many grants were a mosaic of small parcels of land passed for a score or more landlords.[88]

This phenomenon is similarly attested to by the patent rolls relating to Kilnamanagh, which record a succession of land grants to various individuals who did not subsequently take up their estates, due presumably to either those in question selling or passing on their parcels of estate to other assignee owners or Gaelic-Irish residents, or the problem of prior claimants to the respective lands.[89] In 1614, for example, one Francis Edgeworth, an assignee of a certain Sir John Eyres, was granted lands in the barony following the attaintment of one of the O'Dwyers for an unspecified offence.[90] There is no later record in the *Civil Survey* or elsewhere of Edgeworth ever taking possession of his holdings. A similar picture emerges from other examples, including the grants to one

Laurence Esmond of lands in 1617 and 1618 and one William Parsons in 1621, again following the attainments of certain O'Dwyers and others for undisclosed transgressions.[91]

Ranger asserts that the contemporary economic circumstances in Ireland were, in actuality, capitalised on by a select number of opportunistic individuals, who correspondingly "grew more and more powerful and prosperous".[92] He points out, moreover, that their ascendancy continued unabated in the decades preceding the 1641 rebellion, despite "sporadic attempts" on the part of the government to break their power.[93] Lord Deputy Wentworth, for example, wrote despairingly in 1633 that he found the kingdom of Ireland to be dominated by a

> society of strange people, their own privates altogether their study without any regard at all to the public ... and consequently all the crown revenue reduced into fee farms, [with] all defects of title either through fraud or error in drawing assurances from the crown industriously made valid in law by new grants.[94]

This profiteering agenda of New English expansion was not confined to the seventeenth century, of course. A similar picture has been pointed out for the later sixteenth century, in chapter two, in relation to the Munster plantation, wherein it is seen that the execution of its plans quickly degenerated into individual expropriation and extortion of profit, with little visible government control. In this context, despite the careful planning of government plantation efforts in the sixteenth and seventeenth centuries, "the limited resources of government proved unable to enforce them fully or to police the activities of those granted forfeited land".[95] Subsequently, as Gillespie asserts, many grantees were "more concerned to establish themselves as local magnates than to promote the political aims of the plantation schemes".[96] The adventurer class of the early seventeenth century was no different, and Sir Philip Percivall was one of those individuals possessing the means and wealth to, in Lord Deputy Wentworth's despondent words, "purchase what best liked him for his money".[97]

From the early decades of the seventeenth century, Sir Philip Percivall – whose descendants later became established as the earls of Egmont – held the lucrative office of clerk and registrar of the court of wards in Ireland.[98] He also held the appointments of clerk of the crown, prothonotary of the court of common pleas and keeper of the public accounts.[99] In the 1630s, he began to arduously build up an extensive network of properties throughout Ireland, via the remunerative and influential positions he held in government. The bulk of his holdings were seen in Munster, principally in Counties Cork, Tipperary and Waterford. He established a large estate in Burton in north-east Cork having been granted it by letters patent from King Charles I in 1637 and in Tipperary he purchased, leased, and acquired the mortgages and wardships[100] of extensive lands throughout the county.[101]

Numerous other New English individuals attained mortgages to various lands in west Tipperary, in the early seventeenth century, as evidenced by the *Civil Survey*.[102] Elsewhere in Munster, a similar pattern emerges. Indeed, as MacCarthy-Morrogh points out, from the late sixteenth century it had been noted by the New English that their interests in Munster would be most readily strengthened by the advancement of newcomers "into the Irish areas by way of mortgages, for 'those Irish lords are in great poverty and want' and the settlers, 'by that policy win still upon them without force'".[103] He goes on to draw attention to the successful efforts of, for example, Sir Valentine Browne in Kerry and Richard Boyle in Cork in becoming substantial mortgagees.[104]

Notwithstanding the significance of the mortgaging of lands, the evidence from Kilnamanagh indicates that it was at the lease-holding level that the New English most substantially permeated the property market in west County Tipperary in the pre-1641 period, when Percivall and other prominent New English figures acquired leases of large tracts of land.[105] In addition, certain New English individuals of the town of Cashel, in Middlethird barony to the south-east, were also establishing greater influence in the barony in the pre-1641 period, by acquiring the leases of various parish tithes and attached rectory lands.[106] The greatest impact of this permeation of the land market at the lease-holding level was arguably the manner in which their leases served to consolidate the system of a rent-based economy. One Greenvill Halls, for example, secured the lease of lands to the south of Clonoulty parish in Kilnamanagh in 1638, which he later assigned to another New English landowner, Anthony Shertliffe of County Cork, who subsequently rented out the lands to the inhabitants there for a specified yearly rent.[107] Percivall and various other individuals, such as Sir Hardress Waller of Castletown, in neighbouring east County Limerick,[108] were also respectively in possession of substantial holdings by lease in Clanwilliam to the south by 1640.[109] The several individuals concerned held their leases indiscriminately from various Protestant and Catholic owners.[110] Percivall, for example, was a lessee to Philip

O'Dwyer of Dundrum, the chief of Kilnamanagh, in Oughterleague parish to south of the barony.[111]

A number of writers have drawn attention to the effectual infiltration of the adventurer class of the contemporary land market by various other mechanisms.[112] O'Dowd, for example, observes that, in the early seventeenth century, an increasing number of New English entrepreneurs were procuring lands in Gaelic areas "through crown grants of dissolved monastic property and other forfeited estates".[113] Others underline the extensive effects of newcomers purchasing lands from indebted Gaelic-Irish landlords unable to adjust to the changed economic circumstances. Gillespie, for example, has shown how the percentage of lands owned by the Gaelic-Irish in Counties Cavan, Armagh, and Monaghan fell dramatically in the period from 1609 to 1641, due to newcomers either becoming substantial mortgagees or directly purchasing properties.[114] Furthermore, he points out that

> the most successful colonisation scheme of the early seventeenth century, the settlement of Antrim and Down, was managed entirely through purchases of land by private individuals of recent English and Scottish origin from native Irish lords.[115]

Sir Philip Percivall had also purchased specific properties throughout County Tipperary at this point, taking possession of lands in Kilnamanagh, thus, from various lesser O'Dwyer landowners prior to the outbreak of rebellion.[116]

Percivall had also utilised his influential position in government to gain the wardships (possession of minors' estates) of a number of properties throughout the province of Munster.[117] He had procured, for example, the wardship of Connor O'Dwyer of Ballagh in Kilnamanagh in 1637.[118] The series of inquisitions into the holdings, services and succession of deceased persons held during the reigns of James I and Charles I represented "a corollary of the feudal axiom that the king owned all the land in his kingdom".[119] In this context, Percivall was granted the wardship of Connor O'Dwyer following the death of his grandfather, Connor McEdmond O'Dwyer, and subsequent inquisition post-mortem into his estate.[120] Despite, then, that Connor McEdmond O'Dwyer had earlier redefined and secured his holdings in the context of the 'Commission for the Remedy of Defective Titles' (and correspondingly had them regranted by King James I in 1609, as outlined earlier), an outsider in the person of Sir

Philip Percivall was subsequently seen by the O'Dwyers to nevertheless gain charge of his lands and prevent the O'Dwyers from retaining control.

Through a variety of mechanisms, therefore, Percivall had significantly permeated the property market in Kilnamanagh in the late 1630s and early 1640s, and was subsequently recorded as the owner of large tracts of lands in the barony in the terriers accompanying the Down Survey parish maps, c.1654.[121] His prominence in the region can be neatly illustrated by examining the close contact he maintained with another leading New English landowner in the area, Laurence Lord Esmond, regarding the availability of various properties such as the lease of the crown land of Clonoulty parish in late 1640.[122] Having been notified by Esmond of the possibility of the sale of his portion of the lease, Percivall promptly replied "when my money comes in, I'll hearken to the purchase".[123] Although he never did acquire possession of Clonoulty, the important consideration here is to underline his seemingly unrelenting drive for land. His activities, furthermore, emphasise the fluidity of the contemporary land market, and point to the manifest authority and influence which he had acquired in the barony in the pre-1641 period.

Conclusion

The discernible individualistic nature of the land-holding structure emerging in early seventeenth-century Kilnamanagh attests particularly to the impact of the spread of a common-law system of property rights and subsequent opening of a market in land. In this context, the evidence points to Duffy's suggestion that

> the breakdown in Gaelic landholding systems in the early seventeenth century, upon which rested the whole superstructure of the Gaelic social system, signalled the general transformation of Gaelic society in the face of economic forces emanating from the expanding mercantilist English state.[124]

The individualistic agendas of the O'Dwyer landowners reveal the extent to which the Gaelic-Irish freehold system of landownership had been fractured in the pre-1641 period. It indicates, too, how the principle of the 'lordship', as the organising fundamental of society, dominated and administered by the chief and his foremost kinsmen, had rapidly foundered with the consolidation of English legal and socio-economic order. Furthermore, the correspondences of the O'Dwyers with prominent government officials, and their later association with the New English adventurer, Sir Philip Percivall, underline both their knowledge and appreciation of contemporary political and economic currents in society. In early seventeenth-century Kilnamanagh, then, a conventional colonial reading of developments, incorporating exclusive notions of Self and Other, cannot ultimately be sustained.[125] The evidence presented above illustrates conversely how the worlds of the New English 'colonisers' and the Gaelic-Irish 'colonised' were *not* "unitary entities immune to the influence of the other".[126] Shared economic and social spaces were being actively forged in contemporary Irish society, by both the New English and the Gaelic-Irish, but a subsequent key question emerges, however, which forms the initial exploration of chapter four: to what extent were such 'spaces' bounded and ultimately limited by contemporary notions of identity and exclusion?

Notes

[1] *Cal. S.P. Ire., 1603-1606*, p. 161

[2] *Hastings MSS, vol. 4*, p. 25

[3] See, for example: R. Gillespie, 1993, 'Explorers, Exploiters and Entrepreneurs: Early Modern Ireland and its Context, 1500-1700', in: B.J. Graham and L.J. Proudfoot (eds.), *An Historical Geography of Ireland*, Academic Press, London, pp. 123-157; W.J. Smyth, 1990, 'Territorial, Social and Settlement Hierarchies in Seventeenth-Century Kilkenny', in: W. Nolan and K. Whelan (eds.), *Kilkenny: History and Society*, Geography Publications, Dublin, pp. 127-160; M. O'Dowd, 1986, 'Gaelic Economy and Society', in: C. Brady and R. Gillespie (eds.), *Natives and Newcomers: Essays on the Making of Irish Colonial Society, 1534-1641*, Irish Academic Press, Dublin, pp. 120-147; P.J. Duffy, 1981 'The Territorial Organisation of Gaelic Landownership and its Transformation in County Monaghan, 1591-1640', *Irish Geography*, vol. 14, pp. 1-23; W. Nolan, 1979, *Fassadinin: Land, Settlement and Society in South-East Ireland, 1600-1850*, Geography Publications, Dublin; and K.S. Bottigheimer, 1978, 'Kingdom and Colony: Ireland in the Westward Enterprise 1536-1660', in: K.R. Andrews, N.P. Canny and P.E.H. Hair (eds.), *The Westward Enterprise: English Activities in Ireland, The Atlantic and America, 1480-1650*, Liverpool University Press, Liverpool, pp. 45-64

[4] W.J. Smyth, 1985, 'Property, Patronage and Population – Reconstructing the Human Geography of Mid-Seventeenth Century County Tipperary', in: W. Nolan (ed.), *Tipperary: History and Society*, Geography Publications, Dublin, p. 104

[5] R. Gillespie, 1983, 'Thesis Abstract. East Ulster in the Early Seventeenth Century: A Colonial Economy and Society (Ph.D. Thesis, University of Dublin, 1982)', *Irish Economic and Social History*, X, p. 92

[6] See *Cal. S.P. Ire., 1606-1608*, pp. 70-71 for the crown lands and tithes in Co. Tipperary in possession of King James I in 1606.

[7] N.A.I., Chancery Bills, J, 185, p. 32, and N.L.I., D. 3420 and D. 3427

[8] N.A.I., Chancery Bills, B, 133, p. 18

[9] *Ibid.*

[10] B. Cunningham and R. Gillespie, 1990, 'Englishmen in Sixteenth-Century Irish Annals', *Irish Economic and Social History*, XVII, p. 14. Cf. N. Patterson, 1991, 'Gaelic Law and the Tudor Conquest of Ireland: The Social Background of the Sixteenth-Century Recensions of the Pseudo-Historical Prologue to the *Senchas Már*', *Irish Historical Studies*, vol. 27, no. 107, pp. 193-215

[11] J.H. Ohlmeyer, 1998, '"Civilizinge of those Rude Partes": Colonization within Britain and Ireland, 1580-1640s', in: N. Canny (ed.), *The Origins of Empire: British Overseas Enterprise to the Close of the 17th Century*, The Oxford History of the British Empire, vol. 1, Oxford University Press, Oxford, p. 139

[12] *Cal. Carew MSS, 1601-1603*, p. 385. Prominent O'Dwyers were also successively pardoned in the early years of the century for various offences. For pardons administered in the years 1602-1609, see *Fiants Ire., Hen. VIII-Eliz., 1586-1603*, nos. 6706-6707; *Cal. pat. rolls Ire., Jas. I*, pp. 62-63, 87, 95, 149; and N.L.I., D. 3387-3389

THE QUEST FOR SURVIVAL

[13] See V.G. Kiernan, 1993, 'The British Isles: Celt and Saxon', in M. Teich and R. Porter (eds.), *The National Question in Europe in Historical Context*, Cambridge University Press, Cambridge, pp. 1-34; see esp. pp. 6-9. See also *Idem.*, 1980, *State and Society in Europe, 1550-1660*, Basil Blackwell, Oxford, esp. pp. 134-135

[14] O'Dowd, 'Gaelic Economy and Society', p. 132

[15] *Hastings MSS, vol. 4*, p. 25. May 27, 1607, is the date of the underwritten order of the lord deputy, the petition itself being undated. Although the content of the petition is clearly of most importance, the initial request does appear to be made at some point in 1607, given that elsewhere the earl of Ormond also writes of "O'Dwyer's purpose to surrender his lands" for that year; see *Cal. S.P. Ire., 1606-1608*, p. 195

[16] *Hastings MSS, vol. 4*, p. 25

[17] *Ibid.*

[18] For a coherent analysis of the reform agenda of the surrender and regrant agreements in the early Stuart period, see O'Dowd, 'Gaelic Economy and Society', pp. 132-137

[19] *Cal. pat. rolls Ire., Jas. I*, pp. 104-105

[20] *Ibid.*, p. 105. Although there were some rent-style arrangements evident in Kilnamanagh through the course of the late medieval and Tudor periods, as outlined in chapter two, the surrender and regrant of Dermot O'Dwyer represented the first attempt to comprehensively introduce a rent-based economy in the lordship.

[21] Duffy, 'Territorial Organisation of Gaelic Landownership', p. 1

[22] Ohlmeyer, "Civilizinge of those Rude Partes"', p. 141

[23] *Cal. pat. rolls Ire., Jas. I*, pp. 104-105

[24] *Ibid.*, p. 105

[25] *Ibid.*

[26] As O'Dowd notes, however, there is a distinct difficulty in assessing the success of the policy given the "considerable differences between individual agreements" and subsequent danger of generalising; see O'Dowd, 'Gaelic Economy and Society', p. 132. Accordingly, the evidence from the surrender and regrant of Dermot O'Dwyer is herein presented in the localised context. Nevertheless, individual agreements such as O'Dwyer's inform our understanding of the effectiveness of the policy, and have a particular relevancy since very little attention has been given to the "fate of many of the families" who made them; see *ibid.*, p. 136

[27] O'Dowd remarks that "the government was anxious not to upset the internal power balance of the lordship and so tried to arrange terms to suit local circumstances"; see O'Dowd, 'Gaelic Economy and Society', p. 133

[28] *Civil Survey, County Tipperary*, vol. 2, pp. 76-108

[29] R. Gillespie, 1991, *The Transformation of the Irish Economy 1550-1700*, Studies in Irish Economic and Social History 6, The Economic and Social History Society of Ireland, p. 21

[30] M. O'Dowd, 1983, 'Land Inheritance in Early Modern County Sligo', *Irish Economic and Social History*, X, p. 18

[31] M. MacCarthy-Morrogh, 1986, *The Munster Plantation: English Migration to Southern Ireland 1583-1641*, Clarendon Press, Oxford, p. 89; see also pp. 71-88 for a coherent analysis of the complexities of property ownership and legal title in Munster

in the late sixteenth and early seventeenth centuries.

[32] *Cal. S.P. Ire., 1606-1608*, p. 195; *Cal. pat. rolls Ire., Jas. I*, p. 105

[33] A. Clarke, 1970, 'Ireland and the General Crisis', *Past and Present*, no. xlviii, p. 90

[34] Bottigheimer, 'Kingdom and Colony: Ireland in the Westward Enterprise', p. 55

[35] O'Dowd, 'Gaelic Economy and Society', p. 135

[36] *Ibid.*

[37] Gillespie, *Transformation of the Irish Economy*, p. 10

[38] O'Dowd, 'Gaelic Economy and Society', p. 134

[39] V. Treadwell, 1997, 'New Light on Richard Hadsor, I: Richard Hadsor and the Authorship of 'Advertisements for Ireland', 1622/3', *Irish Historical Studies*, vol. 30, no. 119, p. 310. See also J. McLaughlin, 1997, 'New Light on Richard Hadsor, II: Richard Hadsor's 'Discourse' on the Irish State, 1604', *Irish Historical Studies*, vol. 30, no. 119, pp. 337-353 for a useful presentation of the 1604 'Discourse'.

[40] *Cal. pat. rolls Ire., Jas. I*, pp. 156, 198

[41] *Ibid.*, p. 156

[42] *Ibid.*, p. 198. See also *Cal. S.P. Ire., 1611-1614*, pp. 104-105 for a listing of "Fines paid upon Grants past upon the Commissions of Defective Titles and Surrenders" from 1607 to 1611, which included those of the two leading landholders in the Kilnamanagh lordship secondary to the chief, viz. Connor and John O'Dwyer.

[43] *Cal. pat. rolls Ire., Jas. I*, pp. 156, 198. Dermot O'Dwyer's landholding privileges were also guaranteed in other grants administered elsewhere during this period. For example, his rights to rents and services of lands within his lordship were safeguarded in a grant to Walter Lawles (of Kilkenny County) of the manor of Kilfeacle in Clanwilliam barony, to the southern edges of Kilnamanagh, in 1608. It is evident again that the parcels of land protected overlapped the lands specified in his surrender and regrant and those of the aforesaid manor; see *ibid.*, pp. 119-120

[44] Gillespie, 'East Ulster in the Early Seventeenth Century', p. 92. See also Idem., 1985, *Colonial Ulster: The Settlement of East Ulster 1600-1641*, Cork University Press, Cork

[45] *Ibid.*

[46] *Cal. pat. rolls Ire., Jas. I*, pp. 156, 198

[47] O'Dowd, 'Gaelic Economy and Society', p. 144

[48] *Egmont MSS*, vol. 1, pt. 1, p. 147

[49] J.C. Beckett, 1981, *The Making of Modern Ireland 1603-1923*, Faber and Faber, London (first pub. 1966), pp. 34-35

[50] Gillespie, 'East Ulster in the Early Seventeenth Century', p. 93

[51] *Cal. pat. rolls Ire., Jas. I*, pp. 105, 156, 198. See *Cal. Carew MSS, 1603-1624*, pp. 73-74 for a listing of the rents raised by the king's commissioners from 1605 to 1611 by virtue of the 1605 and 1606 commissions, wherein the revenues accrued from the grants to the three leading Kilnamanagh landholders, viz. Dermot, Connor and John O'Dwyer, are included.

[52] The earl of Ormond, who had commissioned Dermot O'Dwyer as sheriff of the liberty of Tipperary for 1599-1600, had continued his close association with the O'Dwyers by appointing another O'Dwyer, Thomas of Ballynemona, sheriff in 1608;

see T. Blake Butler, 1960, 'The Sheriffs of the Liberty of The County Tipperary', *Irish Genealogist*, vol. 3, no. 5, p. 159

[53] *Cal. S.P. Ire., 1615-1625*, p. 3

[54] *Cal. S.P. Ire., 1611-1614*, p. 526

[55] *Cal. S.P. Ire., 1615-1625*, pp. 3, 328-329; Blake Butler, 'Sheriffs of the Liberty of County Tipperary', p. 159

[56] Duffy points out, for example, that in County Monaghan in south Ulster, "the indigenous system seems to have collapsed in the first two decades of the seventeenth century"; see Duffy, 'Territorial Organisation of Gaelic Landownership', p. 19

[57] Gillespie, *Transformation of the Irish Economy*, pp. 21-22

[58] *Ibid.*, p. 23

[59] *Ibid.*

[60] *Ibid.*, p. 24

[61] N. Canny, 1985, 'Migration and Opportunity: Britain, Ireland and the New World', *Irish Economic and Social History*, XII, p. 30

[62] *Idem.*, 1994, 'English Migration into and across the Atlantic during the Seventeenth and Eighteenth Centuries', in: *Idem.* (ed.), *Europeans on the Move: Studies on European Migration, 1500-1800*, Clarendon Press, Oxford, p. 62

[63] M. MacCarthy-Morrogh, 1986, 'The English Presence in Early Seventeenth Century Munster', in: Brady and Gillespie (eds.), *Natives and Newcomers*, p. 172

[64] Duffy, 'Territorial Organisation of Gaelic Landownership', p. 19

[65] *Ibid.*

[66] Gillespie, *Transformation of the Irish Economy*, p. 21

[67] *Ibid.*. In relation to the Old English, Gillespie employs the examples of Counties Roscommon and Sligo to point out that the percentage of Old English landownership in Ireland grew considerably in the period from 1600 to 1641.

[68] N.A.I., Chancery Bills, M, 111, p. 17

[69] N.A.I., Record Commission, 4/10. The lists of inquisitions in Tipperary, contained herein, were part of the proceedings of the chancery court of Ireland and included inquiries into the legal entitlement of fifteen lesser O'Dwyer landowners, dating chiefly to the 1620s and 1630s. Unfortunately, these records (and others relating to elsewhere) are largely, as Sheehan observes, "mere lists of names and dates, with no details at all of the cases"; see A.J. Sheehan, 1983, 'Official Reaction to Native Land Claims in the Plantation of Munster', *Irish Historical Studies*, vol. 23, no. 92, p. 318

[70] See N.A.I., Chancery Bills, AA, 54, pp. 12-13 for the settlement of a discord between members of the O'Dwyers and others regarding lands in Kilnamanagh in 1619 following the death of one Edmond Walsh.

[71] The Gaelic-Irish custom of mortgaging constituted a practice of land acquisition whereby the mortgagee, for a sum of money, took possession of a tract of land legally owned by the mortgagor until the payment was repaid. It frequently amounted to a means of cheaply purchasing land due either to the subsequent attaintment or indebtedness of those mortgaging. For useful comment on the convention of mortgaging, see: MacCarthy-Morrogh, *The Munster Plantation*, pp. 80-81; N. Canny, 1986, 'Protestants, Planters and Apartheid in Early Modern Ireland', *Irish Historical Studies*,

vol. 25, no 98, p. 112; and O'Dowd, 'Gaelic Economy and Society', p. 127

[72] V.G. Kiernan, 1980, *State and Society in Europe, 1550-1650*, Basil Blackwell, Oxford, p. 135

[73] See, for example, *Cal. pat. rolls Ire., Jas. I*, p. 583, wherein O'Dwyer's efforts to secure the mortgage of lands in Counties Tipperary and Limerick in 1624 are recorded. His son, Anthony O'Dwyer, was later conveyed the feoffment of lands in County Waterford in 1633, which again illustrates the involvement of individual members of the O'Dwyers in an expanded land market; see 'Mansfield Papers', intro. J.F. Ainsworth and E. MacLysaght, 1958, *Analecta Hibernica*, 20, pp. 93-94

[74] N.L.I., MFIC Pos. 8302

[75] *Civil Survey, County Tipperary*, vol. 2, pp. 77, 79, 81, 83, 86, 95, 97. O'Dwyer was also a lessee of the Anglican archbishop of Cashel of hierarchy church lands in Oughterleague parish in 1640; see *ibid.*, p. 359

[76] Smyth, 'Property, Patronage and Population', p. 117

[77] He had mortgaged lands to his chief in Castletown and Clonoulty parishes by 1640; see *Civil Survey, County Tipperary*, vol. 2, pp. 77, 97

[78] *Civil Survey, County Tipperary*, vol. 2, pp. 79, 96-98, 102

[79] *Ibid.*, pp. 81, 96-98, 107

[80] *Ibid.*, pp. 9, 47-49, 51-52

[81] Lease of lands from King James I in Clonoulty parish by Philip O'Dwyer of Ballyhyde, 1621: *Cal. pat. rolls Ire., Jas. I*, p. 503

[82] A. Clarke, 1976, 'The Irish Economy, 1600-1660', in: T.W. Moody, F.X. Martin and F.J. Byrne (eds.), *A New History of Ireland III: Early Modern Ireland 1534-1691*, Clarendon Press, Oxford, pp. 170-171. Evident in Kilnamanagh, therefore, is an ineluctable degree of the antithesis of 'continuity and change', which despite being a long-established concept should, nevertheless, as Mitson argues, "not be relegated to a cliché"; see A. Mitson, 1993, 'The Significance of Kinship Networks in the Seventeenth Century: South-West Nottinghamshire', in: C. Phythian-Adams (ed.), *Societies, Cultures and Kinship, 1580-1850 – Cultural Provinces and English Local History*, Leicester University Press, London, p. 70

[83] For commentary on the evolution of the adventurer class in Ireland in the early seventeenth century, see: MacCarthy-Morrogh, 'The English Presence', pp. 171-190; N. Canny, 1982, *The Upstart Earl: A Study of the Social World of Richard Boyle, First Earl of Cork, 1566-1643*, Cambridge University Press, Cambridge; and T.O. Ranger, 1957, 'Richard Boyle and the Making of an Irish Fortune, 1588-1614', *Irish Historical Studies*, vol. 10, no. 39, pp. 257-297

[84] See the comments of Gillespie, *Transformation of the Irish Economy*, pp. 19-23 and Ranger, 'Richard Boyle and the Making of an Irish Fortune', pp. 296-297

[85] *Egmont MSS*, vols. 1-2

[86] G.A. Hayes-McCoy, 1976, 'The Completion of the Tudor Conquest and the Advance of the Counter-Reformation, 1571-1603' in: Moody *et al* (eds.), *A New History of Ireland III*, p. 109

[87] Ranger, 'Richard Boyle and the Making of an Irish Fortune', p. 296

[88] *Ibid.*

[89] Regarding the confusing nature of the documentary evidence of convoluted land conveyances, fines, recoveries, settlements and trusts, see the useful comments of A.A. Dibben, 1968, *Title Deeds: 13th-19th Centuries*, Pamphlet no. 72, The Historical Association, London.

[90] *Cal. pat. rolls Ire., Jas. I*, p. 354

[91] *Ibid.*, pp. 359, 426, 513-514

[92] Ranger, 'Richard Boyle and the Making of an Irish Fortune', p. 297

[93] *Ibid.*, p. 296

[94] Quoted in: *ibid.*, p. 297

[95] Gillespie, *Transformation of the Irish Economy*, p. 20

[96] *Ibid.*

[97] Quoted in: Ranger, 'Richard Boyle and the Making of an Irish Fortune', p. 297

[98] *Egmont MSS*, vol. 2, p. 11

[99] *Ibid.*, p. vi

[100] This was a specific mechanism whereby one skilfully acquired possession of property by procuring the grant of legal guardian (or wardship) to heirs to estates who were in their minority.

[101] *Egmont MSS*, vol. 1, pt. 1, pp. 92, 96-97, 108-109, 113-114; N.L.I., D. 3786 and D. 3918; *Civil Survey, County Tipperary*, vol. 2, pp. 8, 13-14, 95, 101-102, 359, 384, 399

[102] *Civil Survey, County Tipperary*, vol. 2, pp. 20, 51, 55, 59-61

[103] MacCarthy-Morrogh, *The Munster Plantation*, p. 81

[104] *Ibid.*, pp. 81-82

[105] *Civil Survey, County Tipperary*, vol. 2, pp. 8, 13, 95, 359, 384, 399. See also N.L.I., D. 3786 and D. 3918, wherein his efforts to secure leases (sometimes in advance, which is the case for the agreement recorded in N.L.I., D. 3786) of particular lands in the county is revealed. These leases and others were typically for a duration of between 21 and 31 years.

[106] James Hamilton, son to the Anglican archbishop of Cashel, and one George Conway had separately procured leases of the tithes and affiliated religious lands of Donohill, Kilpatrick, Ballintemple, Oughterleague and Moyaliff parishes by 1640; see *Civil Survey, County Tipperary*, vol. 2, pp. 82, 86-87, 90, 105. See also N.L.I., D. 3988 for an indenture recording the transfer of the lease (formerly held by a member of the neighbouring Old English Butlers) to Conway of the tithes, rectories and respective lands of Kilpatrick, Ballintemple, Oughterleague and Moyaliff in 1635.

[107] *Civil Survey, County Tipperary*, vol. 2, pp. 94-95

[108] Percivall maintained regular correspondence with Waller during the late 1630s and early 1640s, regarding the acquisition of lands in west Tipperary and other matters; see *Egmont MSS*, vol. 1, pt. 1, pp. 99-100, 103-104, 117

[109] *Civil Survey, County Tipperary*, vol. 2, pp. 6, 8, 13, 25, 28, 38, 42, 48-49, 52, 56, 60, 363-364. It is important to point out that Clanwilliam barony had been partially included in the Munster plantation and, therefore, a number of New English landowners, such as Gamaliell Waters of Cullen (see *ibid.*, pp. 28, 56, 363-364) had already established themselves there in the opening decades of the seventeenth century and possibly earlier. Hence, the *Civil Survey* records a larger proportion of lands in the

barony in possession (by various legal mechanisms) of Protestant individuals than in Kilnamanagh, where their presence was not as marked. There are eleven Protestants listed in the *Civil Survey* as landowners in Clanwilliam in 1640, whereas in Kilnamanagh only three are recorded; see *ibid.*, pp. 6, 8-10, 13-14, 17, 19-20, 22, 24-28, 38-39, 42, 48-49, 51-52, 55-56, 59-61, 363-364 (Clanwilliam); pp. 94-95, 101-102, 359-361 (Kilnamanagh). Furthermore, there were 180 Englishmen listed as having paid the poll money ordinances in Clanwilliam *c.*1660, while Kilnamanagh saw the lowest number of Englishmen (86) registered in any barony in the county; see *Census Ire., 1659*, pp. 302-304, 325-329. A similar picture emerges from the figures indexing those who paid the hearth taxes of Tipperary at this juncture; see *Hearth Money Records 1665-1666/7*, pp. 36-39, 63-66, 76-77, 119-127, 156-165

[110] These included the earls of Thomond and Ormond, the countess of Ormond, the archbishop of Cashel, the bishop of Emly, the Old English Burkes and Butlers, and the Gaelic-Irish Ryans and O'Dwyers.

[111] *Civil Survey, County Tipperary*, vol. 2, p. 359

[112] See, for example: Gillespie, *Transformation of the Irish Economy*, pp. 21-24; Canny, 'Protestants, Planters and Apartheid', pp. 112-113; O'Dowd, 'Gaelic Economy and Society', p. 143-144; and Duffy, 'Territorial Organisation of Gaelic Landownership', pp. 12-19

[113] O'Dowd, 'Gaelic Economy and Society', p. 143

[114] Gillespie, *Transformation of the Irish Economy*, p. 22

[115] *Ibid.*

[116] *Civil Survey, County Tipperary*, vol. 2, pp. 101-102. See also *ibid.*, p. 14 for lands purchased by Percivall in Clanwilliam barony to the south. Other substantial New English adventurers, such as Richard Boyle, first earl of Cork, also purchased properties in the county during the pre-1641 period; see, for example, *ibid.*, p. 22, for lands purchased by Boyle in Clanwilliam.

[117] *Egmont MSS*, vol. 1, pt. 1, pp. 113-114

[118] *Ibid.*, p. 92

[119] Nolan, *Fassadinin*, p. 247

[120] *Egmont MSS*, vol. 1, pt. 1, p. 92

[121] N.L.I., MFIC Pos. 7384 b.. Percivall's properties were largely concentrated in the more well-endowed lands of the southern and eastern parishes, which also contained the greatest degree of settlement as indicated in the Down Survey barony map of Kilnamanagh illustrated in fig. 2.1.

[122] *Egmont MSS*, vol. 1, pt. 1, pp. 121, 125. Esmond is listed in the *Civil Survey* as the holder of one third of the lease of Clonoulty crown land in 1640; see *Civil Survey, County Tipperary*, vol. 2, pp. 360-361

[123] *Egmont MSS*, vol. 1, pt. 1, p. 121

[124] Duffy, 'Territorial Organisation of Gaelic Landownership', p. 19

[125] For a critical appraisal of the shortcomings of a straightforward 'colonial' interpretation of society, see MacCarthy-Morrogh, 'The English Presence', pp. 281-284. Cf. R. Gillespie, 1993, 'Documents and Sources: Plantation and Profit: Richard Spert's Tract on Ireland, 1608', *Irish Economic and Social History*, XX, pp. 64-65. See

also the recent comments of L.J. Proudfoot, 2000, 'Hybrid Space? Self and Other in Narratives of Landownership in Nineteenth-Century Ireland', *Journal of Historical Geography*, 26, 2, pp. 203-221. Proudfoot's work negates the notions of Self and Other and explores, on the contrary, the useful concept of 'inbetween space' in the context of a problematised colonial setting.

[126] B.S.A. Yeoh, 2000, 'Historical Geographies of the Colonised World', in: B. Graham and C. Nash (eds.), *Modern Historical Geographies*, Prentice Hall, Harlow, p. 165. Yeoh argues that "in the same way that narratives of colonialism have been subject to closer scrutiny and refinement, accounts of the colonised world must also avoid homogenising and essentialising the 'colonised' as a category"; see *ibid.*

Chapter 4

Geographies of Identity and Resistance

> I will handle the matter of religion as nicely as I may, especially in this broken time … matters of treason not tending to religion may be sufficiently proved to convince them; but if it do appear in the least that any part of their punishment proceeds for matter of religion, it will kindle a great fire in this kingdom – *Sir George Carew, President of Munster, 1600* [1]

How prophetic of Sir George Carew above, as he indicates in 1600 the emerging significance of religion as the foremost differentiating constituent in early modern Irish society? Through the course of the seventeenth century, it was increasingly constructed as the basic benchmark for determining notions of 'difference' in colonial society, superseding all other economic, ethnic, or class divisions.[2] It constituted the most conveniently employed mode of representation of an essential component of colonisation – the distinction between the 'coloniser' and the 'colonised' – and was, in effect, as MacCarthy-Morrogh asserts, "the perfect litmus".[3] However, early seventeenth-century Irish society was far more complex in its orientations of allegiance and identity, and, in attempting to locate these intricacies, this chapter seeks to interrogate the tensions and contradictions intrinsic to Gaelic society in contemporary west Tipperary. It examines in more detail the currents of both accommodation and resistance fundamental to the responses of the O'Dwyers to the presence of the New English in the early seventeenth century, and proceeds to demonstrate the complicated and often contradictory negotiation of Gaelic-Irish identity in a 'colonial' context prior to the 1641 rebellion.

A Level of Integration in Pre-1641 Society

In exploring the interaction of the existing population with the New English newcomers in pre-1641 west Tipperary, assessing the extent of the New English settler, or tenant, population represents a foremost concern. To begin with, the evidence is slight, with little information contained in the primary contemporary government records, such as the *Civil Survey*, *State Papers* or

97

Patent Rolls, suggestive of either the numbers of settlers or the nature of their position in society.[4] For this reason, the fragmentary accounts of related developments recorded elsewhere – which, in the context of the present work, include particularly the *Egmont Manuscripts* – are decidedly significant.

A series of correspondences in the *Egmont Manuscripts* indicate that Sir Philip Percivall had introduced a number of New English settlers on the lands in his tenure in south Kilnamanagh and north Clanwilliam in the pre-1641 period.[5] Letters sent to Percivall, dating to 1641, from settlers in the barony refer to him as their "master" and, furthermore, reveal the close contact which the adventurer maintained with his tenants regarding the maintenance, use and transfer of his lands, and the negotiation and sale of his crops and stock.[6] Elsewhere, the *Civil Survey* records that one John Percivall (a likely relative of Sir Philip, although there is no indication of such) inhabited lands leased by Sir Philip in north Clanwilliam, along with his tenants, in 1640.[7] Information contained within the '1641 depositions', too, attest to the establishment of a prominent settler community in the region, wherein the residency of a Protestant minister points to a noted level of settlement effected by 1641.[8] The cumulative evidence, therefore, intimates the existence of a significant settler population in west Tipperary at this juncture. O'Murchadha has presented a similar picture for pre-1641 County Clare, where "the emphasis on landownership figures has meant that an important settler element, subsisting for the most part on leasehold and mortgage arrangements, has largely gone unnoticed".[9]

The exploration of the level of integration attained in pre-1641 society in Kilnamanagh also implores the question of how successful the New English land-owning class was in incorporating the existing population in the increasingly commercialised economic structure. The acquisition of substantial tracts of land by Sir Philip Percivall and others in west Tipperary in the 1630s constituted part of a broader project throughout the country which "helped to create the conditions in which a more commercially-orientated agriculture could develop".[10] Such 'conditions' included a shift in land management techniques and an introduction of new agricultural practices via the establishment of a settler population.[11] In effect, new attitudes "to land and social status, to law and religion, were so different from those of native society that the growing dominance of newcomer social ideas amounted to a social revolution".[12]

How successful was Sir Philip Percivall in disseminating these commercial ideas tantamount to a social revolution? To begin with, as MacCarthy-Morrogh points out, Percivall was a major source of credit for investors, merchants and settlers in Munster.[13] The *Egmont Manuscripts* indicate that he was also extending loans to some of his prominent English tenants in the O'Dwyer lordship of Kilnamanagh in the early 1640s.[14] It is important to note, however, that the emergence of a market economy in west Tipperary in the early seventeenth century was not solely attributable to the New Englishman. As argued in chapter three, a commercialised economy was earlier recognised by the leading O'Dwyer landowners as a necessary component to their survival and, accordingly, positively engaged.[15] Furthermore, the commercialisation of economic activities was not a straightforward transformation. As Gillespie argues, the "ideas of 'redistributive' and 'market' economies are best regarded as poles on a spectrum along which Ireland moved some way during the seventeenth century".[16]

In relation to the integration of the settler community in early seventeenth-century Ireland, Gillespie has utilised the 1608 treatise by the crown advisor on colonisation projects, Richard Spert, to assert that one of the common designs of contemporary English settlement in Ireland, that of preserving political stability, was best achieved by "giving wealth to the natives so that they would have a stake in the new order and be reluctant to overturn it".[17] In the official plantation schemes, a similar aim was "to employ natives and integrate them into the commercial economy" and, hence, maintain control.[18] Such an agenda was identified for west Tipperary in the 1630s, in chapter three, where it was argued that Sir Philip Percivall's close contact with the O'Dwyers regarding the expanding market in land ensured the necessary economic terms of reference between them to effect a level of incorporation at the upper levels of society. The evidence, moreover, from the letters of his tenants illustrate a substantial degree of cooperation between Percivall and lesser Gaelic-Irish and Old English of west Tipperary.[19] It is seen, for example, that the Englishman traded in cattle, sheep and fodder provisions with various individuals of the Ryans, Magraths and Bourckes.[20] Such a positive working relationship and familiarity between Percivall and the existing population is further indicated by a priest in the barony claiming that Sir Philip had "promised him [a] house and garden and the benefit of [a] well, without demanding any rent".[21]

Regarding the nature of interaction between Percivall and the O'Dwyers, it is important to emphasise that the series of correspondences recorded in the *Egmont Manuscripts* expressly divulge shared economic and social terms of reference, which were subsequently employed to negotiate contact between them. This ensured a substantial degree of integration in society, at the landholding level. Furthermore, evidence emerges which illustrates that the O'Dwyers sought to consolidate their position by actively forging stronger links with Percivall. Writing in 1637, Charles O'Dwyer, a substantial landowner in Oughterleague parish, advised the Englishman

> to buy lands in that neighbourhood [of Kilnamanagh], as the inhabitants are so affrighted by the relation of the coming of the Plantation that they will sell upon very easy rates.[22]

Notably, the communication points to the manner in which intended government plantation efforts in the area were resulting in a significant level of social unrest as the O'Dwyers and others were faced with the threat of losing their rights to lands by failing to secure title in an English court.[23] It also illustrates the further economic pressures exerted on the O'Dwyers and other landowners in Kilnamanagh by the expanding capitalist English state, of which the adventurer class was an integral part.[24] Most significantly, however, the correspondence reveals how the O'Dwyers were actively seeking New English landowners to acquire landholdings within their neighbourhood in order to stabilise existing arrangements. O'Murchadha has similarly argued in relation to County Clare how the fourth earl of Thomond and others "encouraged the immigration to [the county] of settlers of English and Dutch origin in the drive to improve and modernize their estates".[25] The enterprise of the O'Brien earls of Thomond, however, must be seen in the context of their standing as powerful magnates and defenders of New English authority in Clare since the mid-sixteenth century; they had been substantially 'anglicised' and had earlier converted to Protestantism.[26] Evidence, therefore, of the innovation of the Gaelic-Irish O'Dwyers has an additional significance to the reading of the period, given that they were Catholic and not as comparatively interconnected in political circles.

The application of the leading O'Dwyer landowners to secure favour with Percivall occurred within the context of their realisation of his power and influence in Irish society; an ascendancy also held in the localised context of Kilnamanagh. He had shown how comprehensively he could acquire lands in the barony through a variety of mechanisms and it also appears that he acquired a level of control of the local magistrate arrangements in the pre-rebellion period.[27] The O'Dwyers' interaction with Percivall typifies their progressive attempts to forge positive perspectives on contemporary political and economic realities; a process which has been argued here to have been occurring from the late sixteenth century. Further evidence of the close and often personal contact which the O'Dwyers had effected with Percivall emerges from a suggestion of Philip O'Dwyer, the chief, of "a match between Sir Philip's daughter and his own kinsman, the lord of Castleconill".[28] Elsewhere, too (as quoted at the beginning of this chapter), O'Dwyer wrote to Percivall thanking him for "the kind expression of [his] love and care".[29]

It is important to stress that the evidence does not present a case of the O'Dwyers merely yielding authority to a powerful and pre-eminent individual in the person of Sir Philip Percivall, but rather reveals that it was a shared and negotiated level of interaction. The Englishman, for example, wrote to the chief of the O'Dwyers, at one point, "apologising for his servant's behaviour" in Kilnamanagh.[30] The cumulative evidence suggests that a significant level of *shared* confidence had been engendered between them in the pre-1641 period. As Mac Cuarta has argued,

> the cultural and social dimensions of colonial interaction were both more pervasive and less clearcut than the politics of Anglo-Irish relations, and the contemporary official discourse of civility and barbarism, might suggest.[31]

He uses the example of the "successful 'New English' colonist", Sir Matthew De Renzy, in King's County and County Wexford to make the point that "the common New English critique of Gaelic culture [such as the frequently cited Spenser, for example] does not give a fully-rounded picture of settler involvement with native culture".[32]

In a comprehensive work examining the Munster plantation, MacCarthy-Morrogh develops Mac Cuarta's argument by emphasising the "modest level of integration" achieved in society, where the "relaxed attitude" and "growing confidence" of the new settlers towards the existing population was demonstrated by their increasingly positive conception of intermarriage and the Irish language, and by their identification with their new homeland.[33] He argues that the "social unity among greater landlords from all backgrounds produced a strong element of stability and surprisingly peaceful conditions in the province after 1603".[34] Elsewhere, he points out that "from their prominent position as landowners some of the natives ... could, and did, exercise a strong local authority".[35] As argued above, similar currents were in motion in contemporary west Tipperary and, as MacCarthy-Morrogh observes, this "pre-1641 balance was forgotten in later years and is perhaps underestimated today because of the implacability of the religious divide from the rebellion onwards".[36] In considering the fluidity of social relations at the contact zone of Kilnamanagh, then, it is important to be mindful that a level of integration with the existing population was needed to effect a colonisation process that reflected both the general government desire to bring about reform and the simultaneous need to compromise an expedient response to complicated localised settings.

Negotiating Identity in a Colonial Context

The study of events unfolding in early modern Irish society is pervaded by considerable debate concerning the underlying ideology and manifestation of the Gaelic-Irish response that evolved in the late sixteenth and early seventeenth centuries. Ellis observes that

> Irish historiography of the Gaelic peoples has [witnessed] a vigorous debate in recent years about the Gaelic response to conquest and colonisation, the question of a 'national consciousness', and the changing nature of the Gaelic mentality.[37]

The essence of the argument has centred on the evidence of contemporary native poetry, which has prompted the presentation of various contradictory theses regarding the fundamental composition of Gaelic-Irish society.[38] Respecting the controversy, the important consideration is that the conflicting arguments submitted have served to illustrate the localism of occurrences in Gaelic-Irish society at this juncture, which provide a useful context to developments unfolding in contemporary Kilnamanagh.[39] Crucially, too, the opposing treatises have also served to further demonstrate the often-antithetical constituents of Gaelic-Irish reactions to New English colonialism in the early modern period.

Regarding the evolving debate on the Gaelic-Irish response, the evidence of the interaction of the O'Dwyers with Sir Philip Percivall provides a valuable testimony to the existence of a positive working relationship between native and newcomer in the pre-1641 period. The entry of the New English at the landholding level is seen to have not produced "an instant polarization of groups on ethnic grounds", and in Kilnamanagh as elsewhere "lines of distinction [between the Gaelic-Irish, Old and New English] continued to be blurred in the early years of the seventeenth century".[40] The Gaelic-Irish, therefore, were not always the victims in the practices of colonisation unfolding in early modern Ireland, as Sheehan points out in relation to the plantation of Munster, and as Morgan observes of contemporary developments in Ulster.[41] As argued above, the leading O'Dwyer landholding families of Kilnamanagh had, from the early seventeenth century, actively sought to advance themselves by accessing the common law to consolidate their respective properties, and by forging positive and mutually advantageous relationships with their most influential New English neighbours.

Developments in early modern west Tipperary, then, serve to illustrate the progressive adaptability of Gaelic-Irish society, which, as Morgan asserts, "proved strong enough to resist any challenges and flexible enough to adapt new ideas, methods and technology for its own end".[42] The pattern of change refutes Dunne's delineation of Gaelic-Irish ideology (extrapolated from the remains of contemporary poetry) as "deeply fatalistic, increasingly escapist and essentially apolitical",[43] and O'Riordan's depiction of a static Gaelic-Irish mentality anchored in the same fashion as the bardic poets by acceptance of the *fait accompli*.[44] Conversely, the political awareness of the O'Dwyers has been shown to have been a consistent and influential feature of a society that recognised the opportunities of the new order and was, in fact, "anxious to take advantage of them".[45]

Patterson presents evidence which illustrates that one of the most important components of the Gaelic learned class, the brehons (traditional lawyers), "supported administrative reforms within the Gaelic lordships, in accord with crown demands, and that they used native jural traditions to support legal change".[46] He concludes, furthermore, that

> [t]he appropriation of Gaelic legal traditions to justify the anglicisation of Irish local government lends further support to the view that Gaelic society and culture responded in diverse ways to the threat of conquest.[47]

Cunningham and Gillespie have also stressed the inherent flexibility of the Gaelic-Irish mentality, drawing attention, for example, to the manner in which the establishment of the presidency of Connacht was not viewed by the Gaelic-

Irish community as "the product of conquest by an outside element but rather in the traditional terms of a new lord arising following the decline or failure of an old line".[48] Furthermore, they emphasise that this positive reception of external administration was accommodated by a common Gaelic-Irish social structure wherein "[d]ynastic collapse and the rise of a new powerful lord were an inbuilt element".[49]

Cunningham and Gillespie submit that the evolving working relationships between the Gaelic-Irish and New English government constituted a "highly successful native Irish attempt to integrate the development of the authority of the English administration in Ireland into the framework of native social and political change".[50] They proceed to outline how the "activities of individual settlers and officials in Connacht were treated similarly", which indicates that the consideration later afforded to Sir Philip Percivall by the O'Dwyers was neither a new feature of Gaelic-Irish society nor unique to west Tipperary.[51] The reactions of the O'Dwyers formed, in effect, part of a succession of unfolding developments in the localities characterised by cooperation and underpinned by individualistic concerns. O'Dowd, for example, draws attention to the experiences of the O'Hara family in County Sligo to highlight that it was not unusual to find the Gaelic-Irish from the later sixteenth century willing "to serve on inquisitions finding land for the crown" or "to act as local officials and members of parliament".[52] In Kilnamanagh, John O'Dwyer – who had earlier participated in the surrender and regrant agreements as outlined in chapter three – was similarly serving on a local grand jury convening at Cashel in 1616.[53] Throughout west Tipperary, moreover, the individualistic agenda of the major Gaelic-Irish landowners is seen to have been a consistent feature of society from the early seventeenth century.

Connecting the above discussion to the question of Gaelic-Irish support of the English crown, Cunningham asserts that

> the idea of loyalty to the crown persisted throughout the early seventeenth century, and even in 1641 at the height of rebellion, Charles I was perceived by the Irish as protector of their liberties.[54]

The notion of allegiance to the crown has been shown above to have been a significant (albeit often contradictory) feature of Gaelic-Irish society in Kilnamanagh from the late sixteenth century. The Gaelic-Irish landholding elite quickly realised the futility of physical resistance, given the rejuvenation of New English political control in the aftermath of the Nine Years War. Conversely, they attempted to reconcile themselves to what Bradshaw points out (in relation to the O'Byrnes of County Wicklow) as "the political realities" of the time, in an effort to fashion "a satisfying public image within those limitations".[55] A number of distinct developments support the notion that the O'Dwyers were similarly disposed to fashion themselves as loyal subjects of the English crown: their dealings with the government (particularly regarding the surrender and regrant agreements); their attempts to present themselves as improving landlords in the English tradition; their appreciation and utilisation of the common law; and the positive working association they forged with Sir Philip Percivall. With the outbreak of rebellion in Tipperary, too, in 1641, the Gaelic-Irish and Old English continued to declare their loyalty to King Charles I. Although the action of professing loyalty to the English crown constituted a customary stratagem of Irish rebels in the early modern period, the cumulative evidence nevertheless reveals "that there was a great deal of cooperation and assimilation on the part of the Catholic Gaelic-Irish with the English administration".[56] Collectively, furthermore, the response of the Gaelic-Irish and Old English of west Tipperary at this juncture typified what Fitzpatrick sees as the attempts of the Catholics of Ireland "to reconcile themselves to the Stuarts as their only defence against the New English".[57]

The Gaelic-Irish and Old English of County Tipperary began to forge closer relationships as events moved closer to rebellion in 1641. Both communities were increasingly drawn together through the course of the medieval period by geographical contiguity and intermarriage. By the seventeenth century, the two were influencing each other in many aspects of political, economic and social life. Caball emphasises, for example, that at this juncture the evidence points to a "mature stage of Anglo-Norman accommodation to Gaelic social norms".[58] O'Dowd, too, stresses that "connections between the Gaelic landed classes and the Old English were strengthened ... as more and more native landowners changed their lifestyles to preserve their landed status".[59] There developed, in effect, a shared notion of progressiveness between the Gaelic-Irish and Old English communities, particularly at the landholding level, as a constituent part of the quest for survival.

The close association of the Gaelic-Irish and Old English reflected how both, as Clarke underlines, "had land and wanted to keep it" and "were prepared to yield obedience in order to do so".[60] In west and mid-Tipperary, immediately prior to the uprising of 1641, the leading Gaelic-Irish and Old English families of the region, including the O'Dwyers, sought an accommodation with the New English administration in Munster by reasserting their loyalty to the crown in an effort to safeguard their respective positions in society.[61] The case of the O'Dwyers illustrates the error in assuming the disloyalty of the Gaelic-Irish and, on the contrary, as O'Dowd points out (by taking the example of the O'Haras of County Sligo and the O'Reillys of County Cavan), "a large number of Gaelic lords were willing to proclaim their loyalty to the crown".[62] The Gaelic-Irish response in Kilnamanagh, furthermore, crucially problematises such dominant narratives that delineate an over-neat relationship of 'coloniser' and 'colonised'. In this area of west County Tipperary, a much more sophisticated and complex picture of society emerges prior to 1641; a society that, in essence, maintained a progressive, if uneven, balance due largely to the prevailing need of the landed classes to survive.

The level of Gaelic-Irish accommodation initiated with New English order reflected an overriding objective to successfully withstand change. Crucially, however, the extent to which some adapted to the presence of an expanded crown administration, whilst others opposed it, ensured that the overall reaction of the Gaelic-Irish incorporated essentially antithetical constituents of conformity and resistance. This mirrored the substantial level of fracture within the Gaelic-Irish polity that has been argued above to have been insidiously occurring from the early seventeenth century. Such conflicting meanings, intrinsic to the Gaelic-Irish response, were concomitant with the onset of the increasingly individualistic legal, economic and political character of the localities. Gaelic-Irish society was fragmented and transformed but it was also in a state of transition wherein an inevitable degree of tension emanated from those who did not have a stake in the new arrangement, particularly the lower levels of society.[63] Gaelic-Irish society certainly changed considerably in the late sixteenth and early seventeenth centuries but elements of the old world nevertheless persisted, often in a contradictory and localised manner, which, in part, explains the complexities and dynamic flux of society prior to the outbreak of rebellion in 1641. Ultimately, 'change' had incorporated the uncertainties, fears and contradictions intrinsic to any society transcended by what Fitzpatrick observes as a "hotchpotch struggle for survival".[64]

The Complexities of the Gaelic-Irish Response

Illuminating the shared spaces of pre-1641 Kilnamanagh society has served to problematise simplified notions of Self and Other in the Irish 'colonial' context. It has also impelled a further exploration of the intricacies of early modern Irish society and the perceivable reasons why the apparent normalcy of relations between 'natives' and 'newcomers' broke down. The conflicting responses of the Gaelic-Irish and Old English, in both opposing *and* accommodating New English hegemony, have not, however, been explicitly recognised in the extant literature of the period. The examination of these essentially antithetical constituents of the response of Catholic Ireland to New English colonialism is, on the contrary, a prerequisite to elucidating the discernible origins of the 1641 rebellion. Accordingly, the evidence that has been presented to illustrate the notable level of cooperation in early seventeenth-century west Tipperary is herewith re-examined to demonstrate the simultaneous conflicting ideologies and forms of resistance fundamental to society. As Cunningham and Gillespie note,

> [t]o demonstrate the power of the process of accommodation is not
> to suggest that the violence which periodically erupted between the
> settlers and native Irish was not motivated by real antagonisms.[65]

To begin with, the assertion of a common agenda of progressiveness by the Gaelic-Irish and Old English landholding elite in the pre-1641 period can also be interpreted as a form of opposition to New English cultural hegemony, via the construction of what Withers observes in the case of the contemporary Scottish Highlands as 'class consciousness'.[66] In County Tipperary, this constituted the attempt by the leading Gaelic-Irish and Old English elites to establish a shared sense of perspective in the face of New English ascendancy. The emerging group identity, incorporating both communities, was further facilitated by the notion of a shared sense of history. The importance of history as a political tool and as a legitimising force in the reassertion of identity was being increasing realised in the early modern period, as underlined by Cunningham:

> [i]n the early part of the seventeenth century there was a revival of
> interest in Irish history among the Old English and Old Irish both to
> clarify and justify their positions in the changing social and political
> order.[67]

Cunningham goes on to employ the works of historical chronologists – notably the *Annals of the Four Masters* by Micheál Ó Cléirigh (and his fellow Franciscan monks) and, more particularly, Geoffrey Keating's influential and widely read *Foras Feasa ar Éirinn* [68] – to illustrate the power of history in the dissemination of political overtones and the formulation of group identification. The production of such histories was part, she asserts, "of the continental trend which had seen a sense of nationality develop as a result of the Reformation and Counter-Reformation".[69] Elsewhere, she draws particular attention to Keating's successful integration of the Old English into the Gaelic national myth and consciousness, and to his interpretation of the past that gave "an aura of antiquity to the counter-reformation reforms being promoted by the secular clergy in the early seventeenth century".[70] The works of Keating – a secular priest trained on the Continent, and based in County Tipperary during the first half of the seventeenth century – enjoyed "unrivalled popularity among all elements of the catholic community in Ireland".[71] His work was also likely to have been influential at the lower orders of society, where the "oral mode of Gaelic literary activity may well have guaranteed a wider audience".[72]

The significance of the emerging sense of integrated identity being diffused by Keating and others – with its inherent notions of nationality and Counter-Reformation influences – for Kilnamanagh and County Tipperary was that it served to increasingly distinguish the Gaelic-Irish and Old English from the New English community and administration. In 1618, for example, Tipperary was feared by the New English administration as "the usual rendezvous of priests and Jesuits and other ill-affected persons".[73] By 1629, it was noted that these agitators and others throughout Munster "constantly looked to Spain", and later, in 1639, a plot was discovered between "some Irish Bishops and the Irish resident in Spain for an insurrection in Ireland".[74] Furthermore, in 1616, the *Egmont Manuscripts* record the fines of various Old English and Gaelic-Irish of west and mid-Tipperary, including leading O'Dwyer landowners, for "refusing to present recusants" at the local grand jury of Cashel, which indicates a significant level of opposition to English discrimination based on anti-Catholicism.[75] As Cunningham and Gillespie point out,

> [p]ersecution on the grounds of religion could not be explained away or rationalised in the way that dynastic evolution, political defeat, or social change had been throughout the sixteenth century.[76]

The construction of a distinctly *Catholic* perspective, incorporating the Gaelic-Irish and Old English, contributed to the emergence in the pre-1641 period of what Caball underlines as "a politicised Irish Catholic national consciousness in direct ideological opposition to the aspirations of the protestant British political ascendancy in Ireland".[77] By early 1641, there was "almost universal discontent in Ireland" (due especially to the extreme, exclusivist actions of the then Lord Deputy, the Earl of Strafford), but the heaviest pressure from the New English administration had typically fallen on the Catholics.[78] Subsequently, there emerged the political antecedents of outright rebellion whereby resistance to New English ascendancy took the form of "a relatively sophisticated constitutional opposition ... led by Catholic lawyers".[79] As Barnard points out,

> [c]oalescing with the opposition of the Catholic landed gentry, it produced in 1640 a campaign against Ireland's subordination to English interests, against its legal basis in the operation of Poynings' law, and against the recent erosion of the Catholics' political power in parliament.[80]

Developments in Ireland in this period must also be seen in the European context of the fight for survival between the major Protestant and Catholic powers.[81] As Carlin highlights, the outbreak of revolt in Ireland and moreover "[t]he fact that the Old English of the Pale joined the rebellion" (as those of west and mid-Tipperary did), confirmed in the minds of English contemporaries that "the rebels' cause was 'Romish, and universall'".[82] Cunningham, too, has commented that

> [t]he renewal of Catholic identity through the activities of the counter-reformation clergy ... indirectly fostered [a] sentiment of opposition to New English Protestantism, in so far as their Catholicism laid open the native Irish and Old English to discrimination on religious grounds.[83]

In this sense, both Catholic and Protestant communities had particular reasons to perceive themselves, as Caball observes, "to be in a state of siege".[84] There was inevitably, he argues, "the potential for conflict inherent in the implications of two national identities embodying mutually exclusive world views".[85] Ultimately, a distinctly different Catholic ideology was being advanced from that of the Protestant community who, similarly – though importantly from a different perspective – "appropriated and developed a particular vision of Ireland's history".[86]

The important notion to consider, at this point, is the extent to which the activities of the established church had been effective in disseminating a New English ideology (which, in essence, equated civility with Protestantism) in early seventeenth-century west Tipperary. To begin with, it is evident that the Anglican church, as Caball stresses in the broader context, "did little to create an ecclesiastical environment congenial to the Gaelic and Gaelicised Anglo-Norman communities".[87] A picture of the poor condition of the established church throughout Ireland in the late sixteenth and early seventeenth centuries emerges from a number of contemporary correspondences. Writing in 1604, Sir John Davies, for example, indicates the gravity of the situation by asserting that the spread of apostasy amongst many English gentlemen, merchants and settlers was due to "the religion and ignorance of their own (Protestant) clergy … more than the insinuation and diligence of the [Catholic] priests and Jesuits".[88]

In contemporary west Tipperary, the abuses of the Anglican archbishop of Cashel, Miler Magrath, were noted by his peers as being particularly destructive to the advancement of the Protestant faith. The Anglican archbishop of Dublin, for example, commented in 1607 that he "discovered such abuses and enormities through [Magrath's] misjudgement (especially in those two dioceses of Cashel and Emely [an area encompassing west and south Tipperary]) as he never could have believed".[89] He warned that these abuses were

> of themselves a sufficient motive to induce the people in those two dioceses of Cashel and Emely … to conceive and think that amongst them (the Protestants) there is no religion.[90]

He lamented, furthermore, that there were "not above six churches in repair in these two dioceses",[91] and noted that few Protestant clergymen were operating in the baronies of Kilnamanagh and Clanwilliam at this time, claiming that "there [was] not one preacher or good minister to teach the subjects their duties to God and His Majesty".[92] The situation in Tipperary, in later years, did not substantially improve. In 1611, there was "[n]o hope" reported of any Protestant representation for Tipperary in the Irish Parliament of that year.[93] In 1626 and later in 1629, King Charles I noted the corruption of the Protestant establishment in the dioceses of Cashel and Emly, wherein the churches were "in great decay".[94] Furthermore, areas such as Kilnamanagh (which had not been directly affected by state-organised plantation efforts) had not witnessed a comprehensive extension of organised Protestant activities and influence in the early seventeenth century. The *Civil Survey*, for example, records that by 1640 there was only one vicar resident in Kilnamanagh, compared with ten in Clanwilliam, wherein the Munster plantation had earlier had a noted impact.[95]

The network of Protestant clergymen was seen to be deficient in many parts of Ireland at this point. This did not mean, as Canny points out, that the state and the established Protestant church "were not sincere in their professed concern to bring the protestant faith to the Irish population at the point when their political dominance in the country was assured".[96] It did, however, reflect a situation wherein the state, for a variety of reasons, was unable to deter the majority of the population from maintaining its practice of Roman Catholicism. Various explanations for the fundamental failure of the Protestant Reformation in Ireland have been submitted.[97] Meigs, for example, argues that "the continuous existence of an institutional Catholic Church in Ireland" was a central factor in the ineffectiveness of Protestant church activities.[98] Caball, too, draws attention to the notion that the "popular association of the Anglican Church in Ireland with a new colonial elite actively shaped indigenous reactions to the religious Reformation".[99] Others have pointed to the impact of Counter-Reformation efforts and Ireland's traditional links with the Continent to account for the unsuccessful advancement of Protestantism.[100] The important consideration, however, is that, as Meigs notes, the "Catholic Reformation was implemented among the vast majority of the Irish people", which was a reality that "[successive] English Protestant governments were simply unable to disrupt permanently".[101]

The principal consequence of the failure of the Reformation in west Tipperary and elsewhere in the pre-1641 period was that the extended political and administrative control of the New English was not underpinned by the consolidation of its intrinsic Protestant ideology in the localities. The corollary of which was the retention of Roman Catholicism by the great majority of the population, which was one of the critical elements that contributed to the emergence of a nascent form of Irish nationality that Caball argues was "predicated upon three factors: insular territorial sovereignty, Gaelic cultural hegemony and allegiance to Roman Catholicism".[102] This essentially pre-empted "an easy incorporation of the Irish within an over-arching British identity",[103] and rendered impossible the "island's assimilation" within the

United Kingdom.[104] Unlike Gaelic Scotland, for example, which by the early seventeenth century was increasingly Calvinist, Gaelic Ireland consistently manifested a "rooted opposition to the Reformation" from the mid-Tudor period.[105] Ultimately, the effective implementation of "Tridentine Roman Catholicism" in the "cultural heritage" of both the Gaelic-Irish and Old English communities conversely "led both to perceive themselves as together forming the historic Irish".[106]

Conclusion

In considering the intricate cultural geographies of pre-1641 west Tipperary, a number of key points emerge that are important to our reading of early modern Irish society. First, a noted level of social and economic integration had been forged due largely to the progressive industry of the leading O'Dwyer landowners. Their close association with Sir Philip Percivall has been underlined as a key indication of the level of shared space between native and newcomer in pre-1641 Irish society. Second, and more generally, particular attention has been drawn to the complexities of the Gaelic-Irish response to New English colonialism; stressing the innovation and political awareness of the Gaelic polity and outlook, but also how it was increasingly transcended by contemporary notions of identity and resistance. Finally, in considering the failure of the New English administration in underpinning their programme of political and socio-economic expansion in the localities with their increasingly integral Protestant ideology, a realisation of the inevitability of conflict between two "mutually exclusive world views" decidedly emerges.[107] Imminent insurrection was writ large on the political, social and cultural landscapes of early 1641, and what follows in chapter five is an interrogation of the ultimately bounded nature of cultural interaction in early modern Ireland that eventually provoked rebellion.

Notes

[1] *Cal. Carew MSS, 1589-1600*, pp. 469-470

[2] See the comments of D. Cairns and S. Richards, 1988, *Writing Ireland: Colonialism, Nationalism and Culture*, Manchester University Press, Manchester, esp. chap. 1. Cf. B. Cunningham and R. Gillespie, 1990, 'Englishmen in Sixteenth-Century Irish Annals', *Irish Economic and Social History*, XVII, pp. 5-21, esp. pp. 19-21

[3] M. MacCarthy-Morrogh, 1986, *The Munster Plantation: English Migration to Southern Ireland 1583-1641*, Clarendon Press, Oxford, p. 282

[4] MacCarthy-Morrogh has shown how the influx of English settlers in early modern Munster was, nevertheless, quite considerable, wherein their numbers rose from 5,000 in 1610 to 22,000 in the 1630s; see M. MacCarthy-Morrogh, 1986, 'The English Presence in Early Seventeenth Century Munster', in: C. Brady and R. Gillespie (eds.), *Natives and Newcomers: Essays on the Making of Irish Colonial Society, 1534-1641*, Irish Academic Press, Dublin, pp. 171-190, esp. pp. 172-173. The motives for British settlers immigrating to Ireland, at this juncture, have been analysed elsewhere by MacCarthy-Morrogh: *Idem.*, *The Munster Plantation*, pp. 279-281. Cf. the comments of R. Gillespie, 1991, *The Transformation of the Irish Economy 1550-1700*, Studies in Irish Economic and Social History 6, The Economic and Social History Society of Ireland, pp. 14-15. Some of the push and pull factors cited include: geographical proximity and ease of passage, particularly between Ulster and the south-west of Scotland, and Munster and South-West England; rising farm rents in Scotland and England; declining fortunes of individuals wishing to consequently recover their respective wealth and standing by migration; and the opportunity of acquiring cheap lands.

[5] *Egmont MSS*, vol. 1, pt. 1, pp. 137, 140-141, 156. Both regions subsequently recorded a high number of Englishmen as having paid the poll money ordinances, *c*.1660; see *Census Ire., 1659*, pp. 303, 325

[6] *Egmont MSS*, vol. 1, pt. 1, pp. 137, 140-141, 156

[7] *Civil Survey, County Tipperary*, vol. 2, p. 8. The Civil Survey also records the presence of a vicar in Moyaliff parish in the year 1640; see *ibid.*, p. 360

[8] T.C.D., MS 821, fo. 221. For discussion of the use and shortcomings of the 1641 depositions, see N. Canny, 1993, 'The 1641 Depositions as a Source for the Writing of Social History: County Cork as a Case Study', in: P. O'Flanagan and C.G. Buttimer (eds.), *Cork: History and Society*, Geography Publications, Dublin, pp. 249-308 and, in the specific context of west Tipperary, J.M. Morrissey, 1996, *Landscape and Society in Seventeenth Century West Tipperary*, Unpublished B.A. Thesis, Trinity College, University of Dublin, pp. 101-105

[9] C.D. O'Murchadha, 1984, 'Thesis Abstract. Land and Society in Seventeenth-Century Clare (Ph.D. Thesis, National University of Ireland, 1982)', *Irish Economic and Social History*, XI, p. 125

[10] D. Woodward, 1973, 'The Anglo-Irish Livestock Trade of the Seventeenth Century', *Irish Historical Studies*, vol. 18, no. 72, p. 490. Similar arguments have been propounded elsewhere; see Gillespie, *Transformation of the Irish Economy*, esp. pp. 19-28 and MacCarthy-Morrogh, 'The English Presence', pp. 171-190, esp. pp. 172-173

[11] For commentary on the impact of the New English adventurer class on contemporary

modes of agricultural production and resource management, see Nolan, 1979, *Fassadinin: Land, Settlement and Society in South-East Ireland*, 1600-1850, Geography Publications, Dublin, esp. chaps. 1-2 and, for a more abridged statement, *Idem.*, 1976, 'Thesis Abstract. The Historical Geography of the Ownership and Occupation of Land in the Barony of Fassadinin, Co. Kilkenny (Ph.D. Thesis, National University of Ireland, 1975)', *Irish Economic and Social History*, III, pp. 75-77. Cf. P.J. Duffy, 1988, 'The Evolution of Estate Properties in South Ulster, 1600-1800', in: W.J. Smyth and K. Whelan (eds.), *Common Ground: Essays on the Historical Geography of Ireland*, Cork University Press, Cork, pp. 110-123. For information concerning the land-use of Co. Tipperary, *c.*1640, see the series of maps, derived from the *Civil Survey*, presented in I. Leister, 1963, *Das Werden der Agrarlandschaft in der Graftschaft Tipperary*, Marburg, Germany.

[12] Cunningham and Gillespie, 'Englishmen in Sixteenth-Century Irish Annals', p. 5. Canny argues, also, that the social and economic practices of the new adventurer class were instrumental in the successful re-establishment of the plantation in Munster in the 1620s and 1630s; see N. Canny, 1986, 'Protestants, Planters and Apartheid in Early Modern Ireland', *Irish Historical Studies*, vol. 25, no 98, p. 112

[13] M. MacCarthy-Morrogh, 1987, 'Credit and Remittance: Monetary Problems in Early Seventeenth-Century Munster', *Irish Economic and Social History*, XIV, p. 19. Cf. Gillespie, *Transformation of the Irish Economy*, pp. 12-14; Gillespie argues that a rapid economic recovery in Munster, in the aftermath of the Nine Years war, was brought about by the successful resettlement of British settlers and a simultaneous, substantial rise in population.

[14] *Egmont MSS*, vol. 1, pt. 1, pp. 140-141

[15] The adaptation of an increasingly commercialised economy also mirrored internal changes within the Gaelic-Irish lordships, particularly the fragmentation of vertical alignments of social order, as argued in chapter three.

[16] Gillespie, *Transformation of the Irish Economy*, p. 26. It is perhaps worth noting that the contrast between 'redistributive' and 'market' agricultural economies may not be as useful for this period and place as that between 'subsistence' and 'capitalist' agricultural economies.

[17] *Idem.*, 1993, 'Documents and Sources: Plantation and Profit: Richard Spert's Tract on Ireland, 1608', *Irish Economic and Social History*, XX, p. 64

[18] *Ibid.*

[19] *Egmont MSS*, vol. 1, pt. 1, pp. 137, 140-141

[20] *Ibid.*

[21] *Ibid.*, p. 137

[22] *Ibid.*, p. 93

[23] As outlined in chapter three, direct pressures were exerted upon numerous O'Dwyer landholders to secure their respective properties in Kilnamanagh through a series of inquisitions into rights of title to lands in the 1620s and 1630s; see N.A.I., Record Commission, 4/10. Furthermore, the crown considered plantation plans for Kilnamanagh and other baronies in north Tipperary in the early 1630s; see *Cal. S.P. Ire., 1625-1632*, pp. 536, 577 and *Cal. S.P. Ire., 1647-1660, Addenda*, p. 160. This important notion will be returned to in chapter five.

[24] Nolan has presented a similar case for Fassadinin barony in north County Kilkenny, where "in the 1630s pressure on the part of the barony still in the possession of the [Gaelic-Irish] O'Brennans intensified"; see Nolan, 'Historical Geography of Fassadinin', p. 75

[25] O'Murchadha, 'Land and Society in Seventeenth-Century Clare', p. 125

[26] G.A. Hayes-McCoy, 1976, 'The Royal Supremacy and Ecclesiastical Revolution, 1534-47', in: T.W. Moody, F.X. Martin and F.J. Byrne (eds.), *A New History of Ireland III: Early Modern Ireland 1534-1691*, Clarendon Press, Oxford, pp. 48-49

[27] A letter from one of Percivall's tenants in Kilnamanagh indicates that he possessed the jurisdiction to "entertain" whom he decided "as serjeant in Clonolta" to the south of the barony; see *Egmont MSS*, vol. 1, pt. 1, p. 140. Evidence of his influence at the local court level is also suggested by another letter from one of his tenants, urging him to "strictly follow at the assizes" a certain case of sheepstealing; see *ibid.*, p. 137

[28] *Egmont MSS*, vol. 1, pt. 1, p. 115

[29] *Ibid.*, p. 149

[30] *Ibid.*, p. 97

[31] B. Mac Cuarta, 1993, 'A Planter's Interaction with Gaelic Culture: Sir Matthew de Renzy, 1577-1634', *Irish Economic and Social History*, XX, p. 1. For similar observations regarding developments elsewhere, cf. H. Morgan, 1988, 'The End of Gaelic Ulster: A Thematic Interpretation of Events between 1534 and 1610', *Irish Historical Studies*, vol. 26, no. 101, pp. 8-32 and T. Bartlett, 1982, 'The O'Haras of Annaghmore *c.*1600-*c.*1800: Survival and Revival', *Irish Economic and Social History*, IX, pp. 34-52. See also the comments of J.H. Ohlmeyer, 1998, ''Civilizinge of those Rude Partes': Colonization within Britain and Ireland, 1580-1640s', in: N. Canny (ed.), *The Origins of Empire: British Overseas Enterprise to the Close of the 17th Century*, The Oxford History of the British Empire, vol. 1, Oxford University Press, Oxford, pp. 141-143

[32] Mac Cuarta, 'A Planter's Interaction with Gaelic Culture', pp. 1, 17

[33] MacCarthy-Morrogh, *The Munster Plantation*, pp. 274-275; see also pp. 276-279

[34] *Ibid.*, p. 278

[35] *Idem.*, 'The English Presence', p. 190

[36] *Idem.*, *The Munster Plantation*, p. 274

[37] S.G. Ellis, 1999, 'The Collapse of the Gaelic World', *Irish Historical Studies*, vol. 31, no. 124, p. 450

[38] For a depiction of essentially insular, passive and apolitical characteristics of early modern Gaelic-Irish society, see, for example: T.J. Dunne, 1980, 'The Gaelic Response to Conquest and Colonisation: The Evidence of the Poetry', *Studia Hibernica*, 20, pp. 7-30; B. Cunningham, 1986, 'Native Culture and Political Change in Ireland, 1580-1640', in: Brady and Gillespie (eds.), *Natives and Newcomers*, pp. 148-170; and M. O'Riordan, 1990, *The Gaelic Mind and the Collapse of the Gaelic World*, Cork University Press, Cork. On the contrary, others have outlined and stressed the progressiveness, innovation and political awareness intrinsic to Gaelic society; see, for instance: B. Bradshaw, 1978, 'Native Reaction to the Westward Enterprise: A Case-Study in Gaelic Ideology', in: K.R. Andrews, N.P. Canny and P.E.H. Hair (eds.), *The Westward Enterprise: English Activities in Ireland, The Atlantic and America, 1480-1650*, Liverpool University Press, pp. 65-80; M. Caball, 1994, 'Providence and Exile in Early Seventeenth-Century Ireland', *Irish Historical Studies*, vol. 29, no. 114, pp. 174-188; and *Idem.*, 1998, 'Faith, Culture and Sovereignty: Irish Nationality and its Development, 1558-1625', in: B. Bradshaw and P. Roberts (eds.), *British Consciousness and Identity: The Making of Britain 1533-1707*, Cambridge University Press, Cambridge, pp. 112-139. For some of the poems in question, see S. O'Tuama and T. Kinsella, 1981, *An Duanaire 1600-*

GEOGRAPHIES OF IDENTITY AND RESISTANCE

1900: Poems of the Dispossessed, Dolmen Press, Dublin.

[39] For a useful overview of the debate, see the comments of M. Caball, 1993, 'The Gaelic Mind and the Collapse of the Gaelic World: An Appraisal', *Cambridge Medieval Celtic Studies*, 25, pp. 87-96

[40] Cunningham, 'Native Culture and Political Change', p. 155

[41] A.J. Sheehan, 1983, 'Official Reaction to Native Land Claims in the Plantation of Munster', *Irish Historical Studies*, vol. 23, no. 92, pp. 297-318; Morgan, 'The End of Gaelic Ulster', pp. 8-32

[42] Morgan, 'The End of Gaelic Ulster', p. 32

[43] Dunne, 'The Gaelic Response', p. 11

[44] O'Riordan, *The Gaelic Mind*, esp. chapter 1

[45] M. O'Dowd, 1986, 'Gaelic Economy and Society', in: Brady and Gillespie (eds.), *Natives and Newcomers*, p. 137. For a coherent analysis of the expedient adaptation of change by the Gaelic-Irish in relation to the surrender and regrant agreements, see *ibid.*, pp. 134-137

[46] N. Patterson, 1991, 'Gaelic Law and the Tudor Conquest of Ireland: The Social Background of the Sixteenth-Century Recensions of the Pseudo-Historical Prologue to the *Senchas Már*', *Irish Historical Studies*, vol. 27, no. 107, p. 193

[47] *Ibid.*, p. 215

[48] Cunningham and Gillespie, 'Englishmen in Sixteenth-Century Irish Annals', p. 15

[49] *Ibid.*

[50] *Ibid.*, p. 17

[51] *Ibid.*

[52] O'Dowd, 'Gaelic Economy and Society', p. 140

[53] *Egmont MSS*, vol. 1, pt. 1, p. 49

[54] Cunningham, 'Native Culture and Political Change', p. 157

[55] Bradshaw, 'Native Reaction to the Westward Enterprise', p. 78

[56] O'Dowd, 'Gaelic Economy and Society', p. 140

[57] B. Fitzpatrick, 1988, *17th Century Ireland: The War of Religions*, New Gill History of Ireland 3, Gill and MacMillan, Dublin, p. 4

[58] Caball, 'Faith, Culture and Sovereignty', p. 130

[59] O'Dowd, 'Gaelic Economy and Society', p. 141

[60] A. Clarke, 1970, 'Ireland and the General Crisis', *Past and Present*, no. xlviii, p. 84

[61] They attempted to present themselves as loyal subjects to Sir William St. Leger, president of Munster, in December 1641; see Carte, *Ormond*, vol. 2, pp. 265-266 and T.C.D., MS 821, fo. 7

[62] O'Dowd, 'Gaelic Economy and Society', p. 139

[63] This tension formed one of the central constituents of the general social unrest that provoked eventual rebellion in Kilnamanagh, and will be considered in detail in chapter five below.

[64] Fitzpatrick, *17th Century Ireland*, p. 4

[65] Cunningham and Gillespie, 'Englishmen in Sixteenth-Century Irish Annals', p. 19

[66] C.W.J. Withers, 1988, *Gaelic Scotland: The Transformation of a Culture Region*, Routledge, London, pp. 328-331. Withers identifies, in theory, three forms of opposition to elite cultural transformation; the other two being 'alternative hegemony' in respect of the retention of religion, language or other cultural characteristics, and 'counter-hegemony' in

the sense of physical resistance.

[67] B. Cunningham, 1986, 'Seventeenth-Century Interpretations of the Past: the Case of Geoffrey Keating', *Irish Historical Studies*, vol. 25, no. 98, p. 116

[68] *A.F.M.*, 7 vols.; G. Keating, *Foras Feasa ar Éirinn: The History of Ireland (c.*1633), ed. D. Comyn and P.S. Dineen, 4 vols., Irish Texts Society, London, 1902-1914

[69] Cunningham, 'Seventeenth-Century Interpretations of the Past', pp. 116-117. Cf. B. Bradshaw, 1993, 'Geoffrey Keating: Apologist of Irish Ireland', in: *Idem.*, A. Hadfield and W. Maley (eds.), *Representing Ireland: Literature and the Origins of Conflict, 1534-1660*, Cambridge University Press, Cambridge, pp. 166-190

[70] Cunningham, 'Native Culture and Political Change', p. 167

[71] *Idem.*, 'Seventeenth-Century Interpretations of the Past', p. 126

[72] Caball, 'Faith, Culture and Sovereignty', p. 137

[73] *Cal. S.P. Ire., 1615-1625*, p. 217

[74] *Cal. S.P. Ire., 1625-1632*, p. 432; *Cal. Clarendon Papers*, vol. 1, p. 184

[75] *Egmont MSS*, vol. 1, pt. 1, p. 49

[76] Cunningham and Gillespie, 'Englishmen in Sixteenth-Century Irish Annals', p. 21

[77] Caball, 'Faith, Culture and Sovereignty', p. 138

[78] P.J. Corish, 1976, 'The Rising of 1641 and the Catholic Confederacy, 1641-5', in: Moody *et al* (eds.), *A New History of Ireland III*, p. 289. See also A. Clarke, 1976, 'The Government of Wentworth, 1632-1640', in: Moody *et al* (eds.), *A New History of Ireland III*, pp. 243-269 and *Idem.*, 1976, 'The Breakdown of Authority, 1640-41', in: Moody *et al* (eds.), *A New History of Ireland III*, pp. 270-288. Cf. M. Perceval-Maxwell, 1994, *The Outbreak of the Irish Rebellion of 1641*, Gill and MacMillan, Dublin

[79] T.C. Barnard, 1975, *Cromwellian Ireland: English Government and Reform in Ireland, 1649-1660*, Oxford University Press, London, p. 2

[80] *Ibid.*

[81] See K.J. Lindley, 1972, 'The Impact of the 1641 Rebellion upon England and Wales, 1641-5', *Irish Historical Studies*, vol. 18, no. 70, pp. 143-176

[82] N. Carlin, 1993, 'Extreme or Mainstream? The English Independents and the Cromwellian Reconquest of Ireland, 1649-1651', in: Bradshaw *et al* (eds.), *Representing Ireland*, p. 211

[83] Cunningham, 'Native Culture and Political Change', p. 170

[84] Caball, 'Providence and Exile', p. 187. For further examination of the role of religion in the Irish historical experience, see the broad collections of essays contained in R.V. Comerford, M. Cullen, J.R. Hill and C. Lennon (eds.), 1990, *Religion, Conflict and Co-Existence in Ireland*, Gill and MacMillan, Dublin. Cf. R. Gillespie, 1998, 'Popular and Unpopular Religion: A View from Early Modern Ireland', in: J.S. Donnelly, Jr. and K.A. Miller (eds.), *Irish Popular Culture, 1650-1850*, Irish Academic Press, Dublin, pp. 30-49

[85] Caball, 'Faith, Culture and Sovereignty', p. 139

[86] A. Ford, 1998, 'James Ussher and the Creation of an Irish Protestant Identity', in: Bradshaw and Roberts (eds.), *British Consciousness and Identity*, p. 184

[87] Caball, 'Faith, Culture and Sovereignty', p. 138

[88] *Cal. S.P. Ire., 1603-1606*, p. 162

[89] *Cal. S.P. Ire., 1606-1608*, p. 235

[90] *Ibid.*, p. 236

[91] *Ibid.*, p. 237

[92] *Ibid.*, p. 242; see also pp. 238-242

[93] *Cal. S.P. Ire., 1611-1614*, p. 165. This may also have been partially due to what Gillespie observes, in relation to contemporary Ulster, as the tendency of the Protestant landlord class (which had been established in Munster by the earlier plantation) to not get involved in the "preoccupations of the central government, such as electoral politics, save when it was necessary"; see R. Gillespie, 1984, 'The Origins and Development of an Ulster Urban Network, 1600-41', *Irish Historical Studies*, vol. 24, no. 93, p. 17

[94] *Cal. pat. rolls Ire., Chas. I*, p. 153; see also *Cal. S.P. Ire., 1625-1632*, p. 458

[95] *Civil Survey, County Tipperary*, vol. 2, pp. 360, 364-367

[96] Canny, 'Protestants, Planters and Apartheid', p. 110. For a comprehensive analysis of the developments and progress of the Protestant and Nonconformist churches in early modern Ireland, see the works of: A. Ford, 1987, *The Protestant Reformation in Ireland, 1590-1641*, Studies in the Intercultural History of Christianity, Verlag Peter Lang, Frankfurt am Main; J. Murray, 1993, 'The Church of Ireland: A Critical Bibliography, 1536-1992, Part I: 1536-1603', *Irish Historical Studies*, vol. 28, no. 112, pp. 345-352; and A. Ford, 1993, 'The Church of Ireland: A Critical Bibliography, 1536-1992, Part II: 1603-41', *Irish Historical Studies*, vol. 28, no. 112, pp. 352-358

[97] For general commentary, see R. MacKenny, 1993, *Sixteenth Century Europe: Expansion and Conflict*, MacMillan History of Europe, MacMillan Press Ltd., Basingstoke, esp. chaps. 5-8, 12 and S.G. Ellis, 1998, *Ireland in the Age of the Tudors, 1447-1603: English Expansion and the End of Gaelic Rule*, Longman, London, chaps. 8-9. Cf. S.A. Meigs, 1994, 'Thesis Abstract. Constantia in Fide: The Persistence of Traditional Religion in Early Modern Ireland, 1400-1690 (Ph.D. Thesis, Northwestern University, Evanston, 1993)', *Irish Economic and Social History*, XXI, pp. 82-83, A. Ford, 1986, 'The Protestant Reformation in Ireland', in: Brady and Gillespie (eds.), *Natives and Newcomers*, pp. 50-74, and C. Lennon, 1986, 'The Counter-Reformation in Ireland, 1542-1641', in: Brady and Gillespie (eds.), *Natives and Newcomers*, pp. 75-92

[98] Meigs, 'Constantia in Fide', p. 82

[99] Caball, 'Faith, Culture and Sovereignty', p. 132

[100] Cf. N. Canny, 1987, 'The Formation of the Irish Mind: Religion, Politics and Gaelic Irish Literature, 1580-1750', in: C.H.E. Philpin (ed.), *Nationalism and Popular Protest in Ireland*, Past and Present Publications, Cambridge University Press, Cambridge, pp. 50-79, esp. pp. 54-65, Caball, 'Faith, Culture and Sovereignty', pp. 112-139, esp. pp. 131-137, and Cunningham, 'Native Culture and Political Change', pp. 148-170, esp. pp. 165-170

[101] Meigs, 'Constantia in Fide', p. 82

[102] Caball, 'Faith, Culture and Sovereignty', pp. 112-113

[103] *Ibid.*, p. 112

[104] See B. Bradshaw, 1998, 'The English Reformation and Identity Formation in Wales and Ireland', in: Bradshaw and Roberts (eds.), *British Consciousness and Identity*, p. 111

[105] Ellis, 'The Collapse of the Gaelic World', p. 465

[106] Bradshaw, 'The English Reformation', p. 111

[107] Caball, 'Faith, Culture and Sovereignty', p. 139

Chapter 5

The 1641 Rebellion:
Defining the 'Coloniser' and the 'Colonised'

> I have received your letter, and thank you for the kind expression of your love and care. Here is no stirring, God be praised, in this province, but everyone preparing of men and arms according [to] their ability, the Lord President and Council of Munster having sent letters to all men of note in the county to make a return of what they can furnish – *Philip O'Dwyer to Sir Philip Percivall, November 16, 1641* [1]

> We have lost 3,000*l.*stock by rebels in Killemanagh and Clanwilliam... Mr. Philip O'Dwyer is keeping what he can for you, but Edmund O'Dwyer of Ballymone has taken at least four hundred sheep and put them upon Ballytemple and Ballybrowngh. He intends to keep the land, and has spoiled your servants' gardens and taken their corn... This loss is not your worship's alone, but every English gentleman in these parts has lost all – *Richard Stokes to his master, Sir Philip Percivall, December 17, 1641* [2]

Writing in late 1641, Philip O'Dwyer, the last chief of Kilnamanagh, demonstrates once again above the industry of the leading land-owning interests in the barony to survive by the consistent adoption of a discerning and progressive outlook on contemporary political realities. O'Dwyer appears to be steadfastly standing loyal to the crown; his close contact with Sir Philip Percivall mirroring the significant level of integration attained in pre-rebellion society. Why, then, did such relations subsequently break down so dramatically in December of 1641, when English tenants in the region were, as reported above, subjected to attack? Why, by the end of the month, moreover, had O'Dwyer and a number of other leading Gaelic-Irish and Old English landowners in mid-Tipperary spearheaded an attack on the town of Cashel and captured it? The offensive signalled the beginning of the 1641 rebellion throughout Munster, but was, despite its apparent abrupt manifestation, the culmination of a series of specific and interrelated developments in contemporary society, which are explored below.

A Sense of Difference

Early modern Ireland may not have been a colony in the strictest sense. As MacCarthy-Morrogh argues, until the late sixteenth century, at least, it was "more a rebellious feudal fief".[3] The evidence presented above from contemporary west Tipperary, indeed, draws particular attention to antithetical features of accommodation and resistance in society and space that do not conform to any conventional colonial model. However, despite having demonstrated the problematic nature of the ideas of Self and Other as conceptual tools in examining early modern Irish society, it is, nevertheless, vitally important to emphasise the presence of a constructed English notion of difference increasingly evident in political and cultural interaction as the early modern period progressed.

The exclusivism of the New English regime – most readily contrived and legitimised on religious grounds – was a phenomenon which was not confined to the English government of the seventeenth century. It had, as outlined in chapter two, manifested itself at various junctures in the later sixteenth century and especially in times of government emergency.[4] By the close of the sixteenth century, the country had effectively come to be regarded as a colony by serving English officials, which "in turn led these officials to the belief that only extreme measures would provide a remedy for the endemic instability that had characterized that country's political history".[5] Underpinning such beliefs were "English doubts about the short-term outcome of the struggle between righteousness (English State Protestantism) and superstitious idolatry (Catholicism)".[6] This is evident in the works of early modern English writers such as Fynes Moryson, for example, wherein the "image of the Catholic Church militant and triumphant" is ever-present as a haunting possibility.[7] As a result, as Cairns and Richards assert,

> the response of the New English was to draw cultural and religious indicators together to efface in their own minds the differences separating Old English and Native Irish and to lump them together as 'other'.[8]

Further exploration of the notion of English superiority and racialism in early modern Ireland reveals a succession of contemporary correspondences by prominent officials and writers which depict Roman Catholicism as the hated and feared embodiment of 'otherness'. In 1600, for example, Sir George Carew refers to the "traitorly priests" as the "chiefest firebrands" of the "unnatural treasons" of the country.[9] The association of Catholicism, moreover, with the threat of intrigue and interference in Ireland's affairs by England's continental enemies, particularly Spain (dating primarily from the 1580s), was a consistent feature of colonial writing and propaganda throughout the seventeenth century.[10] Sir John Davies, for instance, writes in 1604 that the Counter-Reformation Jesuits and priests were primarily sent to Ireland to "withdraw the subject from his allegiance and so serve the turn of Tyrone and the King of Spain".[11] Sir George Carew, using the examples of Counties Tipperary and Kilkenny, had in 1601 earlier claimed that the missionary works of the Jesuits masked a broader design to "raise up the spirits of the ill-affected to revolt" and to "assure the coming of Spanish aids".[12] This correlation, furthermore, between Roman Catholicism and treason strengthened rather than abated as the 1641 rebellion approached.[13]

Catholic church activities, then, were equated with treachery and foreign involvement, which served to legitimise the continual framework of exclusivism. The sense of difference was seen to be particularly influential in the construction of group identity. Through the course of the early seventeenth century, as O'Sullivan notes, even the Old English of the Pale – traditionally regarded as the most loyal subjects of the English crown in Ireland – had, by failing to conform to the established church,

> compromised that loyalty to such a degree that within a short time after the outbreak of insurrection in Ulster in 1641 they too were to be classed as 'Irish rebels', a charge, though hotly disputed, they were never to shake loose from.[14]

Maley develops this point by drawing attention to an anonymous treatise penned at the end of the sixteenth century, which reveals

> a sustained polemic which promotes the New English colonisers as the sole legitimate heirs of English rule ... categorises Ireland's indigenous peoples as incapable of self-government... [and legitimises a] determined exclusion of all other cultural groups inhabiting the island from so-called civil society.[15]

He argues that from this point the 'exclusion' of all other groups was "dependent upon religious persuasion rather than professions of loyalty" and that 'Catholic' and 'Irish' had attained the same meaning, signifying the "ultimate threat to God's Englishmen".[16]

In considering the connection between the exclusive nature of early modern New English colonial thought and the workings of colonisation in practice, the role of religion in the differentiation of competing groups is an interesting one. The workings and significance of religious differentiation in early modern Irish and British societies have been explored by numerous authors. In relation to Ireland, for example, Canny has examined how the legitimising theories of difference – religious and otherwise – fundamental to the plantation effort served inevitably to "provide the several competing groups in early modern Ireland with a sense of well-being and purpose which contributed to the development of group identification".[17] In the English context, Marotti has argued that a constructed notion of anti-Catholicism lay at the origin of English nationalism and that

> [i]n the sixteenth and seventeenth centuries English identity was defined as Protestant, so Roman Catholicism, especially in its post-Tridentine, Jesuit manifestations was cast as the hated and dangerous antagonist.[18]

Such religious and intellectual currents ultimately transcended both the Gaelic-Irish and Old English quest for accommodation in Kilnamanagh and elsewhere in early modern Ireland. In actuality, this meant that the essential components of this process of survival became re-constituted as a polarised struggle between the basic groups of 'Irish Papist' and 'English Protestant', as delineated, for example, in the *Civil Survey*.[19]

The agency of religion, however, as a key determinant on political and social events unfolding is less clear-cut than many authors have argued. MacCarthy-Morrogh, for example, suggests that "religion was the ultimate divider".[20] Clearly though, as argued above, religion was not the only constituent in the evolving dynamics of seventeenth-century Irish society. Bottigheimer notes, for instance, that in searching for "a turning point in the early modern religious history of Ireland, we find instead a sequence of swinging movements which gradually and almost unintentionally produce cleavage".[21] Religion could certainly be utilised as a rallying cry as the Ulster Confederacy proved en route to the Battle of Kinsale, and when "combined with political and social tensions at a time of economic crisis" it could become an "explosive issue".[22] However, religious differentiation is arguably best seen as reinforcing what Bottigheimer observes as "older conflicts of a political or cultural nature".[23]

The ongoing (re)negotiation of what was an increasingly 'othered' Catholic Irish identity and reaction in early seventeenth-century Kilnamanagh occurred within this over-arching framework of difference. One outcome for Kilnamanagh and elsewhere, as Cairns and Richards have stressed, was that the

> understanding of the Native Irish and Old English held by the New English required the latter to treat the former as subjects fit only for domination – hence the comparatively insignificant attempts that were made at conversion to Protestantism.[24]

As events moved closer to rebellion in the mid seventeenth-century, this racialist sense of difference increasingly manifested itself in the form of discrimination regarding participation in the political sphere and entry into public offices. The exclusion of Catholics from the various levels of the legal profession, for example, accelerated prior to 1641.[25] The pre-1641 period, too, saw a gradual decline in the number of Old English and Gaelic-Irish Catholics holding high civic or bureaucratic posts. In the earlier part of the century, the sheriffs serving the liberty of the Tipperary had not been exclusively New Englishmen; a member of the O'Dwyers, as outlined earlier, officiating in 1608. Similarly, elsewhere in Munster, the New English had not at this time dominated the commissions of the peace.[26] Subsequently, however, a marked exclusivism emerged in the 1620s and 1630s. The period witnessed a determined drive by the New English state apparatus to centralise and consolidate political and administrative control across the island in the hands of the New English Protestant element.[27] Earlier, in 1616, the system whereby the sheriff of the liberty of Tipperary had "exercised his office without taking the oath of supremacy" had been checked.[28] The later dissolution of the liberty and the jurisdictional power of Ormond in 1620, as outlined earlier, also formed an essential component of the process of consolidation throughout Munster. Similar developments elsewhere in the province meant that, by 1640, the New English minority therein had managed to contrive a Protestant representative majority in parliament.[29]

Ultimately, then, political and ideological discrimination and exclusion counterbalanced the social and economic process of accommodation and integration in pre-1641 society in west Tipperary. It is important to stress that both processes were, in effect, occurring simultaneously, which further complicated the arena of contestation over time. Partially, the evidence from Kilnamanagh furthers the notion that integration in society in Munster, prior to the 1641 rebellion, was more effective and fruitful than has often been maintained. It points, moreover, to MacCarthy-Morrogh's contention that to "slot Munster into the English colonial system is to give a misleading impression of the internal nature of the province", which he believes was "akin to a slightly raffish county on the English borders".[30] This English provincial analogy, however, can be taken too far. As Clark points out, the process of settlement in Ireland, in the early modern period, was significantly different from that of the expansion of state control over the English border counties:

> compared with the increasingly cohesive character of county society in England and Wales – with the growing sense of a county community, and of quarter sessions as the county 'parliament' – provincial officials in Ireland had to contend with the three-cornered rivalry of New English, Old English and native Irish landowners.[31]

Racialist hostility, too, among the New English towards the Catholic Irish was "almost certainly growing in the early seventeenth century, fuelled by the Irish risings under Elizabeth".[32] Such aggression was seen in County Tipperary immediately prior to the 1641 rebellion, when the discriminatory actions of Sir William St. Leger, president of the province, reveal a marked antagonism towards the Gaelic-Irish and Old English, predicated on religious and racialist grounds.[33]

The notion of superiority, therefore – most readily legitimised and represented in religious terms – was an essential component in facilitating the mainstay of New English interest in the localities in Ireland: the monopolisation of power.[34] The necessity of exclusiveness, furthermore, constituted a widespread conviction of the New English administration of Munster in the pre-1641 period. Contemporary correspondences preserved in the *Egmont Manuscripts* between Sir William St. Leger, president of the province, and his intimate friend Sir Philip Percivall, for example, reveal the extent of this exclusiveness fundamental to New English ideology and government. Respecting the efforts to control the escalating sense of tension in the localities in Munster in 1641 with the aid of loyal Gaelic-Irish and Old English landholding elites (including the O'Dwyers), St. Leger's remarks crucially demonstrate a fundamental prejudice based on a religious axiom of difference:

> had I arms, I could draw together three or four thousand good protestants, on whom we might have relied; but to put all our strength of arms into the hands of another religion, religion being the pretence of the war, is a thing, I confess, beyond my understanding.[35]

Elsewhere, too, he is seen to have rebuked those responsible for "putting the King's arms into the *Papists'* hands" whilst assuring Sir Philip Percivall that his castles were "safe in the hands of honest *Englishmen*".[36] Another prominent New Englishman in contemporary Munster, Richard Boyle, first earl of Cork, demonstrated in 1636 what MacCarthy-Morrogh observes as "the dark fears of a classic embattled settler":[37]

> I dare not venture for my cure upon the Physicians of this kingdom who though some of them are learned and experienced, yet they are all of a contrary religion to me.[38]

The Breakdown of Order

Such intellectual and religious currents in society as outlined above were important in County Tipperary in that they formed some of the impetus and underlying ideologies driving ideas of resistance and identity that were a constituent part of the process of Gaelic-Irish and Old English opposition to, and ultimate insurrection against, New English rule. In the broader context, as Caball submits,

> the prolonged English conquest and its religious ancillary, the protestant reform movement, were significant factors in propelling, by way of reaction, the development of a revised and dynamic Irish identity in the late sixteenth and early seventeenth centuries.[39]

Preceding the uprising of 1641, there developed "a politicised Irish Catholic national consciousness in direct ideological opposition to the aspirations of the protestant British political ascendancy in Ireland".[40] Indeed, as Bradshaw argues, a "dimension of nationalism" was a consistent feature of Catholic political opposition to New English hegemony from the mid-Tudor period.[41] He proceeds to assert that from this point the Old English, particularly, "sought to adapt English political and constitutional institutions for the purpose of constructing an authentically national Irish polity", and that "this was the outlook of those who [thereafter] sought to resist the aggressive colonialism of the new English by constitutional means".[42] Treadwell, furthermore, has utilised the early seventeenth-century treatises presented to King James I by the Old English crown counsel for Irish affairs, Richard Hadsor, to highlight that there were a series of attempts by the Old English to construct a valid platform to assert their central belief (shared by the Gaelic-Irish), that

> the king's government in Ireland should express the common interest of Old and New English, loyal Catholics and Protestants, and apply the principles of the common law which Ireland shared with England.[43]

Such overarching ideological and political currents increasingly transcended the contested and dynamic social spaces of west Tipperary as New English hegemony became progressively more exclusivist in character. As Fanon observes, through history, the 'colonised' is "treated as an inferior but not convinced of his inferiority", and the Gaelic-Irish and Old English of west Tipperary ultimately reacted similarly to New English suppositions of superiority.[44]

It is important to underline that, at this juncture, many old tensions between the Old English and Gaelic-Irish persisted, particularly "over whether or not to compromise with the English administration".[45] In the immediate pre-1641 period, both communities appeared to act in a united fashion in defence of their liberties in Kilnamanagh and surrounding baronies by asserting a common perspective in the face of New English ascendancy and by later joining the rebellion. Elsewhere in the country, however, "the [Gaelic-Irish] rebels cursed the Old English openly" and, in this sense, old tensions and contradictions in Irish society remained.[46] Lennon, too, comments that "bitter divisions" between the Old English and Gaelic-Irish Catholics continued in the post-1641 period, which "reveal the extent to which commitment to a common faith failed to obliterate deep cultural differences".[47]

Evolving developments in the seventeenth century, however, increasingly resulted in closer associations being forged between Catholics of both heritages that were frequently driven by the exclusivist actions and policies of the New English government. Barnard, for example, points out that Sir Thomas Wentworth, earl of Strafford (lord deputy of Ireland, 1633-1641), by "treating the Irish Catholics as a homogenous group of doubtful loyalty, helped to create such a group".[48] The Gaelic-Irish of Kilnamanagh, together with Catholics throughout the country, were "marked out as 'only half subjects', as James I had earlier described them, and in consequence they were exposed to various discriminations, particularly when the executive power was strong".[49] In 1629, for example, King Charles I directed his lord deputy, Lord Falkland, to issue a "proclamation against the Roman priests" and apprehend all "titulary Bishops".[50] The associations, moreover, of Catholicism with allegiance to Rome and Protestantism with loyalty to the crown had become axioms; the king, for instance, advised his lord deputy "*Papist* tenants shall be evicted if possible from the episcopal lands and they shall be settled with *British* tenants".[51]

Government plantation plans in the 1630s served to engender even further the growing state of tension and disquiet in the localities.[52] Bottigheimer points out that prior to this "only open rebellion had exposed [the Catholics] to such harsh treatment", and that it was the "implications of the plantation rather than its actuality which was unsettling, for Ireland was swept by rebellion before any extensive colonization could take place".[53] The purpose and intention of plantation policies were, indeed, to have a crucial impact on the actions of established Gaelic-Irish and Old English landowners throughout Ireland. As Kearney argues, the "significance of the plantation of Connacht [which never did take place] lay in the fear which it created".[54] In a similar manner to the anxiety caused by the commission for defective titles, impending plantation plans "threatened to cause large-scale changes in the ownership of land", and for the first time "old English proprietors and those Gaelic-Irish who had come to terms with the English government during Elizabeth's reign were faced with the threat of Plantation".[55] The policy of Lord Deputy Wentworth towards the landed interests and especially his administration's threats of land confiscations were ultimately disastrous in the effect they created on tenurial insecurity and ensuing social tension across the country.[56]

The prospect of plantation in Kilnamanagh and elsewhere in north and west Tipperary had been stated overtly in government circles from the early 1630s:

[p]eople talk of planting the territories of Ormond, Arra, Ownymullrian [Owney and Arra], Ikerrin, and Kilnamanagh. The King's title is good and the gentry there are ready for a plantation.[57]

By late 1630, the king had issued a draft to the lord justices in Ireland outlining his plans to plant territories throughout the county of Tipperary in order to secure the area and his subjects from "ill-affected persons", and to foster "true religion".[58] Such open plantation policies gave rise to an inevitable degree of anxiety and restlessness in west Tipperary. With the threat of confiscations in the barony,[59] the leading O'Dwyer landholders attempted to forge closer economic and social relations with the influential New Englishman, Sir Philip Percivall, in an effort to mitigate the impact of intended official plantation programmes on the stability of society in the localities.[60] As one contemporary observed, the "freeholders [would] be greatly frightened if they hear that the whole matter is to be settled in England".[61] It was the disquiet emanating from such fears that constituted the chief concern of both the government and the Gaelic-Irish landholding elites as the region inched closer to insurrection in the late 1630s. Ultimately, this source of tension was not controlled by either and formed, subsequently, one of the most significant components of the process of outright rebellion in 1641.

Throughout the early seventeenth century, County Tipperary witnessed a consistent, and often considerable, level of social unrest. In addition to the effect of intended plantation plans, a source of further disquiet proved to be erstwhile Gaelic-Irish and Old English landowners, dispossessed of their estates in earlier plantation schemes. From the late sixteenth century these individuals, particularly, were resentful of the New English, whom they believed to have twisted the law "in favour of a minority as well as to have intruded on territories to which they had no claim apart from that of occupation by force".[62] They subsequently constituted a significant threat to government administration in the localities in Tipperary. In 1619, for example, the lord deputy, Sir Oliver St. John Gogarty, wrote to the Privy Council concerning robberies carried out by the "idle gentlemen" of the county and encouraged the notion that they be allowed to go into foreign service in Poland, declaring that "it would be an ease to the kingdom if some foreign prince were to draw 10,000 of them to a war abroad".[63] An additional factor in the escalating social tension in the pre-1641 period was the prevalence of militant Counter-Reformation activities. As outlined earlier, the county had been equated with the threat of Jesuit intrigue from the early seventeenth century and, in later years, this picture had not improved.[64] By the early 1630s, for example, it had come to be represented as "a receptacle, den, and common thoroughfare for all leaud and ill-affected persons flying from every [province] to infect our other loving subjects".[65]

The permeation, too, of the New English entrepreneurial class at the influential landholding and political levels and the simultaneous lessening in power of the Gaelic-Irish lords inevitably engendered economic pressures within a society adjusting to a new socio-economic order. O'Dowd observes, for example, that in the pre-1641 period there emerged the necessity to

> pay crown rents and composition dues; to secure letters patent for land and other administrative documents such as pardons; to pursue law suits in local courts ... and also to pay for the new English fashions and lifestyle adopted by increasing numbers of Gaelic lords.[66]

As a related point, the increased power of New Englishmen in the towns added to what O'Dowd sees as the "uneasy relationship" that existed between rural Gaelic Ireland and the urban centres.[67] Gillespie submits, furthermore, that due to the "overriding concern of the central government throughout the early seventeenth century" of governing the localities, the towns came to play a "vital role" in the New English monopolisation of power, particularly via the "careful control" of Protestant representation in the ruling administration.[68] The focus of the subsequent outbreak of rebellion in Tipperary, and throughout the island in 1641, became the capture of the prominent neighbouring municipality, owing evidently to the clear strategic reasons but due also to towns such as Cashel being seen by the Gaelic-Irish as a bulwark of New English authority and domination, as evidenced by the contemporary writings of the Ormond biographer, Thomas Carte, and the 1641 depositions.[69]

For various reasons, then, County Tipperary experienced a marked outbreak of robberies and pillaging, particularly in the 1620s and 1630s.[70] In 1629, Lord Deputy Falkland, reported to the English Privy Council of the "dangerous state" of Tipperary and enclosed an important letter from a member of the *Gaelic-Irish* community divulging the seriousness of the situation on the ground.[71] Crucially, the correspondence exposes the prevalence of robberies and looting in the county, and the lack of lawful administrative procedure in local government. Most significantly, however, the letter suggests that the most critical constituent in the breakdown of control was the failure of those Gaelic-Irish participating in the new legal and political order to construct a concerted and unified perspective within the new arrangement. The extent of division and uncertainty inherent in Gaelic society at this juncture, for example, is indicated by the manner in which one individual's attempts to administrate lawful procedures were impeded by another from his own community that "did not carry them out".[72]

Respecting the notion of fracture in Gaelic society, Ellis observes that

> [b]y the time of the 1641 rising, political discourse in Ireland was conducted predominantly within the framework of an English-style kingdom of Ireland with little support for the restoration of a traditional Gaelic high kingship.[73]

He points out, furthermore, that the anglicisation of Irish Gaeldom was "devastatingly successful" in relation to "the land settlements, systems of law and administration, language and culture".[74] It was this fracture in society that resurfaced in the early 1640s, prior to outright rebellion, when the members of the O'Dwyers with a stake in the new arrangement and in a position of authority were unsuccessful in their attempts to control their subordinates.[75] In essence, their efforts to engage and accommodate the new order ultimately failed to incorporate Gaelic-Irish society at large.

The disruption of traditional Gaelic society was, in effect, a principal cause of unrest and eventual rebellion in west Tipperary and throughout the country. Many Gaelic-Irish lords, by reaching an accommodation with the New English administration in an effort to survive, simultaneously created a confused and contradictory polity within their respective lordships, which resulted in them being discredited in the eyes of their traditional followers. O'Dowd outlines, for example, how the chief of the O'Haras in County Sligo in the early seventeenth century, having recognised and utilised "the advantages of contact with the Dublin government ... was also anxious to receive traditional Gaelic recognition of his position".[76] Furthermore, as Bottigheimer stresses, the surrender and regrant agreements "attributed to Gaelic lords rights over their lands which, in Irish custom, they did not have".[77] He goes on to highlight that subsequent to the lessening of respect from their subordinates, their "followers and clansmen, instead of supporting their lords' allegiance to the English king, turned against them as betrayers of traditional and tribal responsibilities".[78] In this respect, there is, of course, a distinct irony in the manner in which by conforming, in an attempt to survive, the Gaelic-Irish ensured paradoxically their own demise.

The failure of the landholding class in west County Tipperary to assert its traditional governing role over its subordinates in the immediate pre-1641 period is evident from a number of contemporary correspondences and writings. Carte, for example, records a significant degree of dissension and hostility emanating from the lower orders of society as the outbreak of rebellion approached.[79] The escalating unrest was seen to manifest itself in the shape of physical disturbances such as pillaging and robberies directed primarily at New English tenants.[80] In November of 1641, for example, Carte refers to "some petty robberies committed by loose fellows in some Irish parishes" throughout Munster.[81] Later, in mid-December, he catalogues

> some robberies committed in the County of Tipperary by a rabble of
> the common sort and a parcel of young fellows of the baronies of
> Eliogurty, Killemanna, Clanwilliam and Middlethyrde".[82]

The *Egmont Manuscripts* also record a general collapse in social and economic order in Tipperary in late 1641, which was intensified by the outbreak of rebellion in Ulster in late October.[83] A complete breakdown in the economy was seen with the outbreak of robberies, spoiling of crops and stock and the retention of rents throughout west and mid-Tipperary.[84]

The deteriorating conditions in Munster through the course of November and December 1641 are outlined in a series of contemporary correspondences between Sir William St. Leger, president of Munster, and Sir Philip Percivall.[85] Carte documents further difficulties encountered by the leading landowners of the county to secure the control of their subordinates in late 1641:

> the gentry of Tipperary, [given the] aptness of the vulgar sort (under
> colour thereof) to plunder their English neighbours, laboured all
> they could within their respective districts and neighbourhoods for
> a while to correct their insolence... several gentlemen of quality in
> the county ... by fair words and sermons, diverted them from ...
> offering violence to any body.[86]

As quoted at the beginning of this chapter, Philip O'Dwyer, the last chief of Kilnamanagh, also attempted to maintain control by defending the properties of Sir Philip Percivall but was ultimately thwarted in his efforts by other members of the O'Dwyers, who continued to plunder and spoil; thus reflecting the absence of either a unified or stable Gaelic-Irish polity in the pre-1641 period.[87]

In 1641, the leading O'Dwyers and others were attempting to stabilise a society that had, in actuality, been insidiously fragmented from the early seventeenth century. For example, whilst some of the principal O'Dwyers had forged close relations with Sir Philip Percivall, others had, on occasions, actively opposed his presence in the barony; as highlighted by the manner in which numerous O'Dwyers levied rents from his lands in the wardship of Ballagh in the late 1630s.[88] Ellis argues that Gaelic-Irish society's make-up had always been characterised by substantial rifts, and that "[o]nly a tiny minority of Irish people had enjoyed any kind of rights under it".[89] Canny points out, too, that the peasants' position in society was often an uncertain and precarious one.[90] With the lessening of the traditional subjugation of the lower orders of society – which must have occurred with the reform of the lordships – there subsequently emerged a new impediment to both the New English and Gaelic-Irish control of the localities.[91] This notion was confirmed in relation to Kilnamanagh and elsewhere when the outbreak of revolt was initially seen to be dominated by the lower orders of society.[92] The O'Dwyer landholding classes, however, continued to attempt to maintain control in late 1641 despite the fact that, as St. Leger commented, there came "such bloody news out of [those] parts that it [would be] enough to fright away all timorous men, and to stir up and encourage all ill-affected persons to rebellion".[93]

Exclusion and Rebellion: Delimiting Irish Society

What, then, were the circumstances that brought about the insurrection of the landholding classes?[94] To begin with, by examining briefly the geographies of fear in contemporary west Tipperary, one quickly gets the sense of overwhelming anxiety permeating both Catholic and Protestant communities. The Catholic gentry increasingly imagined that New English "distrusting of their loyalty, and destroying of their reputations, was the preface to a design of taking away their lives".[95] To this end, evidence emerges that suggests that such beliefs equated to the most readily discernible by the Catholic community at large, given the New English administration's severe and exclusive actions in government. As Carte observes, the governors in Ireland such as St. Leger were "the likeliest persons in it to get by the troubles of the Kingdom, and to raise their own fortunes by the ruin of those of private Gentlemen".[96] He submits, furthermore, that the Catholics had "much reason" to think that

> the Lords Justices really wished the Rebellion to spread, and more Gentlemen of estates be involved in it, [so] that the forfeitures might be greater, and a general plantation be carried on by a new set of English Protestants all over the Kingdom, to the ruin and expulsion of all the old English and natives that were Roman Catholicks.[97]

Due to a lack of further evidence, it is difficult to assess the extent to which such fearful beliefs reflected a design of the New English administration in Munster to instigate rebellion or general discontent. In any case, there were, as argued, clearly a range of other factors involved. The important consideration, however, is that such fears actually existed in the Catholic community.

There were, of course, similar fears in the Protestant community. Evident from correspondences contained in the *Egmont Manuscripts*, for example, is a sense that the New English community in Munster perceived themselves to be in a perpetual state of siege.[98] Such a cycle of fear was not new to Irish society. In 1629, for example, Lord Deputy Falkland received a report from a New English settler in Tipperary outlining how "the Justices do more harm than good" as none "dare challenge the people whom [they] suspect [of misdemeanours]".[99] The unrest was subsequently accentuated by calls for the authority of an external Provost Marshal,[100] whose presence in the county the lord deputy later commented constituted the "greatest terror" and brought about the repression of disorders by the execution of "far more people than ever".[101] The confiscation of estates, too, had been a prominent fear of the landed classes throughout the 1630s when, as outlined above, intended government plantation plans engendered a substantial level of social unrest.[102] In essence, as Canny submits, the interaction of "indigenous and planter communities" created a "type of hybrid culture" which fostered a sense of restlessness whereby "in moments of crisis the fears and prejudices of one religious community tended to feed off those of the other".[103]

Such 'fears and prejudices' were seen to be profoundly influential in Munster in late 1641 in precipitating racialist rhetoric and conduct of senior government officials such as St. Leger.[104] In Kilnamanagh, this served inevitably to fuel the severe actions of English troops in response to the outbreak of physical disturbances perpetrated by the lower levels of society in December 1641.[105] Carte records how St. Leger and the troops under his command responded to social disorder by pursuing a reign of terror across the province of Munster and executing numerous individuals, many of which were claimed to be innocent, particularly in Kilnamanagh.[106] Carte's account of developments are corroborated by the president's own reports to Sir Philip Percivall outlining the justification for his actions and the number of killings.[107] He believed, for example, that

> if the traitors had been but roughly handled (if but as I have dealt with them with what poor force I had) surely they could never have attained this superiority over us.[108]

As Carte observes, St. Leger was "a brave, gallant, and honest man, but somewhat too rough and fiery in his temper".[109] His actions served, ultimately, to alienate the land-owning classes of Munster – many of which had "shewn themselves zealous to oppose [the rebellion] and had tendered their service for that end" – by his subsequent "hasty and rough manner of treating them".[110]

In the immediate aftermath of the extreme actions of St. Leger's troops in west and mid-Tipperary in December 1641, the leading Gaelic-Irish and Old English gentry of the region (including Philip O'Dwyer, the last chief of Kilnamanagh) presented their concerns to St. Leger:

> [t]hey observed to the President how generally the people were exasperated by those inconsiderate cruelties, running distractedly from house to house; and that they were on the point of gathering together in great numbers, not knowing what they had to trust to, and what was likely to be their fate.[111]

Their presentation of concerns was marked especially by their determined efforts to present themselves as loyal subjects:

they told him that they waited upon his Lordship to be informed how affairs stood, and that they coveted nothing more than to serve his Majesty, and preserve the peace; and desired that he would be pleased to qualify them for it with authority and arms, in which case they would not fail to suppress the rabble, and secure the peace of the County.[112]

The response of St. Leger, however, appeared to reflect the evident exclusiveness of contemporary New English government in Ireland:

[t]he president did not receive their representation and offer, in the manner they expected; but in a hasty furious manner answered them, that they were all Rebels and he would not trust one soul of them, but thought it more prudent to hang the best of them.[113]

This hugely consequential outburst marked firmly the full extent of the 'Othering' of the Catholic Irish by the New English administration in Munster and inevitably guaranteed the outbreak of the 1641 rebellion in the province.

Subsequent to St. Leger's failure to incorporate the elite members of Gaelic-Irish and Old English society of west and mid Tipperary as loyal subjects of King Charles I, Carte records how the 1641 rebellion "like a torrent, overspread at once all Munster".[114] In west Tipperary, Gaelic-Irish and Old English alike "were still in great ferment" and "could not sleep safely in their own houses, whilst Cashel was a receptacle for the President's troops to come thither, and from thence to rush in amongst them and destroy them".[115] The rising broke out in the county on 31 December when a number of Gaelic-Irish and Old English gentry, spearheaded by Philip O'Dwyer, the last chief of Kilnamanagh, led an attack on Cashel and seized it.[116]

O'Dwyer and the other leaders, even in the midst of rebellion, attempted to construct a position from which they could assert their loyalty to the crown. It was the New English *administration* they had lost faith in, and they were anxious to present themselves as defenders of King Charles I, as evidenced by a number of testimonies recorded in the 1641 depositions.[117] The 1641 offensive in Tipperary, however, disguised a substantial degree of division within Gaelic society. The extent to which, for example, the leading O'Dwyers and others were required to curb the plundering and killing of Protestant settlers in the town by a "rabble" of the lower orders reveals the degree to which they had lost effective control over their subordinates.[118] Comparable difficulties were encountered by members of the Butler gentry in restraining the rampaging of their followers in the taking of key towns in neighbouring County Kilkenny.[119] Similar frictions in Gaelic society were evident in the progress of the rebellion in County Kerry.[120] In the broader context, as O'Dowd argues, the "massacres of 1641 provided the first substantial evidence of the loosening of the lords' control over the localities".[121] The landholding classes had been reluctant to join the insurrection and, in an effort to maintain legitimacy to their actions, endeavoured to disassociate themselves from the outrages of the lower orders when they did;[122] that they had to do so at all, however, reflected the clear divisions inherent in Gaelic-Irish society by the mid-seventeenth century.

Conclusion

> [I]mpolitick acts of cruelty, exercised without a just distinction between the innocent and the guilty; a practice attended with very unhappy consequences in the course of the troubles of Ireland.[123]

Carte conveys above a foreboding sense of the profound effect the rebellion in Tipperary would come to have on the interaction of native and newcomer or (more pertinently, at this juncture) 'Irish Papist' and 'English Protestant' in the future. There were a number of important factors precipitating the outbreak of disturbances in the localities including particularly the earlier fragmentation and disruption of the Gaelic-Irish polity and the subsequent failure of the elite members of society in re-imagining and re-configuring vertical alignments of social order. The outbreak of rebellion in Ulster inevitably affected developments in Tipperary, too, but as Yeoh points out, the "contingent nature of resistance should also be noted, its emergence and dissolution inextricably linked to the specific context".[124] The leading O'Dwyers continued to attempt to reconcile both their position and those of their patrons to the crown administration in Munster as late as mid-December 1641. Ultimately, however, they faced the culmination of the fundamental exclusiveness of New English rule: the complete breakdown of any integration earlier achieved.

In bringing this chapter to a close, it is important to emphasise the significance of the process of Gaelic-Irish accommodation to English social and economic order in the pre-1641 period, despite the subsequent outbreak of rebellion. I have argued above that the breakdown in social order mirrored partly, paradoxically, how successful the transformation of the upper levels of Gaelic-Irish society had earlier been. The O'Dwyers of Kilnamanagh, however, in their efforts to survive faced negotiation with an exclusivist New English administration in Munster which neither considered them loyal nor part of its vision of the future. A citizen of Cashel later testified in the 1641 depositions that, in capturing the town, Philip O'Dwyer, the chief, declared to the English Protestants that they "might thank the Lord President of Munster for the case they were in, regarding his lordship killed so many honest men in the country for nothing".[125] St. Leger had clearly not taken the advice earlier tendered to him regarding the maintenance of peace in the province:

> to use those Lords and gentlemen very courteously, extolling the merits of that province ... and the great confidence his majesty hath of their loyalty, whereof in the last wars they gave good testimony.[126]

He had, on the contrary, demonstrated the limited extent to which integration could ever take place in the context of exclusivist government rhetoric and activities. The rebellion had not yet begun, for example, when Sir Philip Percivall – who, at one point, had negotiated a significant level of shared economic and social links with the Gaelic-Irish of west Tipperary – left for England and abandoned a society in transition of which he was once a prominent figure.[127] Ultimately, the shared space engendered between Percivall and the O'Dwyers was bounded by a fundamental notion of difference.

Notes

[1] *Egmont MSS*, vol. 1, pt. 1, p. 149

[2] *Ibid.*, p. 156

[3] M. MacCarthy-Morrogh, 1986, *The Munster Plantation: English Migration to Southern Ireland 1583-1641*, Clarendon Press, Oxford, p. 282

[4] On this point, see A.J. Sheehan, 1984, 'Attitudes to Religious and Temporal Authority in Cork in 1600: A Document from Laud MS 612', *Analecta Hibernica*, 31, p. 63

[5] N. Canny, 1988, *Kingdom and Colony: Ireland in the Atlantic World 1560-1800*, John Hopkins University Press, Baltimore, p. 31

[6] D. Cairns and S. Richards, 1988, *Writing Ireland: Colonialism, Nationalism and Culture*, Manchester University Press, Manchester, p. 7

[7] G. Kew, 1998, 'The Irish Sections of Fynes Moryson's Unpublished Itinerary', *Anelecta Hibernica*, 37, p. 8

[8] Cairns and Richards, *Writing Ireland*, p. 7

[9] *Cal. S.P. Ire., 1600-1601*, p. 5

[10] B. O'Buachalla, 1996, *Aisling Ghéar: Na Stíobhartaigh agus an tAos Léinn, 1603-1788*, An Clochomhar, Baile Átha Cliath, caibidil 1

[11] *Cal. S.P. Ire., 1603-1606*, p. 162

[12] *Cal. S.P. Ire., 1600-1601*, p. 425

[13] See, for example: *Cal. S.P. Ire., 1603-1606*, p. 442; *Cal. S.P. Ire., 1606-1608*, pp. 309-310; *Cal. S.P. Ire., 1611-1614*, pp. 429-430; and *Cal. S.P. Ire., 1615-1625*, p. 22

[14] H. O'Sullivan, 1992, 'Thesis Abstract. Landownership Changes in the County of Louth in the Seventeenth Century (Ph.D. Thesis, University of Dublin, 1992)', *Irish Economic and Social History*, XIX, p. 81

[15] 'The Supplication of the Blood of the English Most Lamentably Murdered in Ireland, Cryeng Out of the Yearth for Revenge (1598)', intro. W. Maley, 1995, *Analecta Hibernica*, 36, p. 5

[16] *Ibid.*, p. 4

[17] N. Canny, 1986, 'Protestants, Planters and Apartheid in Early Modern Ireland', *Irish Historical Studies*, vol. 25, no 98, p. 114

[18] A.F. Marotti, 1997, 'Southwell's Remains: Catholicism and Anti-Catholicism in Early Modern England', in: C.C. Brown and A.F. Marotti (eds.), *Texts and Cultural Change in Early Modern England*, MacMillan Press Ltd., Houndmills, Basingstoke, p. 37

[19] *Civil Survey, County Tipperary*, vol. 2

[20] MacCarthy-Morrogh, *The Munster Plantation*, p. 283

[21] K.S. Bottigheimer, 1978, 'Kingdom and Colony: Ireland in the Westward Enterprise 1536-1660', in: K.R. Andrews, N.P. Canny and P.E.H. Hair (eds.), *The Westward Enterprise: English Activities in Ireland, The Atlantic and America, 1480-1650*, Liverpool University Press, Liverpool, p. 54

[22] B. Cunningham and R. Gillespie, 1990, 'Englishmen in Sixteenth-Century Irish Annals', *Irish Economic and Social History*, XVII, p. 21

[23] Bottigheimer, 'Kingdom and Colony: Ireland in the Westward Enterprise', pp. 54-55

[24] Cairns and Richards, *Writing Ireland*, p. 7

[25] C. Kenny, 1987, 'The Exclusion of Catholics from the Legal Profession in Ireland, 1537-

1829', *Irish Historical Studies*, vol. 25, no. 100, pp. 337-357; see esp. pp. 342-347

[26] MacCarthy-Morrogh, *The Munster Plantation*, p. 273

[27] For contemporary developments in Munster, see *ibid.*, pp. 273-274, 281-284. For Ulster, cf. R. Gillespie, 1983, 'Thesis Abstract. East Ulster in the Early Seventeenth Century: A Colonial Economy and Society (Ph.D. Thesis, University of Dublin, 1982)', *Irish Economic and Social History*, X, pp. 92-94

[28] *Egmont MSS*, vol. 1, pt. 1, p. 47

[29] MacCarthy-Morrogh, *The Munster Plantation*, p. 273

[30] *Idem.*, 1986, 'The English Presence in Early Seventeenth Century Munster', in: C. Brady and R. Gillespie (eds.), *Natives and Newcomers: Essays on the Making of Irish Colonial Society, 1534-1641*, Irish Academic Press, Dublin, p. 190

[31] P. Clark, 1987, 'Review Article. Planters and Plantations', *Irish Economic and Social History*, XIV, p. 65

[32] *Ibid.*

[33] See *Egmont MSS*, vol. 1, pt. 1, pp. 143-144, 147-154, Carte, *Ormond*, vol. 2, pp. 265-266, and T.C.D., MS 821, fo. 7

[34] Ellis' suggestion that all Irishmen "enjoyed with Englishmen the same free status as the king's subjects" since the formation of the "new English Kingdom of Ireland in 1541" does not account for this underlying sense of superiority and difference; see S.G. Ellis, 1999, 'The Collapse of the Gaelic World', *Irish Historical Studies*, vol. 31, no. 124, p. 469

[35] *Egmont MSS*, vol. 1, pt. 1, p. 148

[36] *Ibid.*, p. 150 (my emphases)

[37] MacCarthy-Morrogh, *The Munster Plantation*, p. 283

[38] Quoted in: *ibid.*

[39] M. Caball, 1998, 'Faith, Culture and Sovereignty: Irish Nationality and its Development, 1558-1625', in: B. Bradshaw and P. Roberts (eds.), *British Consciousness and Identity: The Making of Britain 1533-1707*, Cambridge University Press, Cambridge, p. 112

[40] *Ibid.*, p. 138

[41] B. Bradshaw, 1979, *The Irish Constitutional Revolution of the Sixteenth Century*, Cambridge University Press, Cambridge, p. 287

[42] *Ibid.*, p. 288

[43] V. Treadwell, 1997, 'New Light on Richard Hadsor, I: Richard Hadsor and the Authorship of 'Advertisements for Ireland', 1622/3', *Irish Historical Studies*, vol. 30, no. 119, p. 311

[44] F. Fanon, 1967, *The Wretched of the Earth*, trans. C. Farrington, Penguin, Harmondsworth, p. 42

[45] T.C. Barnard, 1975, *Cromwellian Ireland: English Government and Reform in Ireland, 1649-1660*, Oxford University Press, London, p. 3

[46] R. Gillespie, 1986, 'The End of an Era: Ulster and the Outbreak of the 1641 Rising', in: Brady and Gillespie (eds.), *Natives and Newcomers*, p. 213. Some of the reasons for this were the Gaelic-Irish viewing the Old English world as somehow still foreign and in collusion with the New English regime.

[47] C. Lennon, 1986, 'The Counter-Reformation in Ireland, 1542-1641', in: Brady and Gillespie (eds.), *Natives and Newcomers*, p. 91

[48] Barnard, *Cromwellian Ireland*, p. 3

[49] P.J. Corish, 1976, 'The Rising of 1641 and the Catholic Confederacy, 1641-5' in: T.W. Moody,

THE 1641 REBELLION

F.X. Martin and F.J. Byrne (eds.), *A New History of Ireland III: Early Modern Ireland 1534-1691*, Clarendon Press, Oxford, p. 289. See also the contemporary accounts of government discrimination against Catholics recorded in Carte, *Ormond*, vol. 2, p. 263

[50] *Cal. S.P. Ire., 1625-1632*, p. 458

[51] *Ibid.* (my emphases)

[52] K.S. Bottigheimer, 1971, *English Money and Irish Land: The 'Adventurers' in the Cromwellian Settlement of Ireland*, Clarendon Press, Oxford, p. 26

[53] *Ibid.*

[54] H.F. Kearney, 1959, *Strafford in Ireland, 1633-1641: A Study in Absolutism*, Manchester University Press, Manchester, p. 102

[55] *Ibid.*. For further commentary on the effects of seventeenth-century government plantation policies, see A. Clarke with R. Dudley Edwards, 1976, 'Pacification, Plantation, and the Catholic Question, 1603-23', in: Moody *et al* (eds.), *A New History of Ireland III*, pp. 187-232

[56] Cf. Gillespie, 'The End of an Era', pp. 194-196 and A. Clarke, 1976, 'Selling Royal Favours, 1624-32', in: Moody *et al* (eds.), *A New History of Ireland III*, pp. 233-242, esp. pp. 240-242

[57] Lord Esmonde to Lord Dorchester, 1630: *Cal. S.P. Ire., 1625-1632*, p. 536

[58] *Cal. S.P. Ire., 1647-1660, Addenda*, p. 160

[59] As outlined in chapter three, direct pressures were exerted upon numerous O'Dwyer landholders to secure their respective properties through a series of inquisitions into rights of title to specific lands throughout Kilnamanagh from 1617 to 1637; see N.A.I., Record Commission, 4/10

[60] See *Egmont MSS*, vol. 1, pt. 1, pp. 85, 93, 95, 97, 115

[61] Lord Esmonde to Lord Dorchester, 1630: *Cal. S.P. Ire., 1625-1632*, p. 577

[62] D.B. Quinn, 1966, 'The Munster Plantation: Problems and Opportunities', *Cork Historical Society Journal*, LXXI, p. 33

[63] *Cal. S.P. Ire., 1615-1625*, pp. 262-263

[64] See the comments of R. Gillespie and B. Cunningham, 1991, 'Holy Cross Abbey and the Counter Reformation in Tipperary', *Tipperary Historical Journal*, 4, pp. 170-180

[65] *Cal. S.P. Ire., 1647-1660, Addenda*, p. 160

[66] M. O'Dowd, 1986, 'Gaelic Economy and Society', in: Brady and Gillespie (eds.), *Natives and Newcomers*, p. 143

[67] *Ibid.*, p. 131

[68] R. Gillespie, 1984, 'The Origins and Development of an Ulster Urban Network, 1600-41', *Irish Historical Studies*, vol. 24, no. 93, p. 17. See also the comments of A.J. Sheehan, 1986, 'Irish Towns in a Period of Change, 1558-1625', in: Brady and Gillespie (eds.), *Natives and Newcomers*, pp. 93-119, esp. pp. 103-105 and R.H. Buchanan, 1986, 'Towns and Plantations, 1500-1700', in: W. Nolan (ed.), *The Shaping of Ireland: The Geographical Perspective*, The Mercier Press, Cork, pp. 84-98, esp. pp. 93-95

[69] Carte, *Ormond*, vol. 2, pp. 262, 266; T.C.D., MS 821, fos. 7, 234, 255. See also N.A.I., Co 2450-2451, pp. 2-50 for a charter of Cashel dating to 1637, wherein the extension of New English government jurisdiction and authority in the city and environs is indicated.

[70] See *Cal. S.P. Ire., 1615-1625*, p. 217 and *Cal. S.P. Ire., 1625-1632*, p. 433

[71] *Cal. S.P. Ire., 1625-1632*, pp. 435-436

[72] *Ibid.*, p. 436

[73] Ellis, 'The Collapse of the Gaelic World', p. 467

[74] *Ibid.*, p. 469
[75] Cf., for example, *Egmont MSS*, vol. 1, pt. 1, p. 149 and p. 156
[76] O'Dowd, 'Gaelic Economy and Society', p. 138
[77] Bottigheimer, *English Money and Irish Land*, p. 6
[78] *Ibid.*. In Kilnamanagh, in 1631, some members of the O'Dwyers refused to pay their rents and services to the earl of Ormond; see N.L.I., D. 3791
[79] Carte, *Ormond*, vol. 2, pp. 263-266
[80] *Ibid.*. See also T.C.D., MS 821, fo. 221
[81] Carte, *Ormond*, vol. 2, p. 264
[82] *Ibid.*, p. 265
[83] *Egmont MSS*, vol. 1, pt. 1, pp. 143, 152-153. MacCarthy-Morrogh places great emphasis on the effect of the Ulster rising on events unfolding in Munster, and goes so far as to suggest that a "new amalgamation" of society therein "might have evolved had not the province been sucked into the wider struggle after 1641"; see MacCarthy-Morrogh, *The Munster Plantation*, p. 286. Insurrection in Ulster was certainly a substantial contributing factor to the precipitation of rebellion throughout the country, but the uprising elsewhere, such as in Munster – whose Gaelic-Irish and Old English communities did not rise in arms until late December of 1641 – had also specific localised origins which, in the extant literature, have received scant attention; see the comments of O'Dowd, 'Gaelic Economy and Society', pp. 139-140. Cf. N. Canny, 1995, 'What Really Happened in Ireland in 1641?', in: J.H. Ohlmeyer (ed.), *Ireland from Independence to Occupation 1641-1660*, Cambridge University Press, Cambridge, pp. 24-42
[84] *Egmont MSS*, vol. 1, pt. 1, pp. 152-157
[85] *Ibid.*, pp. 143, 153-154
[86] Carte, *Ormond*, vol. 2, p. 266
[87] *Egmont MSS*, vol. 1, pt. 1, pp. 149, 156
[88] *Ibid.*, p. 92
[89] Ellis, 'The Collapse of the Gaelic World', p. 467
[90] N. Canny, 1976, *The Elizabethan Conquest of Ireland: A Pattern Established*, Harvester Press, Hassocks, Sussex, pp. 17-18
[91] O'Dowd draws attention to evidence supporting this notion in the contemporary satire *Pairlement Chloinne Tomáis*; see O'Dowd, 'Gaelic Economy and Society', pp. 144-145 and *Pairlement Chloinne Tomáis*, ed. N.J.A. Williams, Dublin Institute for Advanced Studies, Dublin, 1981, PCT I, pp. 1-98
[92] T.C.D., MS 821, fos. 7, 12 , 234, 255; Carte, *Ormond*, vol. 2, p. 266
[93] *Egmont MSS*, vol. 1, pt. 1, p. 143
[94] Canny stresses that in attempting to elucidate the "true character of the revolt" the question of how the property-owning elites experienced a "change of heart" in late 1641 "requires special attention"; see N. Canny, 1993, 'The 1641 Depositions as a Source for the Writing of Social History: County Cork as a Case Study', in: P. O'Flanagan and C.G. Buttimer (eds.), *Cork: History and Society*, Geography Publications, Dublin, pp. 274, 277
[95] *Ibid.*, p. 266. A similar picture emerges throughout Munster at this time; see J.C. Beckett, 1981, *The Making of Modern Ireland 1603-1923*, Faber and Faber, London (first pub. 1966), p. 87
[96] Carte, *Ormond*, vol. 2, pp. 262-263
[97] *Ibid.*, p. 263
[98] *Egmont MSS*, vol. 1, pt. 1, pp. 142-157

[99] *Cal. S.P. Ire., 1625-1632*, p. 433

[100] *Ibid.*, p. 436

[101] *Ibid.*, p. 450

[102] In 1637, for example, a number of O'Dwyer landowners had taken control of the lands of Connor O'Dwyer of Ballagh, whose wardship had earlier been granted to Sir Philip Percivall – see *Egmont MSS*, vol. 1, pt. 1, p. 92

[103] N. Canny, 1987, 'The Formation of the Irish Mind: Religion, Politics and Gaelic Irish Literature, 1580-1750', in: C.H.E. Philpin (ed.), *Nationalism and Popular Protest in Ireland*, Past and Present Publications, Cambridge University Press, Cambridge, p. 77

[104] *Egmont MSS*, vol. 1, pt. 1, pp. 142-143, 148-157

[105] Withers observes a similar pattern in the contemporary Scottish Highlands, the process mirroring a "renewed assertion of authority in the form of military force, by 'rule' not hegemony"; see C.W.J. Withers, 1988, *Gaelic Scotland: The Transformation of a Culture Region*, Routledge, London, p. 328

[106] Carte, *Ormond*, vol. 2, pp. 264-266

[107] *Egmont MSS*, vol. 1, pt. 1, pp. 143, 153-154; see also pp. 149-152

[108] *Ibid.*, p. 154

[109] Carte, *Ormond*, vol. 2, p. 264

[110] *Ibid.*

[111] *Ibid.*, p. 265

[112] *Ibid.*, pp. 265-266

[113] *Ibid.*, p. 266

[114] *Ibid.*, pp. 263-264

[115] *Ibid.,,* p. 266

[116] *Ibid.*; T.C.D., MS 821, fos. 7, 12, 221, 255, 234

[117] One Archibald Campbell of Cashel, for example, testified that he heard "divers of the gentry say that they had a good warrant under the Great Seal for what they did … and that it was the Queen's Commission and the King's toleration [they were acting upon], and that the Parliament in England was the only cause of it"; see T.C.D., MS 821, fo. 12. See also *ibid.*, fo. 7, wherein again the determined agenda of the landholding gentry to present themselves as loyal subjects, in an effort to maintain their respective positions in society, is evident.

[118] Carte, *Ormond*, vol. 2, pp. 266-267; T.C.D., MS 821, fos. 234, 255

[119] Carte, *Ormond*, vol. 2, pp. 267-268

[120] Canny, 'The Formation of the Irish Mind', pp. 76-77

[121] O'Dowd, 'Gaelic Economy and Society', p. 147

[122] A strong sense of the eagerness of the landholding classes to distance themselves from the plundering of their subordinates emerges from the depositions. One English witness at Cashel, for example, testified that the leader of the rebellion, Philip O'Dwyer, had one of his following hanged subsequent to the murder of citizens in the town; see T.C.D., MS 821, fo. 255

[123] Carte, *Ormond*, vol. 2, p. 267

[124] B.S.A. Yeoh, 2000, 'Historical Geographies of the Colonised World', in: B. Graham and C. Nash (eds.), *Modern Historical Geographies*, Prentice Hall, Harlow, p. 164

[125] T.C.D., MS 821, fo. 7

[126] Sir John Bath to the president of Munster, *c*.1633: *Cal. S.P. Ire., 1647-1660, Addenda*, p. 308

[127] *Egmont MSS*, vol. 1, pt. 1, p. 156

Chapter 6

Conclusion:
Locating Early Modern Irish Society

This work has explored the intrinsic ambiguities of the resistance of a little-known but not untypical Gaelic-Irish family to New English colonialism in early modern Ireland. It has sought to sift out the diverse, interlocking and conflicting practices of accommodation and resistance which transcended society in a multiplicity of ways. In interrogating the various sites of cultural interaction at the political, economic and social levels, the hybrid and heterogeneous nature of early modern Irish society has distinctly emerged. This has been recognised as a prerequisite to further elucidating the complex and contradictory reasons for the breakdown of social order in the late 1630s and subsequent outbreak of the 1641 rebellion.

The O'Dwyers of Kilnamanagh in west Tipperary encountered aspects of New English colonialism in a variety of conflicting ways. Their actions were characterised by fundamental contradictions, reflective of a fragmented Gaelic polity and ideology, as they endeavoured to resist, come to terms with, and eventually situate themselves in the new legal, political and socio-economic order of successive New English administrations. By underlining the ambiguous nature of the contact zone in early modern Irish society, the overarching imperative of a 'quest for survival' clearly emerges. This has referred specifically to the manner in which the leading O'Dwyers and a number of their subordinates redefined their landholdings and related societal positions in the context of the common law and English social norms. By revealing the Gaelic-Irish knowledge and appreciation of contemporary political and economic currents in society, and demonstrating the progressiveness of their contact with prominent English figures and government officials, the inadequacies of a conventional colonial reading of developments have been underlined. The interaction of the O'Dwyers with the prominent New Englishman, Sir Philip Percivall, furthermore, has been cited as particularly indicative of the shared space negotiated and constructed between native and newcomer in early modern Irish society.

The piecemeal nature of contemporary English government in Ireland ensured a significant level of integration with the existing population, which was negotiated principally by the upper levels of society sharing economic and social terms of reference. These spaces of betweenness, however, are shown to have not reflected a broader, pluralistic design of early modern English colonial thought but, rather, the extent to which the Gaelic-Irish had recognised, and acted on, the necessity of re-defining their legal, social and economic order. This process of accommodation, moreover, is argued to have been ultimately limited by a constructed sense of difference in the visioning and practice of English colonialism in Ireland. It is important to reiterate that the various practices of New English colonialism that the Gaelic-Irish of west Tipperary were responding to were themselves not bereft of contradiction. Although not the central focus of this work, the Self in colonial and post-colonial discourse also needs to be destabilised to account for the fluidity and ambiguities of practices of colonialism. As Young notes,

> [a]lthough much emphasis is placed on the specific particularity of different colonized cultures, this tends to be accompanied by comparatively little historical work on the diversity of colonialism and imperialism, which were nothing if not heterogeneous, often contradictory, practices.[1]

In early modern Ireland, the responses of the Gaelic-Irish cut across and transmuted the practices of New English colonialism emerging in a variety of ways. As Lester argues, "indigenous responses, which were themselves multifaceted," were also "constitutive of the manifest power relations" which informed the discourse and practices of colonialism.[2] Recognising the interconnections (in addition to the conflicts) between the worlds of the coloniser and the colonised allows the construction of a multiplicity of historico-geographical accounts of the spaces and practices of colonialism.[3]

The responses of the O'Dwyers to the activities of the New English were wholly more complex and dynamic than that allowed by any simplified reading of colonial subjugation and resistance. It is important, however, to not lose sight of the practices of colonialism (religious and cultural differentiation and the threat of plantation, for example), however nascent and often contradictory, which inevitably served to induce elements of Gaelic-Irish accommodation. The attempted construction of an alternative Gaelic polity and identity comprised part of the evolving, contradictory forms of resistance to New English hegemony emerging in early modern Ireland.[4]

What, then, were the key themes in the fracture of pre-1641 society and subsequent deterioration of social order? Two factors are submitted to have been pivotal to the breakdown of order. Firstly, it is suggested that a critical degree of incorporation of the elite members of Gaelic-Irish society into the English political, social and economic system engendered an insidious disintegration of Gaelic ideology and social order. Fragmented and ambiguous, the Gaelic polity is shown to have been increasingly inflected by individualistic agendas of the Gaelic-Irish themselves, which were concomitant with the consolidation of an English legal and economic structure, and subsequent opening of a market in land. The second central element in the breakdown of society is argued to have been the emergence of exclusivist religious and intellectual currents, increasingly underpinning practices of New English colonialism in early modern Ireland. In the Gaelic-Irish quest for survival and accommodation, the negotiation of shared spaces between native and newcomer is demonstrated to have been bounded by an underlying sense of difference. This manifested itself in west Tipperary in the manner in which the entrepreneurial enterprise of Sir Philip Percivall, in facilitating a level of social and economic interaction with the landholding classes, was ultimately superseded by the more radical and racialist rhetoric and actions of Sir William St. Leger, in prompting eventual insurrection.

> In terms of Irish historiography, what is most remarkable about the collapse of the Gaelic world in the [early modern period] is that its passing has hardly been noticed as such, let alone properly analysed.[5]

Ellis alludes above to the dearth of studies respecting the fragmentation of Gaelic-Irish society in the early modern period. Due largely to the unpromising nature of the sources and prevalence of powerful and exclusive metanarratives (as outlined in chapter one), there is a marked lack of understanding of the intricate and contradictory emergence of the conflicting ideologies and identities of early modern Irish society. This has a particular resonance today in the imagined homogeneity of the Republic of Ireland and confusion of identity in Northern Ireland.[6] This work has, in part, been inspired by a determination to understand and conceptualise the conflicting meanings of early modern Irish society as a means to recognise and underline the legitimacy of myriad representations of the past. As outlined in chapter one, it advocates the premise that a variety of versions of Ireland's histories can be situated in a broader historical discourse which explicitly celebrates notions of particularity, heterogeneity and contradiction.

In drawing together the disparate themes of this work, it is important to stress the ambiguous nature of early modern Irish society. A particular concern throughout has been the necessity of explicitly recognising the heterogeneous nature of the sites of cultural interaction as a prerequisite to the further exploration of the perceivable reasons for the subsequent breakdown in social order. A further key challenge has been the conceptualisation of the emergence of contemporary society's fundamental ambiguities, which mirror both the shared and bounded spaces and identities of early modern Ireland. There is a distinct difficulty in conceptualising the pattern of change, which was, in essence, a contradictory one and warrants an explicit recognition of such. The conflicting responses of the Gaelic-Irish in both opposing *and* accommodating the New English colonial enterprise have not been explicitly recognised in the extant literature of the period but form a prerequisite to elucidating the manner in which New English hegemony was negotiated and challenged. Throughout this work, the imperative has been to visualise a dual process of accommodation and differentiation in contemporary society.[7]

The problem of conceptualising the emergence of modern Ireland becomes even more difficult for later centuries. How can one represent traumas such as the catastrophic consequences for the O'Dwyers in the aftermath of the Cromwellian conquest in the early 1650s? Their subsequent executions, transplantations to Connacht, dispersal to the armies of Continental Europe and sweeping loss of properties and status present a unique set of interpretive difficulties. Many O'Dwyers were to remain in Kilnamanagh, of course. They were to form part of the evolving world of resistance in the hidden Ireland of the later seventeenth century and beyond, which brought about the liberation of an historical consciousness of oppression ultimately necessary for the overthrow of the Protestant ascendancy.

It is particularly important that the violence, oppression and trauma of Ireland's past are not overlooked in any critical (re)consideration of the Irish experience of English colonialism. Writing the diverse and often conflicting narratives of Ireland's past must necessarily involve an engagement with particularity and contradiction, as advocated in chapter one. In interrogating a past coloured by social upheaval and political controversy, and inflected by the search for historical antecedents for the legitimacies of contemporary contested identities, the challenge for Irish historical consciousness lies in the construction of multiple legitimate narratives that cut across, contest, transcend and inform each other in myriad ways.

It is important to recognise and interrogate the traumas of Ireland's past without descending into the pitfalls of metanarratives that subsume the very intricacies, contradictions and shared and contested spaces which make such histories so revealing and consequential for the understanding of the present. The recognition of the validity of myriad representations of the past, and the acceptance of the inherent contradictions of time, must ultimately generate a more nuanced historical geography of ideas. In the frontispiece, Kennelly would appear to ask who will solve the problem of historical consciousness?[8] Perhaps it is more appropriate to first ask who will accept the problem of historical consciousness? It is only then that the abounding array of conflicting meanings, contestations and traumas of the past, which constitute the nebulous heterogeneity of the present, can be explored, challenged and fruitfully debated.

Notes

[1] R.J.C. Young, 2001, *Postcolonialism: An Historical Introduction*, Blackwell, Oxford, p. 15

[2] A. Lester, 1998, *Colonial Discourse and the Colonisation of Queen Adelaide Province, South Africa*, Historical Geography Research Series, 34, HGRG, London, p. 10. Cf. Anne McClintock, 1995, *Imperial Leather: Race, Gender and Sexuality in the Colonial Contest*, Routledge, London, chap. 1

[3] For an excellent overview of how colonial and postcolonial studies have been broadened, diversified and sometimes limited by the postcolonial critique, see A.D. King, 1999, '(Post)colonial Geographies: Material and Symbolic', *Historical Geography*, 27, pp. 99-118. Cf. A. Lester, 1998, "'Otherness' and the Frontiers of Empire: The Eastern Cape Colony, 1806-c.1850', *Journal of Historical Geography*, 24, 1, pp. 2-19. Lester underlines some of the shortcomings of "the postcolonial approaches to situations of colonial contact" such as the "tendency to abstract conceptions of 'otherness' from the enormous variety of historical contexts in which they were created", resulting in a "kind of 'meta-narrative'" which views the coloniser and the colonised as "monolithic, opposing forces"; see *ibid.*, p. 2

[4] Yeoh argues that "paying attention to forms of resistance beyond the most explicit and heroic manifestations, allows us to appreciate the fluid, unstable nature of power relations"; see B.S.A. Yeoh, 2000, 'Historical Geographies of the Colonised World', in: B.J. Graham and C. Nash (eds.), *Modern Historical Geographies*, Prentice Hall, Harlow, p. 150

[5] S.G. Ellis, 1999, 'The Collapse of the Gaelic World', *Irish Historical Studies*, vol. 31, no. 124, p. 469

[6] See the comments of B.J. Graham, 1994, 'No Place of the Mind: Contested Protestant Representations of Ulster', *Ecumene*, 1 (3), pp. 259-260. Cf. *Idem.*, 2000, 'The Past in Place: Historical Geographies of Identity', in: *Idem.* and Nash (eds.), *Modern Historical Geographies*, pp. 75, 85-88

[7] As Yeoh points out, "in the colonised world, it is important to not only recognise that there were a panoply of resistances inhabiting different spaces but also to underscore the way they connect, collide, diverge, transmute, sometimes in unexpected ways, and often moving 'in' and 'out' of spaces of domination"; see Yeoh, 'Historical Geographies of the Colonised World', p. 151

[8] B. Kennelly, 'Who Will Solve It?', quoted in: T.B. Barry, R. Frame and K. Simms (eds.), 1995, *Colony and Frontier in Medieval Ireland*, Hambledon Press, London, p. x

Bibliography

Manuscript Sources

National Archives of Ireland, Dublin

This work has utilised a diverse collection of documents housed in the N.A.I. (MSS nos. are random and are presented individually in the footnotes) relating to a succession of land transfers, disputes and settlements dating to the early seventeenth century. Other records respecting contemporary land inquisitions and chancery court proceedings have also been employed.

National Library of Ireland, Dublin

Many of the documents consulted in the N.L.I. (again the MSS nos. are random; they are presented separately in the footnotes) have been in relation to specific individuals, including various earls of Ormond and members of the O'Dwyers. The Down Survey barony and parish maps of Kilnamanagh and the genealogical record of the O'Dwyers are also preserved herein.

Library of Trinity College Dublin, Manuscripts Department

Trinity houses the records of the examination for the inquiry of cruelties and losses suffered in the 1641 rebellion known as the 1641 depositions (T.C.D., MS 821). Herein, notable developments of the 1641 rebellion in the barony of Kilnamanagh are recorded, including the perceivable agendas of insurrection of those involved and the condition of Protestant settlers living in the environs of Cashel.

Printed Sources

Annals of the Kingdom of Ireland, by the Four Masters, from the Earliest Period to the Year 1616, vols. 4-6, ed. and trans. J. O'Donovan, 1851, Third Edition intro. K.W. Nicholls, De Burca Rare Books, Dublin, 1990

BIBLIOGRAPHY

Calendar of the Carew Manuscripts Preserved in the Archiepiscopal Library at Lambeth, 1515-1624, 6 vols., ed. J.S. Brewer and W. Bullen, P.R.O., London, 1867-1873

Calendar of the Clarendon State Papers Preserved in the Bodleian Library, vol. 1, ed. O. Ogle and W.H. Bliss, Clarendon Press, Oxford, 1872

Calendar of Ormond Deeds, vol. 4-6 (1509-1603), ed. E. Curtis, I.M.C., Dublin, 1937-1943

Calendar of the Patent and Close Rolls of Chancery in Ireland, 3 vols. (Henry VIII-Elizabeth, Elizabeth and Charles I), ed. J. Morrin, P.R.O., London, 1861-1863

Calendar of the State Papers Relating to Ireland, 1509-1670, 24 vols., P.R.O., London, 1860-1912

A Census of Ireland, c.1659 (With Supplementary Material from the Poll Money Ordinances 1660-1661), ed. S. Pender, I.M.C., Dublin, 1939

The Civil Survey, A.D. 1654-1656, County of Tipperary, Vol. 2, Western and Northern Baronies, ed. R.C. Simington, I.M.C, Dublin, 1934

The Irish Fiants of the Tudor Sovereigns, Henry VIII-Elizabeth, 1521-1603, 3 vols., intro. K.W. Nicholls, Edmund Burke, Dublin, 1994

The Irish Patent Rolls of James I: Facsimile of the Irish Record Commissioners' Calendar Prepared Prior to 1830, intro. M.C. Griffith, I.M.C., Dublin, 1966

'Mansfield Papers', intro. J.F. Ainsworth and E. MacLysaght, 1958, *Analecta Hibernica*, 20, pp. 92-125

The Red Book of Ormond, ed. N.B. White, I.M.C., Dublin, 1932

Report on the Manuscripts of the Earl of Egmont, 2 vols., H.M.C., London, 1905-09

Report on the Manuscripts of the Late Reginald Rawden Hastings, Esq., of the Manor House, Ashby de la Zouch, vol. 4, ed. F. Bickley, H.M.C., London, 1947

Tipperary's Families: Being the Hearth Money Records for 1665-6-7, ed. T. Laffan, James Duffy and Co. Ltd., Dublin, 1911

BIBLIOGRAPHY

Contemporary Works

T. Carte, *History of the Life of James, First Duke of Ormond, from his Birth in 1610 to his Death in 1688*, vol. 2, F. Bettenham, London, 1736

J. Davies, *A Discovery of the True Causes Why Ireland was Never Entirely Subdued and Brought Under Obedience of the Crown of England until the Beginning of His Majesty's Happy Reign* (1612), reprint. J.G. Barry, Irish University Press, Shannon, 1969

J. Derricke, *The Image of Irelande* (1581), reprint. J. Small, Adam and Charles Black, Edinburgh, 1883

Giraldus Cambrensis (Gerald of Wales), *Topographia Hibernica (The History and Topography of Ireland)* (1188-1189), trans. J.J. O'Meara, Penguin, Harmondsworth, 1982

Idem., *Expugnatio Hibernica (The Conquest of Ireland)* (1188-1189), ed. and trans. A.B. Scott and F.X. Martin, Royal Irish Academy, Dublin, 1978

G. Keating, *Foras Feasa ar Éirinn: The History of Ireland* (c.1633), ed. D. Comyn and P.S. Dineen, 4 vols., Irish Texts Society, London, 1902-1914

A. Ortelius, 1573, *Theatrum Orbis Terrarum* (additamentum), Neptune Gallery, Dublin

Pairlement Chloinne Tomáis, ed. N.J.A. Williams, Dublin Institute for Advanced Studies, Dublin, 1981

E. Spenser, *A View of the Present State of Ireland* (c.1596), ed. W.L. Renwick, Clarendon Press, Oxford, 1970

Idem., 'A Brief Note of Ireland' (c.1598), reprint. E.A. Greenlaw *et al.* (eds.), *The Works of Edmund Spenser: A Variorum Edition*, vol. 10, pp. 233-245, 11 vols., John Hopkins University Press, Baltimore, 1932-1949vv

'The Supplication of the Blood of the English Most Lamentably Murdered in Ireland, Cryeng Out of the Yearth for Revenge (1598)', intro. W. Maley, 1995, *Analecta Hibernica*, 36, pp. 1-77

BIBLIOGRAPHY

Secondary Works

F.H.A. Aalen, 1978, *Man and the Landscape in Ireland*, Academic Press, London

Idem., 1989, 'Imprints of the Past', in: D. Gillmor (ed.), *The Irish Countryside*, Wolfhound Press, Dublin, pp. 83-120

S.C. Aitken, 1997, 'Analysis of Texts: Armchair Theory and Couch-Potato Geography', in: R. Flowerdew and D. Martin (eds.), *Methods in Human Geography*, Longman, Harlow, pp. 197-212

J.H. Andrews, 1988, 'Jones Hughes' Ireland: A Literary Quest', in: W.J. Smyth and K. Whelan (eds.), *Common Ground: Essays on the Historical Geography of Ireland presented to T. Jones Hughes*, Cork University Press, Cork, pp. 1-21

J. Appleton, 1975, *The Experience of Landscape*, John Wiley and Sons, New York

D. Armitage, 1998, 'Literature and Empire', in: N. Canny (ed.), *The Origins of Empire: British Overseas Enterprise to the Close of the 17ᵗʰ Century*, The Oxford History of the British Empire, vol. 1, Oxford University Press, Oxford, pp. 99-123

Atlas of the Parishes of Cashel and Emly, Thurles, Co. Tipperary, 1970

D.J. Baker, 1993, 'Off the Map: Charting Uncertainty in Renaissance Ireland', in: B. Bradshaw, A. Hadfield and W. Maley (eds.), *Representing Ireland: Literature and the Origins of Conflict, 1534-1660*, Cambridge University Press, Cambridge, pp. 76-92

T.C. Barnard, 1975, *Cromwellian Ireland: English Government and Reform in Ireland, 1649-1660*, Oxford University Press, London

T.B. Barry, 1993, 'Late Medieval Ireland: The Debate on Social and Economic Transformation, 1350-1550', in: B.J. Graham and L.J. Proudfoot (eds.), *An Historical Geography of Ireland*, Academic Press, London, pp. 99-122

Idem., 1995, 'The Last Frontier: Defence and Settlement in Late Medieval Ireland', in: T.B. Barry, R. Frame and K. Simms (eds.), *Colony and Frontier in Medieval Ireland*, Hambledon Press, London, pp. 217-228

BIBLIOGRAPHY

T. Bartlett, 1982, 'The O'Haras of Annaghmore *c*.1600-*c*.1800: Survival and Revival', *Irish Economic and Social History*, IX, pp. 34-52

J.C. Beckett, 1976, *The Anglo-Irish Tradition*, Faber and Faber, London

Idem., 1981, *The Making of Modern Ireland 1603-1923*, Faber and Faber, London (first pub. 1966)

T. Blake Butler, 1953, 'Seneschals of the Liberty of Tipperary', *Irish Genealogist*, vol. 2, no. 10, pp. 294-303

Idem., 1959, 'The Sheriffs of the Liberty of The County Tipperary', *Irish Genealogist*, vol. 3, no. 4, pp. 120-123

Idem., 1960, 'The Sheriffs of the Liberty of The County Tipperary', *Irish Genealogist*, vol. 3, no. 5, pp. 158-161

A. Blunt and C. McEwan (eds.), 2002, *Postcolonial Geographies*, Continuum, London

K.S. Bottigheimer, 1971, *English Money and Irish Land: The 'Adventurers' in the Cromwellian Settlement of Ireland*, Clarendon Press, Oxford

Idem., 1978, 'Kingdom and Colony: Ireland in the Westward Enterprise 1536-1660', in: K.R. Andrews, N.P. Canny and P.E.H. Hair (eds.), *The Westward Enterprise: English Activities in Ireland, The Atlantic and America, 1480-1650*, Liverpool University Press, Liverpool, pp. 45-64

D.G. Boyce and A. O'Day (eds.), 1996, *Modern Irish History: Revisionism and the Revisionist Controversy*, Routledge, London

B. Bradshaw, 1978, 'Native Reaction to the Westward Enterprise: A Case-Study in Gaelic Ideology', in: Andrews *et al* (eds.), *The Westward Enterprise*, pp. 65-80

Idem., 1979, *The Irish Constitutional Revolution of the Sixteenth Century*, Cambridge University Press, Cambridge

Idem., 1988, 'Robe and Sword in the Conquest of Ireland', in: C. Cross, D. Loades and J.J. Scarisbrick (eds.), *Law and Government under the Tudors*, Cambridge University Press, Cambridge, pp. 139-162

BIBLIOGRAPHY

Idem., 1989, 'Nationalism and Historical Scholarship in Modern Ireland', *Irish Historical Studies*, vol. 26, no. 104, pp. 329-351

Idem., 1993, 'Geoffrey Keating: Apologist of Irish Ireland', in: Bradshaw *et al* (eds.), *Representing Ireland*, pp. 166-190

Idem., 1998, 'The English Reformation and Identity Formation in Wales and Ireland', in: *Idem.* and P. Roberts (eds.), *British Consciousness and Identity: The Making of Britain 1533-1707*, Cambridge University Press, Cambridge, pp. 43-111

C. Brady, 1986, 'Court, Castle and Country: The Framework of Government in Tudor Ireland', in: *Idem.* and R. Gillespie (eds.), *Natives and Newcomers: Essays on the Making of Irish Colonial Society, 1534-1641*, Irish Academic Press, Dublin, pp. 22-49

Idem., 1989, 'Thomas Butler, Earl of Ormond (1531-1614) and Reform in Tudor Ireland', in: *Idem.*, (ed.), *Worsted in the Game: Losers in Irish History*, Lilliput Press, Dublin, pp. 49-59

Idem., 1989, 'The Road to the View: On the Decline of Reform Thought in Tudor Ireland', in: P. Coughlin (ed.), *Spenser and Ireland: An Interdisciplinary Perspective*, Cork University Press, Cork, pp. 25-45

Idem., 1994, *The Chief Governors: The Rise and Fall of Reform Government in Tudor Ireland 1536-1588*, Cambridge University Press, Cambridge

Idem., 1996, 'England's Defence and Ireland's Reform: The Dilemma of the Irish Viceroys, 1541-1641', in: B. Bradshaw and J. Morrill (eds.), *The British Problem, c.1534-1707: State Formation in the Atlantic Archipelago*, MacMillan Press Ltd., Basingstoke, pp. 89-117

G. Bridge, 1997, 'Guest Editorial. Towards a Situated Universalism: On Strategic Rationality and 'Local Theory'', *Environment and Planning D: Society and Space*, 15, pp. 633-639

Idem., 2000, 'Rationality, Ethics, and Space: On Situated Universalism and the Self-Interested Acknowledgement of 'Difference', *Environment and Planning D: Society and Space*, 18, pp. 519-535

BIBLIOGRAPHY

R.H. Buchanan, 1984, 'Historical Geography of Ireland Pre-1700', *Irish Geography*, supplement to vol. 17, pp. 129-148

Idem., 1986, 'Towns and Plantations, 1500-1700', in: W. Nolan (ed.), *The Shaping of Ireland: The Geographical Perspective*, The Mercier Press, Cork, pp. 84-98

W.F.T. Butler, 1917, *Confiscations in Irish History*, Talbot Press, Dublin

Idem., 1925, *Gleanings from Irish History*, Longmans, Green, London

M. Caball, 1993, 'The Gaelic Mind and the Collapse of the Gaelic World: An Appraisal', *Cambridge Medieval Celtic Studies*, 25, pp. 87-96

Idem., 1994, 'Providence and Exile in Early Seventeenth-Century Ireland', *Irish Historical Studies*, vol. 29, no. 114, pp. 174-188

Idem., 1998, 'Faith, Culture and Sovereignty: Irish Nationality and its Development, 1558-1625', in: Bradshaw and Roberts (eds.), *British Consciousness and Identity*, pp. 112-139

C.T. Cairns, 1987, *Irish Tower Houses: A County Tipperary Case Study*, Athlone, Co. Westmeath

D. Cairns and S. Richards, 1988, *Writing Ireland: Colonialism, Nationalism and Culture*, Manchester University Press, Manchester

D. Cairns, 1991, 'Recent Irish Histories', *History Workshop Journal*, 31, pp. 156-162

M. Callanan, 1938, *Records of Four Tipperary Septs,* O'Gorman Ltd., Galway

B.N.S. Campbell, 1990, 'People and Land in the Middle Ages, 1066-1500', in: R.A. Dodgshon and R.A. Butlin (eds.), *An Historical Geography of England and Wales*, Second Edition, Academic Press, London, pp. 69-122

N. Canny, 1976, *The Elizabethan Conquest of Ireland: A Pattern Established*, Harvester Press, Hassocks, Sussex

Idem., 1978, 'The Permissive Frontier: The Problem of Social Control in English Settlements in Ireland and Virginia 1550-1650', in: Andrews *et al* (eds.), *The Westward Enterprise*, pp. 17-44

BIBLIOGRAPHY

Idem., 1982, *The Upstart Earl: A Study of the Social World of Richard Boyle, First Earl of Cork, 1566-1643*, Cambridge University Press, Cambridge

Idem., 1985, 'Migration and Opportunity: Britain, Ireland and the New World', *Irish Economic and Social History*, XII, pp. 7-32

Idem., 1986, 'Protestants, Planters and Apartheid in Early Modern Ireland', *Irish Historical Studies*, vol. 25, no 98, pp. 105-115

Idem., 1987, *From Reformation to Restoration: Ireland 1534-1660*, Helicon Ltd., Dublin

Idem., 1987, 'The Formation of the Irish Mind: Religion, Politics and Gaelic Irish Literature, 1580-1750', in: C.H.E. Philpin (ed.), *Nationalism and Popular Protest in Ireland*, Past and Present Publications, Cambridge University Press, Cambridge, pp. 50-79

Idem., 1987, 'Identity Formation in Ireland: The Emergence of the Anglo-Irish', in: *Idem.* and A. Pagden (eds.), *Colonial Identity in the Atlantic World*, Princeton University Press, Princeton, pp. 159-212

Idem., 1988, *Kingdom and Colony: Ireland in the Atlantic World 1560-1800*, John Hopkins University Press, Baltimore

Idem., 1993, 'The 1641 Depositions as a Source for the Writing of Social History: County Cork as a Case Study', in: P. O'Flanagan and C.G. Buttimer (eds.), *Cork: History and Society*, Geography Publications, Dublin, pp. 249-308

Idem., 1993, 'The Attempted Anglicization of Ireland in the Seventeenth Century: An Exemplar of "British History"', in: R.G. Asch (ed.), *Three Nations – A Common History: England, Scotland, Ireland and British History c.1600-1920*, Universitatsverlag Dr. Brockmeyer, Bochum, pp. 49-82

Idem., 1994, 'English Migration into and across the Atlantic during the Seventeenth and Eighteenth Centuries', in: *Idem.* (ed.), *Europeans on the Move: Studies on European Migration, 1500-1800*, Clarendon Press, Oxford, pp. 39-75

Idem., 1995, 'What Really Happened in Ireland in 1641?', in: J.H. Ohlmeyer (ed.), *Ireland from Independence to Occupation 1641-1660*, Cambridge University Press, Cambridge, pp. 24-42

BIBLIOGRAPHY

N. Carlin, 1993, 'Extreme or Mainstream? The English Independents and the Cromwellian Reconquest of Ireland, 1649-1651', in: Bradshaw *et al* (eds.), *Representing Ireland*, pp. 209-226

J. Carty (ed.), 1951, *Ireland from the Flight of the Earls to Grattan's Parliament 1607-1782: A Documentary Record*, C.J. Fallon Ltd., Dublin

S.T. Cavanagh, 1993, ''The fatal destiny of that land': Elizabethan Views of Ireland', in: Bradshaw *et al* (eds.), *Representing Ireland*, pp. 116-131

P. Clark, 1987, 'Review Article. Planters and Plantations', *Irish Economic and Social History*, XIV, pp. 62-66

A. Clarke, 1970, 'Ireland and the General Crisis', *Past and Present*, no. xlviii, pp. 79-99

Idem., 1976, 'The Irish Economy, 1600-1660', in: T.W. Moody, F.X. Martin and F.J. Byrne (eds.), *A New History of Ireland III: Early Modern Ireland 1534-1691*, Clarendon Press, Oxford, pp. 168-186

Idem. with R. Dudley Edwards, 1976, 'Pacification, Plantation, and the Catholic Question, 1603-23', in: Moody *et al* (eds.), *A New History of Ireland III*, pp. 187-232

A. Clarke, 1976, 'Selling Royal Favours, 1624-32', in: Moody *et al* (eds.), *A New History of Ireland III*, pp. 233-242

Idem., 1976, 'The Government of Wentworth, 1632-1640', in: Moody *et al* (eds.), *A New History of Ireland III*, pp. 243-269

Idem., 1976, 'The Breakdown of Authority, 1640-41', in: Moody *et al* (eds.), *A New History of Ireland III*, pp. 270-288

R.V. Comerford, M. Cullen, J.R. Hill and C. Lennon (eds.), 1990, *Religion, Conflict and Co-Existence in Ireland*, Gill and MacMillan, Dublin

P.J. Corish, 1976, 'The Rising of 1641 and the Catholic Confederacy, 1641-5', in: Moody *et al* (eds.), *A New History of Ireland III*, pp. 289-316

A. Cosgrove, 1981, *Late Medieval Ireland 1370-1541*, Helicon Ltd., Dublin

BIBLIOGRAPHY

T. Cresswell, 1996, *In Place / Out of Place: Geography, Ideology and Transgression*, University of Minnesota Press, Minneapolis

W. Cronon, 1994, 'Comment. Cutting Loose or Running Around', *Journal of Historical Geography*, 20, 1, pp. 38-43

J. Crush, 1994, 'Post-Colonialism, De-Colonisation and Geography', in: A. Godlewska and N. Smith (eds.), *Geography and Empire*, Blackwell, Oxford, pp. 333-350

B. Cunningham, 1986, 'Seventeenth-Century Interpretations of the Past: The Case of Geoffrey Keating', *Irish Historical Studies*, vol. 25, no. 98, pp. 116-128

Idem., 1986, 'Native Culture and Political Change in Ireland, 1580-1640', in: Brady and Gillespie (eds.), *Natives and Newcomers*, pp. 148-170

Idem. and R. Gillespie, 1990, 'Englishmen in Sixteenth-Century Irish Annals', *Irish Economic and Social History*, XVII, pp. 5-21

S. Daniels, 1989, 'Marxism, Culture and the Duplicity of Landscape', in: R. Peet and N. Thrift (eds.), *New Models in Geography, Vol. 2*, Unwin Hyman, London, pp. 196-220

Idem., 1993, *Fields of Vision: Landscape Imagery and National Identity in England and the U.S.*, Polity Press, Cambridge

D. Demeritt, 1994, 'Ecology, Objectivity and Critique in Writings on Nature and Human Societies', *Journal of Historical Geography*, 20, 1, pp. 22-37

A.A. Dibben, 1968, *Title Deeds: 13th-19th Centuries*, Pamphlet no. 72, The Historical Association, London

F. Driver and R. Samuel, 1995, 'Editorial. Rethinking the Idea of Place', *History Workshop Journal*, 39, pp. v-vii

R.W. Dudley Edwards and M. O'Dowd, 1985, *Sources for Early Modern Irish History, 1534-1641*, Cambridge University Press, Cambridge

P.J. Duffy, 1981 'The Territorial Organisation of Gaelic Landownership and its Transformation in County Monaghan, 1591-1640', *Irish Geography*, vol. 14, pp. 1-23

BIBLIOGRAPHY

Idem., 1988, 'The Evolution of Estate Properties in South Ulster, 1600-1800', in: Smyth and Whelan (eds.), *Common Ground*, pp. 110-123

Idem., D. Edwards and E. FitzPatrick (eds.), 2001, *Gaelic Ireland c.1250-c.1650: Land, Lordship and Settlement*, Four Courts Press, Dublin

J. Duncan, 1980, 'The Superorganic in American Cultural Geography', *Annals of the Association of American Geographers*, 70 (2), pp. 181-198

Idem., 1990, *The City as Text: The Politics of Landscape Interpretation*, Cambridge University Press, Cambridge

Idem. and D. Ley, 1993, 'Representing the Place of Culture', in: *Idem.* (eds.), *Place / Culture / Representation*, Routledge, London, pp. 1-21

J. Duncan and D. Cosgrove, 1995, 'Editorial. Colonialism and Postcolonialism in the Former British Empire', *Ecumene*, 2 (2), pp. 127-128

J. Duncan, 1999, 'Complicity and Resistance in the Colonial Archive: Some Issues of Method and Theory in Historical Geography', *Historical Geography*, 27, pp. 119-128

T.J. Dunne, 1980, 'The Gaelic Response to Conquest and Colonisation: The Evidence of the Poetry', *Studia Hibernica*, 20, pp. 7-30

Idem., 1992, 'New Histories: Beyond "Revisionism"', *Irish Review*, 12, pp. 1-12

C. Durston, 1986, '"Let Ireland Be Quiet': Opposition in England to the Cromwellian Conquest in Ireland', *History Workshop Journal*, 21, pp. 105-112

S.G. Ellis, 1985, *Tudor Ireland: Crown, Community and the Conflict of Cultures 1470-1603*, Longman, London

Idem., 1986, *Reform and Revival, English Government in Ireland 1470-1534*, Studies in History 47, Royal Historical Society, The Boydell Press, Woodbridge

Idem., 1986, 'Nationalist Historiography and the English and Gaelic Worlds in the Late Middle Ages', *Irish Historical Studies*, vol. 25, no. 97, pp. 1-18

BIBLIOGRAPHY

Idem., 1991, 'Historiographical Debate. Representations of the Past in Ireland: Whose Past and Whose Present?', *Irish Historical Studies*, vol. 27, no. 108, pp. 289-308

Idem., 1996, 'Writing Irish History: Revisionism, Colonialism, and the British Isles', *Irish Review*, 19, pp. 1-21

Idem., 1998, *Ireland in the Age of the Tudors, 1447-1603: English Expansion and the End of Gaelic Rule*, Longman, London

Idem., 1999, 'The Collapse of the Gaelic World', *Irish Historical Studies*, vol. 31, no. 124, pp. 449-469

C.A. Empey and K. Simms, 1975, 'The Ordinances of the White Earl and the Problem of Coign and Livery in the Later Middle Ages', *Proceedings of the Royal Irish Academy*, vol. 75, sec. C, pp. 161-188

C.A. Empey, 1985, 'The Norman Period: 1185-1500', in: W. Nolan (ed.), *Tipperary: History and Society*, Geography Publications, Dublin, pp. 71-91

E. Estyn Evans, 1942, *Irish Heritage: The Landscape, the People and their Work*, Dundalgan Press, Dundalk

Idem., 1981, *The Personality of Ireland: Habitat, Heritage and History* (Revised Edition), Blackstaff, Belfast

F. Fanon, 1967, *The Wretched of the Earth*, trans. C. Farrington, Penguin, Harmondsworth

B. Fitzpatrick, 1988, *17th Century Ireland: The War of Religions*, New Gill History of Ireland 3, Gill and MacMillan, Dublin

A. Ford, 1986, 'The Protestant Reformation in Ireland', in: Brady and Gillespie (eds.), *Natives and Newcomers*, pp. 50-74

Idem., 1987, *The Protestant Reformation in Ireland, 1590-1641*, Studies in the Intercultural History of Christianity, Verlag Peter Lang, Frankfurt am Main

Idem., 1993, 'The Church of Ireland: A Critical Bibliography, 1536-1992, Part II: 1603-41', *Irish Historical Studies*, vol. 28, no. 112, pp. 352-358

BIBLIOGRAPHY

Idem., 1998, 'James Ussher and the Creation of an Irish Protestant Identity', in: Bradshaw and Roberts (eds.), *British Consciousness and Identity*, pp. 184-212

J.W. Foster, 1991, *Colonial Consequences: Essays in Irish Literature and Culture*, Lilliput Press, Dublin

R.F. Foster, 1986, 'We are all Revisionists Now', *Irish Review*, 1, pp. 1-5

Idem., 1989, *Modern Ireland 1600-1972*, Penguin, London

R. Frame, 1990, *The Political Development of the British Isles 1100-1400*, Clarendon Press, Oxford

C. Geertz, 1973, *The Interpretation of Cultures*, Basic Books, New York

R. Gillespie, 1983, 'Thesis Abstract. East Ulster in the Early Seventeenth Century: A Colonial Economy and Society (Ph.D. Thesis, University of Dublin, 1982)', *Irish Economic and Social History*, X, pp. 92-94

Idem., 1984, 'The Origins and Development of an Ulster Urban Network, 1600-41', *Irish Historical Studies*, vol. 24, no. 93, pp. 15-29

Idem., 1985, *Colonial Ulster: The Settlement of East Ulster 1600-1641*, Cork University Press, Cork

Idem., 1986, 'The End of an Era: Ulster and the Outbreak of the 1641 Rising', in: Brady and Gillespie (eds.), *Natives and Newcomers*, pp. 191-213

Idem., 1991, *The Transformation of the Irish Economy 1550-1700*, Studies in Irish Economic and Social History 6, The Economic and Social History Society of Ireland

Idem. and B. Cunningham, 1991, 'Holy Cross Abbey and the Counter Reformation in Tipperary', *Tipperary Historical Journal*, 4, pp. 170-180

Idem., 1993, 'Documents and Sources: Plantation and Profit: Richard Spert's Tract on Ireland, 1608', *Irish Economic and Social History*, XX, pp. 62-71

Idem., 1993, 'Explorers, Exploiters and Entrepreneurs: Early Modern Ireland and its Context, 1500-1700', in: Graham and Proudfoot (eds.), *An Historical Geography of Ireland*, pp. 123-157

BIBLIOGRAPHY

Idem., 1998, 'Popular and Unpopular Religion: A View from Early Modern Ireland', in: J.S. Donnelly, Jr. and K.A. Miller (eds.), *Irish Popular Culture, 1650-1850*, Irish Academic Press, Dublin, pp. 30-49

Idem., 1998, 'Documents and Sources: A Manor Court in Seventeenth Century Ireland', *Irish Economic and Social History*, XXV, pp. 81-87

J. Gillingham, 1993, 'The English Invasion of Ireland', in: Bradshaw *et al* (eds.), *Representing Ireland*, pp. 24-42

B.J. Graham and L.J. Proudfoot, 1993, 'A Perspective on the Nature of Irish Historical Geography', in: *Idem.* (eds.), *An Historical Geography of Ireland*, pp. 1-18

B.J. Graham, 1993, 'The High Middle Ages: *c.*1100 to *c.*1350', in: *Idem.* and Proudfoot (eds.), *An Historical Geography of Ireland*, pp. 58-98

Idem., 1994, 'No Place of the Mind: Contested Protestant Representations of Ulster', *Ecumene*, 1 (3), pp. 257-281

Idem., 1997, 'Ireland and Irishness: Place, Culture and Identity', in: *Idem.* (ed.), *In Search of Ireland: A Cultural Geography*, Routledge, London, pp. 1-15

Idem., 2000, 'The Past in Place: Historical Geographies of Identity', in: *Idem.* and C. Nash (eds.), *Modern Historical Geographies*, Prentice Hall, Harlow, pp. 70-99

A. Hadfield, 1993, 'Briton and Scythian: Tudor Representations of Irish Origins', *Irish Historical Studies*, vol. 28, no. 112, pp. 390-408

Idem. and J. McVeagh (eds.), 1994, *Strangers to that Land: British Perceptions of Ireland from the Reformation to the Famine*, Colin Smythe, Gerard's Cross, Bucks.

A. Hadfield, 1997, *Edmund Spenser's Irish Experience: Wild Fruit and Salvage Soyl*, Clarendon Press, Oxford

Idem., 1998, *Literature, Travel and Colonial Writing in the English Renaissance 1545-1625*, Clarendon Press, Oxford

S. Hall, 1997, 'Cultural Identity and Diaspora', excerpts reprint. in: L. MacDowell (ed.), *Undoing Place? A Geographical Reader*, Routledge, London, pp. 231-242

BIBLIOGRAPHY

M. Hallinan (ed.), 1993, *Tipperary County: People and Places*, Kincora Press, Dublin

R.C. Harris, 1996, 'Classics in Human Geography Revisited. R.C. Harris, 1971, 'Theory and Synthesis in Historical Geography', *Canadian Geographer*, 15, pp. 157-172: Author's Response', *Progress in Human Geography*, vol. 20, no. 2, pp. 199-201

G.A. Hayes-McCoy, 1976, 'The Royal Supremacy and Ecclesiastical Revolution, 1534-47', in: Moody *et al* (eds.), *A New History of Ireland III*, pp. 39-68

Idem., 1976, 'Conciliation, Coercion and the Protestant Reformation, 1547-71', in: Moody *et al* (eds.), *A New History of Ireland III*, pp. 69-93

Idem., 1976, 'The Completion of the Tudor Conquest and the Advance of the Counter Reformation, 1571-1603', in: Moody *et al* (eds.), *A New History of Ireland III*, pp. 94-141

M. Heffernan, 1997, 'Editorial. The Future of Historical Geography', *Journal of Historical Geography*, 23, 1, pp. 1-2

G. Henderson, 1998, 'Review Article. "Landscape is Dead, Long Live Landscape": A Handbook for Sceptics', *Journal of Historical Geography*, 24, 1, pp. 94-100

M. Hennessy, 1985, 'Parochial Organisation in Medieval Tipperary', in: Nolan (ed.), *Tipperary: History and Society*, pp. 60-70

Idem., 1988, 'The Priory and Hospital of New Gate: The Evolution and Decline of a Medieval Monastic Estate', in: Smyth and Whelan (eds.), *Common Ground*, pp. 41-54

S. Hutton and P. Stewart, 1991, 'Introduction: Perspectives on Irish History and Social Studies', in: *Idem.* (eds.), *Ireland's Histories: Aspects of State, Society and Ideology*, Routledge, London, pp. 1-10

J.M. Jacobs, 1996, *Edge of Empire: Postcolonialism and the City*, Routledge, London

L. Jardine, 1993, 'Encountering Ireland: Gabriel Harvey, Edmund Spenser, and English Colonial Ventures', in: Bradshaw *et al* (eds.), *Representing Ireland*, pp. 60-75

BIBLIOGRAPHY

T. Jones Hughes, 1970, 'Town and Baile in Irish Place-Names', in: N. Stephens and R. Glasscock (eds.), *Irish Geographical Studies in Honour of E. Estyn Evans*, Queen's University Belfast, Belfast, pp. 244-258

Idem., 1984, 'Historical Geography of Ireland from *circa* 1700', *Irish Geography*, supplement to vol. 17, pp. 149-166

Idem., 1985, 'Landholding and Settlement in County Tipperary in the Nineteenth Century', in: Nolan (ed.), *Tipperary: History and Society*, pp. 339-366

C. Katz, 1996, 'Towards Minor Theory', *Environment and Planning D: Society and Space*, 14, pp. 487-499

H. Kearney, 1991, 'The Irish and Their History', *History Workshop Journal*, 31, pp. 149-155

H.F. Kearney, 1959, *Strafford in Ireland, 1633-1641: A Study in Absolutism*, Manchester University Press, Manchester

D. Kennedy, 1996, 'Imperial History and Post-Colonial Theory', *Journal of Imperial and Commonwealth History*, 24, pp. 345-363

C. Kenny, 1987, 'The Exclusion of Catholics from the Legal Profession in Ireland, 1537-1829', *Irish Historical Studies*, vol. 25, no. 100, pp. 337-357

G. Kew, 1998, 'The Irish Sections of Fynes Moryson's Unpublished Itinerary', *Anelecta Hibernica*, 37, pp. 1-137

D. Kiberd, 1997, 'Modern Ireland: Postcolonial or European?', in: S. Murray (ed.), *Not on any Map: Essays on Postcoloniality and Cultural Nationalism*, University of Exeter Press, Exeter, pp. 81-100

V.G. Kiernan, 1980, *State and Society in Europe, 1550-1660*, Basil Blackwell, Oxford

Idem., 1987, 'The Emergence of a Nation', in: Philpin (ed.), *Nationalism and Popular Protest*, pp. 16-49

Idem., 1993, 'The British Isles: Celt and Saxon', in M. Teich and R. Porter (eds.), *The National Question in Europe in Historical Context*, Cambridge University Press, Cambridge, pp. 1-34

BIBLIOGRAPHY

A.D. King, 1999, '(Post)colonial Geographies: Material and Symbolic', *Historical Geography*, 27, pp. 99-118

I. Leister, 1963, *Das Werden der Agrarlandschaft in der Graftschaft Tipperary*, Marburg, Germany

C. Lennon, 1986, 'The Counter-Reformation in Ireland, 1542-1641', in: Brady and Gillespie (eds.), *Natives and Newcomers*, pp. 75-92

A. Lester, 1998, ''Otherness' and the Frontiers of Empire: The Eastern Cape Colony, 1806-*c*.1850', *Journal of Historical* Geography, 24, 1, pp. 2-19

Idem., 1998, *Colonial Discourse and the Colonisation of Queen Adelaide Province, South Africa*, Historical Geography Research Series No. 34, HGRG, Royal Geographical Society, London

Idem., 2000, 'Historical Geographies of Imperialism', in: Graham and Nash (eds.), *Modern Historical Geographies*, pp. 100-120

Idem., 2002, 'British Settler Discourse and the Circuits of Empire', *History Workshop Journal*, 51 (1), pp. 24-48

K.J. Lindley, 1972, 'The Impact of the 1641 Rebellion upon England and Wales, 1641-5', *Irish Historical Studies*, vol. 18, no. 70, pp. 143-176

D. Lowenthal, 1975, 'Past Time, Present Place: Landscape and Memory', *The Geographical Review*, 65, pp. 1-36

Idem., 1979, 'Age and Artifact: Dilemmas and Appreciation', in: D.W. Meinig (ed.), *The Interpretation of Ordinary Landscapes*, Oxford University Press, New York, pp. 103-128

J. Lydon, 1987, 'The Impact of the Bruce Invasion, 1315-27', in: A. Cosgrove (ed.), *A New History of Ireland II, Medieval Ireland, 1169-1534*, Clarendon Press, Oxford, pp. 275-302

J. Lydon, 1998, *The Making of Ireland: From Ancient Times to the Present*, Routledge, London

BIBLIOGRAPHY

M. MacCarthy-Morrogh, 1986, *The Munster Plantation: English Migration to Southern Ireland 1583-1641*, Clarendon Press, Oxford

Idem., 1986, 'The English Presence in Early Seventeenth Century Munster', in: Brady and Gillespie (eds.), *Natives and Newcomers*, pp. 171-190

Idem., 1987, 'Credit and Remittance: Monetary Problems in Early Seventeenth-Century Munster', *Irish Economic and Social History*, XIV, pp. 5-19

B. Mac Cuarta, 1993, 'A Planter's Interaction with Gaelic Culture: Sir Matthew de Renzy, 1577-1634', *Irish Economic and Social History*, XX, pp. 1-17

M. MacCurtain, 1972, *Tudor and Stuart Ireland*, The Gill History of Ireland 7, Gill and MacMillan, Dublin

Idem., 1988, 'A Lost Landscape: The Geraldine Castles and Tower Houses of the Shannon Estuary', in: J. Bradley (ed.), *Society and Settlement in Medieval Ireland*, Boethius Press, Kilkenny, pp. 429-444

R. Mackenney, 1993, *Sixteenth Century Europe: Expansion and Conflict*, Macmillan History of Europe, MacMillan Press Ltd., Basingstoke

W. Maley, 1993, 'How Milton and Some Contemporaries Read Spenser's *View*', in: Bradshaw *et al* (eds.), *Representing Ireland*, pp. 191-208

D.G. Marnane, 1985, *Land and Violence: A History of West Tipperary from 1660*, Fitzpatrick Bros., Tipperary

Idem., 1997, 'Writing the Past: Tipperary History and Historians', *Tipperary Historical Journal*, 10, pp. 1-41

A.F. Marotti, 1997, 'Southwell's Remains: Catholicism and Anti-Catholicism in Early Modern England', in: C.C. Brown and A.F. Marotti (eds.), *Texts and Cultural Change in Early Modern England*, MacMillan Press Ltd., Basingstoke, pp. 37-65

F.X. Martin, 1987, 'Introduction: Medieval Ireland', in: Cosgrove (ed.), *A New History of Ireland II*, pp. xlix-lxii

BIBLIOGRAPHY

D. Massey, 1997, 'A Global Sense of Place', reprint. in: T. Barnes and D. Gregory (eds.), *Reading Human Geography: The Poetics and Politics of Inquiry*, Arnold, London, pp. 315-323

M. McCarthy, 1999, 'Cross-Sectional Reconstructions of Historic Urban Landscapes: An Examination of the Nature and Comprehensiveness of a Mid-Seventeenth-Century Survey and Valuation", *Irish Archives*, 6 (1), pp. 3-13

Idem., 2000, 'Turning a World Upside Down: The Metamorphosis of Property, Settlement and Society in the City of Cork during the 1640s and 1650s', *Irish Geography*, 33 (1), pp. 37-55

Idem., 2002, 'Writing Ireland's Historical Geographies', *Journal of Historical Geography*, 28, 4, pp. 534-553

Aileen McClintock, 1988, 'The Earls of Ormond and Tipperary's Role in the Governing of Ireland (1603-1641)', *Tipperary Historical Journal*, 1, pp. 159-172

Anne McClintock, 1995, *Imperial Leather: Race, Gender and Sexuality in the Colonial Contest*, Routledge, London

J. McGurk, 1997, *The Elizabethan Conquest of Ireland (The 1590s Crisis)*, Manchester University Press, Manchester

J. McLaughlin, 1997, 'New Light on Richard Hadsor, II: Richard Hadsor's 'Discourse' on the Irish State, 1604', *Irish Historical Studies*, vol. 30, no. 119, pp. 337-353

S.A. Meigs, 1994, 'Thesis Abstract. Constantia in Fide: The Persistence of Traditional Religion in Early Modern Ireland, 1400-1690 (Ph.D. Thesis, Northwestern University, Evanston, 1993)', *Irish Economic and Social History*, XXI, pp. 82-83

D.W. Meinig, 1982, 'Geographical Analysis of Imperial Expansion', in: A.R.H. Baker and M. Billinge (eds.), *Period and Place: Research Methods in Historical Geography*, Cambridge University Press, Cambridge, pp. 56-75

F. Mitchell, 1986, *The Shell Guide to Reading the Irish Landscape*, Country House, Dublin

BIBLIOGRAPHY

A. Mitson, 1993, 'The Significance of Kinship Networks in the Seventeenth Century: South-West Nottinghamshire', in: C. Phythian-Adams (ed.), *Societies, Cultures and Kinship, 1580-1850 – Cultural Provinces and English Local History*, Leicester University Press, London, pp. 24-77

N.S. Momaday, 1987, 'Personal Reflections', in: C. Martin (ed.), *The American Indian and the Problem of History*, Oxford University Press, New York, pp. 156-161

T.W. Moody, 1976, 'Early Modern Ireland', in: Moody *et al* (eds.), *A New History of Ireland III*, pp. xxxix-lxiii

H. Morgan, 1988, 'The End of Gaelic Ulster: A Thematic Interpretation of Events between 1534 and 1610', *Irish Historical Studies*, vol. 26, no. 101, pp. 8-32

Idem., 1996, 'British Policies before the British State', in: Bradshaw and Morrill (eds.), *The British Problem*, pp. 66-88

Idem., (ed.), 1999, *Political Ideology in Ireland, 1541-1641*, Four Courts Press, Dublin

J. Morrissey, 1996, *Landscape and Society in Seventeenth Century West Tipperary*, Unpublished B.A. Thesis, Trinity College, University of Dublin

Idem., 2000, *Encountering Colonialism: Gaelic-Irish Responses to New English Expansion in Early Modern West Tipperary, c.1541-1641*, Unpublished Ph.D. Thesis, University of Exeter

D.A. Murphy, 1994, *The Two Tipperarys*, Regional Studies in Political and Administrative History No. 1, Relay, Nenagh, Co. Tipperary

J. Murray, 1993, 'The Church of Ireland: A Critical Bibliography, 1536-1992, Part I: 1536-1603', *Irish Historical Studies*, vol. 28, no. 112, pp. 345-352

C. Nash and B. Graham, 2000, 'The Making of Modern Historical Geographies', in: Graham and Nash (eds.), *Modern Historical Geographies*, pp. 1-9

C. Nash, 2002, 'Genealogical Identities', *Environment and Planning D: Society and Space*, 20, pp. 27-52

BIBLIOGRAPHY

P. Neville-Sington, 1997, "A Very Good Trumpet': Richard Hakluyt and the Politics of Overseas Expansion', in: Brown and Marotti (eds.), *Texts and Cultural Change*, pp. 66-81

A. Nic Ghiollamhaith, 1995, 'Kings and Vassals in Later Medieval Ireland', in: Barry *et al* (eds.), *Colony and Frontier*, pp. 201-216

K.W. Nicholls, 1972, *Gaelic and Gaelicised Ireland in the Middle Ages*, Gill and MacMillan, Dublin

Idem., 1982, 'Review Article. Anglo-French Ireland and After', *Peritia*, 1, pp. 370-403

Idem., 1987, 'Gaelic Society and Economy in the High Middle Ages', in: Cosgrove (ed.), *A New History of Ireland II*, pp. 397-438

M. Nicholls, 1999, *A History of the Modern British Isles, 1529-1603: The Two Kingdoms*, Blackwell, Oxford

W. Nolan, 1976, 'Thesis Abstract. The Historical Geography of the Ownership and Occupation of Land in the Barony of Fassadinin, Co. Kilkenny (Ph.D. Thesis, National University of Ireland, 1975)', *Irish Economic and Social History*, III, pp. 75-77

Idem., 1979, *Fassadinin: Land, Settlement and Society in South-East Ireland*, 1600-1850, Geography Publications, Dublin

Idem., 1982, *Tracing the Past: Sources for Local Studies in the Republic of Ireland*, Geography Publications, Dublin

B. O'Buachalla, 1996, *Aisling Ghéar: Na Stíobhartaigh agus an tAos Léinn, 1603-1788*, An Clochomhar, Baile Átha Cliath

C. O'Danachair, 1977-1979, 'Irish Tower Houses and their Regional Distribution', *Béaloideas*, 45-47, pp. 158-163

M. O'Dowd, 1983, 'Land Inheritance in Early Modern County Sligo', *Irish Economic and Social History*, X, pp. 5-18

Idem., 1986, 'Gaelic Economy and Society', in: Brady and Gillespie (eds.), *Natives and Newcomers*, pp. 120-147

BIBLIOGRAPHY

M. O'Dwyer, 1933, *The O'Dwyers of Kilnamanagh: The History of an Irish Sept*, John Murray, London

M. Ogborn, 1996, 'History, Memory and the Politics of Landscape and Space: Work in Historical Geography from Autumn '94 to Autumn '95', *Progress in Human Geography*, vol. 20, no. 2, pp. 222-229

J.H. Ohlmeyer, 1998, '"Civilizinge of those Rude Partes': Colonization within Britain and Ireland, 1580-1640s', in: Canny (ed.), *Origins of Empire*, pp. 124-147

C.D. O'Murchadha, 1984, 'Thesis Abstract. Land and Society in Seventeenth-Century Clare (Ph.D. Thesis, National University of Ireland, 1982)', *Irish Economic and Social History*, XI, pp. 125-126

M. O'Riordan, 1990, *The Gaelic Mind and the Collapse of the Gaelic World*, Cork University Press, Cork

A.R. Orme, 1970, *The World's Landscapes 4: Ireland*, Longman, London

H. O'Sullivan, 1992, 'Thesis Abstract. Landownership Changes in the County of Louth in the Seventeenth Century (Ph.D. Thesis, University of Dublin, 1992)', *Irish Economic and Social History*, XIX, pp. 81-82

S. O'Tuama and T. Kinsella, 1981, *An Duanaire 1600-1900: Poems of the Dispossessed*, Dolmen Press, Dublin

C. Parker, 1995, 'The Internal Frontier: The Irish in County Waterford in the Later Middle Ages', in: Barry *et al* (eds.), *Colony and Frontier*, pp. 139-154

N. Patterson, 1991, 'Gaelic Law and the Tudor Conquest of Ireland: The Social Background of the Sixteenth-Century Recensions of the Pseudo-Historical Prologue to the *Senchas Már*', *Irish Historical Studies*, vol. 27, no. 107, pp. 193-215

M. Perceval-Maxwell, 1994, *The Outbreak of the Irish Rebellion of 1641*, Gill and MacMillan, Dublin

C. Phythian-Adams, 1993, 'Editorial Foreword', in *Idem.* (ed.), *Societies, Cultures and Kinship*, pp. xi-xv

BIBLIOGRAPHY

T. Ploszajska, 2000, 'Historiographies of Geography and Empire', in: Graham and Nash (eds.), *Modern Historical Geographies*, pp. 121-145

P.C. Power, 1989, *History of South Tipperary*, Mercier Press, Cork

T.P. Power, 1993, *Land, Politics and Society in 18th Century Tipperary*, Clarendon Press, Oxford

M.L. Pratt, 1992, *Imperial Eyes: Travel Writing and Transculturation*, Routledge, London

L.J. Proudfoot, 1993, 'Regionalism and Localism: Religious Change and Social Protest, *c.*1700 to *c.*1900', in: Graham and Proudfoot (eds.), *An Historical Geography of Ireland*, pp. 185-218

Idem., 2000, 'Hybrid Space? Self and Other in Narratives of Landownership in Nineteenth-Century Ireland', *Journal of Historical Geography*, 26, 2, pp. 203-221

D.B. Quinn, 1966, *The Elizabethans and the Irish*, Cornell University Press, Ithaca

Idem., 1966, 'The Munster Plantation: Problems and Opportunities', *Cork Historical Society Journal*, LXXI, pp. 19-40

Idem. and K.W. Nicholls, 1976, 'Ireland in 1534', in: Moody *et al* (eds.), *A New History of Ireland III*, pp. 1-38

T.O. Ranger, 1957, 'Richard Boyle and the Making of an Irish Fortune, 1588-1614', *Irish Historical Studies*, vol. 10, no. 39, pp. 257-297

S. Regan, 1992, 'Ireland's Field Day', *History Workshop Journal*, 33, pp. 25-37

J. Reinhard Lupton, 1993, 'Mapping Mutability: or, Spenser's Irish Plot', in: Bradshaw *et al* (eds.), *Representing Ireland*, pp. 93-115

E. Richards, 1985, *A History of the Highland Clearances Volume 2: Emigration, Protest, Reasons*, Beckenham

S. Richards, 1991, 'Polemics on the Irish Past: The 'Return to the Source' in Irish Literary Revivals', *History Workshop Journal*, 31, pp. 120-135

BIBLIOGRAPHY

P. Routledge, 1997, 'A Spatiality of Resistances: Theory and Practice in Nepal's Revolution of 1990', in: S. Pile and M. Keith (eds.), *Geographies of Resistance*, Routledge, London, pp. 68-86

J. Ruane, 1992, 'Colonialism and the Interpretation of Irish Historical Development', in: M. Silverman and P.H. Gulliver (eds.), *Approaching the Past: Historical Anthropology through Irish Case Studies*, Columbia University Press, New York, pp. 293-323

E. Said, 1979, *Orientalism: Western Conceptions of the Orient*, Vintage, New York

Idem., 1989, 'Representing the Colonised: Anthropology's Interlocutors', *Critical Inquiry*, 15, pp. 205-225

Idem., 1993, *Culture and Imperialism*, Routledge, London

A. Sayer and M. Storper, 1997, 'Guest Editorial. Ethics Unbound: For a Normative Turn in Social Theory', *Environment and Planning D: Society and Space*, 15, pp. 1-17

S. Sharkey, 1997, 'Irish Cultural Studies and the Politics of Irish Studies', in: J. McGuigan (ed.), *Cultural Methodologies*, Sage, London, pp. 155-177

A.J. Sheehan, 1983, 'Official Reaction to Native Land Claims in the Plantation of Munster', *Irish Historical Studies*, vol. 23, no. 92, pp. 297-318

Idem., 1984, 'Attitudes to Religious and Temporal Authority in Cork in 1600: A Document from Laud MS 612', *Analecta Hibernica*, 31, pp. 61-68

Idem., 1986, 'Irish Towns in a Period of Change, 1558-1625', in: Brady and Gillespie (eds.), *Natives and Newcomers*, pp. 93-119

A. Simms, 1988, 'Core and Periphery in Medieval Europe: The Irish Experience in a Wider Context', in: Smyth and Whelan (eds.), *Common Ground*, pp. 22-40

K. Simms, 1995, 'Frontiers in the Irish Church – Regional and Cultural', in: Barry *et al* (eds.), *Colony and Frontier*, pp. 177-200

W.G. Skehan, 1993, *Cashel and Emly Heritage*, Abbey Books, Portlaoise, Co. Laois

BIBLIOGRAPHY

B. Smith, 1988, 'The Concept of the March in Medieval Ireland: The Case of Uriel', *Proceedings of the Royal Irish Academy*, vol. 88, sec. C, pp. 257-269

W.J. Smyth, 1983, 'Landholding Changes, Kinship Networks and Class Transformation in Rural Ireland: A Case-Study from County Tipperary', *Irish Geography*, vol. 16, pp. 16-35

Idem., 1985, 'Property, Patronage and Population – Reconstructing the Human Geography of Mid-Seventeenth Century County Tipperary', in: Nolan (ed.), *Tipperary: History and Society*, pp. 104-138

Idem., 1988, 'Society and Settlement in Seventeenth Century Ireland: The Evidence of the 1659 Census', in: *Idem.* and Whelan (eds.), *Common Ground*, pp. 55-83

Idem., 1990, 'Territorial, Social and Settlement Hierarchies in Seventeenth-Century Kilkenny', in: W. Nolan and K. Whelan (eds.), *Kilkenny: History and Society*, Geography Publications, Dublin, pp. 127-160

Idem., 1992, 'Making the Documents of Conquest Speak: The Transformation of Property, Society and Settlement in 17th Century Counties Tipperary and Kilkenny', in: Silverman and Gulliver (eds.), *Approaching the Past*, pp. 236-290

Idem., 1993, 'The Making of Ireland: Agendas and Perspectives in Cultural Geography', in: Graham and Proudfoot (eds.), *An Historical Geography of Ireland*, pp. 399-438

Idem., 1997, 'A Plurality of Irelands: Regions, Societies and Mentalities', in: Graham (ed.), *In Search of Ireland*, pp. 19-42

N. Thomas, 1994, *Colonialism's Culture: Anthropology, Travel and Government*, Polity Press, Cambridge

V. Treadwell, 1997, 'New Light on Richard Hadsor, I: Richard Hadsor and the Authorship of 'Advertisements for Ireland', 1622/3', *Irish Historical Studies*, vol. 30, no. 119, pp. 305-336

Y.-F. Tuan, 1977, *Space and Place: The Perspective of Experience*, University of Minnesota Press, Minneapolis

BIBLIOGRAPHY

Idem., 1979, 'Thought and Landscape', in: Meinig (ed.), *Interpretation of Ordinary Landscapes*, pp. 89-102

J.A. Watt, 1987, 'Approaches to the History of Fourteenth-Century Ireland', in: Cosgrove (ed.), *A New History of Ireland II*, pp. 303-313

Idem., 1987, 'Gaelic Polity and Cultural Identity', in: Cosgrove (ed.), *A New History of Ireland II*, pp. 314-351

Idem., 1987, 'The Anglo-Irish Colony under Strain, 1327-99', in: Cosgrove (ed.), *A New History of Ireland II*, pp. 352-396

D. Wishart, 1997, 'The Selectivity of Historical Representation', *Journal of Historical Geography*, 23, 2, pp. 111-118

C.W.J. Withers, 1988, *Gaelic Scotland: The Transformation of a Culture Region*, Routledge, London

H. Wood, 1919, *A Guide to the Public Records Deposited in the P.R.O. of Ireland*, I.M.C., Dublin

Idem., 1938, 'The Tragedy of the Irish Public Records', *Irish Genealogist*, vol. 1, no. 3, pp. 67-71

D. Woodward, 1973, ' The Anglo-Irish Livestock Trade of the Seventeenth Century', *Irish Historical Studies*, vol. 18, no. 72, pp. 489-515

B.S.A. Yeoh, 2000, 'Historical Geographies of the Colonised World', in: Graham and Nash (eds.), *Modern Historical Geographies*, pp. 146-166

R.J.C. Young, 2001, *Postcolonialism: An Historical Introduction*, Blackwell, Oxford

Index

Significant information in notes is indexed in the form 123n.45, ie note 45 on page 123.

INDEX

O'Haras of Sligo 104, 106, 130
Ohlmeyer, J.H. 73
O'Kennedys of Ormond 33, 55
Old English
    on frontier 28–35
    and Gaelic-Irish 33–4, 43, 60–1n.46, 126–7
    Gaelicisation 33–4, 66n.114
    identity construction 107–8
    and New English 126–7
    power of 43–7
O'Mulryans of Owny 43, 55
O'Murchadha, C.D. 98, 100
O'Neill, Hugh 54–5
Order of Knights Templars 28
O'Riordan, M. 103
Orme, A.R. 3
Ormond, earls of
    and earls of Desmond 45–6
    and New English 56
    and O'Dwyers 30, 44–5
    powers of 43–4, 54
    see also Butler family
Ormond, James Butler, 1st earl of 30
Ormond, James Butler, 2nd earl of 30
Ormond, Thomas Butler, 10th earl of 46, 78, 91n.52
Ormond, Walter Butler, 11th earl of 78
Ortelius, Abraham, map of Ireland 35, *37*
O'Sullivan, H. 121

pardons, O'Dwyers 47, 49–50, 64n.88
Parsons, William 84
Patterson, N. 103
Percivall, John 98
Percivall, Sir Philip
    landholdings 84–5, 86–7, 95nn.116,121
    and O'Dwyers 88, 99–101, 105, 112, 119, 132, 143
    position of 82–3, 98, 115n.27, 124–5, 131–2, 137, 145
Perrot, Sir John 45, 49
place, sense of 8–10